THE
LOVING
HEART
— OF —
FATHER GOD

KATHRYN BLACKWELL

Copyright © 2020
All Rights Reserved
Printed in the United States of America

All rights reserved under International Copyright Law. This book or parts thereof may not be reproduced in any form, stored in a retrieval system or transmitted in any form by any means – electronic, mechanical, photocopy, recording, or otherwise – without the express written permission of the author or the publisher.

Unless otherwise indicated, all scripture quotations, references and definitions are from the Authorized King James Version © 1987; The New King James Version © 1982 by Thomas Nelson, Inc.; The New International Version 1973, 1978, 1984 by International Bible Society by the Zondervan Corporation; The Amplified Bible Old Testament © 1962, 1964, 1965, 1987 by the Zondervan Corporation; The Amplified New Testament © 1954, 1958, 1987 by the Lockman Foundation; The Message. Copyright © 1993, 1994, 1995, 1996, 2000, 2001, 2002. Used by permission of NavPress Publishing Group. All rights reserved; M.G. Easton M.A., D.D., Illustrated Bible Dictionary, Third Edition, published by Thomas Nelson, 1897.

THE LOVING HEART OF FATHER GOD

Kathryn Blackwell
kathryn.blackwell1925@gmail.com

ISBN 978-1-949027-68-6
Print Edition

Published by: Publish Affordably | 773-783-2981
Chicago, Illinois

ACKNOWLEDGMENTS

I am especially thankful for Amy Braily who graciously accepted the daunting task of typing reams of handwritten pages for submission to the publisher.

For confidant and friend Tony Lickwar for his continued encouragement and support.

For Pastors Dr. Ron Johnson, Jr. who reviewed the work for content and biblical accuracy and to his wife Marion Johnson Livingstones Fellowship Church, for their spiritual leadership and loving pastoral care.

THE LOVING HEART OF FATHER GOD

TABLE OF CONTENTS

THE LOVING HEART OF FATHER GOD

Revealed Through:
Familiar Illustrations of Family Relationships v

Revealed Through:
God's Written Word, the Bible,
God's Love Letter to Mankind 1

The Exciting Climax of
God's Creative Activity 28

Israel, God's Firstborn:
The Birth of a New Nation 42

God Is Good 61

The Miracle of Physical Conception Revealed from
Conception to Delivery 76

Spiritual Conception 93

Blessings from the Womb 103

When I See The Blood 130

Supernatural Deliverance 146

Cry of the Newborn 179

Examine Your Heart 211

Who and Whose Are You? 235

Jesus Loves You 259

Gifts to the Newborn 269

Past, Present, Future 282

A Family Affair 288

INTRODUCTION

REVEALED THROUGH: FAMILIAR ILLUSTRATIONS OF FAMILY RELATIONSHIPS

This is what the Lord says: "As a mother comforts her child, so will I comfort you..." (Isaiah 66:13 NIV).

This familiar illustration represents the compassionate care of a loving mother for her fretting child. The baby now rests and nestles peacefully in her comforting arms. It is soothed and consoled as she softly sings to it songs of love. The child, in turn, contentedly responds with sounds of satisfaction and delight. This image of the self-sacrificial loving care of a devoted mother simply reflects the amazingly true character of Father God and the reality of His maternal heart.

There is a God in heaven who is the only eternal, true, and living God. He wants you to know Him and experience all the ways He can and will be of benefit to you. He earnestly desires to draw you into a close personal relationship with Him. He will receive you without regard to your past or present condition. You will find the peace and rest that you have been seeking from all other unreliable and ineffective sources.

He longs to communicate and express His everlasting and unconditional love for you. As you listen to His voice, He will reveal His plans to bless you and keep you in His care. Receive and return His love as you submit and surrender to Him in genuine and unreserved dependence on His grace and mercy.

Believe, receive, and accept with eager expectation all that He freely offers.

This is the Lord's answer to His chosen people, the nation of Israel, when they believed He had forgotten or forsaken them: "Can a woman forget her nursing child, and have no compassion on the son of her womb? Even these may forget, but I will not forget you" (Isaiah 49:15 NASB).

There exists a very special, intimate bond between a nursing mother and her child that is unlike any other human interaction. She has conceived, carried, nurtured, and sheltered the newborn that came forth from her own body. After delivery, she diligently provides for its every need. However, an earthly mother may be guilty of neglect or failure to care for her child. In rare instances, she may even abandon the child if she becomes overburdened by the unfortunate circumstances of life. She may be greatly distracted by the stress of family responsibilities.

But God, who is all-knowing, continually thinks about you. He always has you and your welfare on His mind and in His heart. At all times and in every instance, He has the utmost regard for all that concerns or troubles you. His thoughts toward you were, and are, and will always be for your good. He is carefully attentive to all aspects of your life. He will always be with you and for you, divinely acting on your behalf.

The Psalmist David expresses his confidence in the Lord's faithfulness: "Although my father and mother have forsaken me, yet the Lord will take me up (adopt me as His child)" (Psalm 27:10 AMPC). God will never abandon those who are His own. He will assume complete responsibility for the eternal care of those who are accepted and received into His family. He is more than willing and able to fulfill His promises to supply your every need, not only in this present life but forever, throughout eternity. He remains faithful in every situation and will never give up on you or desert you. He will lovingly draw you to Himself and never let you go.

As a result of human weaknesses and frailties, your natural father and mother may not live up to your expectations. They may fail in their parental roles. However, there is a God who is steadfast and sure. His love for you never fails. He is ever faithful to keep his promises when you connect through faith to His word of truth and the reality of His merciful heart. The result is the assurance of joy, peace, and the abiding security of your relationship with Him.

Or perhaps you had a loving, caring father and mother who did not leave you during their natural lifetimes, but you were separated from them by death or distance. No matter your situation, the only eternal living God promises to be near and available to you, wherever you are or whatever your situation.

Again, the Psalmist writes, "Just as a father has compassion on his children, so the Lord has compassion on those who fear Him" (Psalm 103:13 NASB). The word "fear" often expresses terror or dread, or refers to a very unpleasant emotional response. But in this Scripture, the word "fear" has an entirely different meaning: to respect, to reverence, to be awe-inspired, and to regard greatly.

Many people see God only as a disagreeable, angry tyrant or ruler, someone or something continually needing to be appeased or pacified. They view him as one who is not easily satisfied but is angrily "out to get you" and to give you the punishment you deserve. But this psalm speaks of God's compassion: the tenderhearted, gentle, unconditional love of a concerned father who wants the very best for his children.

"When Israel was a child, then I loved him . . . Yet I taught Ephraim to walk, taking them by the arms or taking them up in my arms, but they did not know that I healed them" (Hosea

11:1,3 AMPC). This Scripture speaks of the Northern Kingdom of the nation of Israel, a group of ten tribes also known as Ephraim. It depicts a father tenderly and patiently caring for his child as he teaches him to walk. Instead of responding with grateful obedience and giving thanks for His gracious bountiful blessings, they were disloyal and served other lifeless pagan gods. After God's correction and discipline, they repented and were restored back to Him from their wayward ways. They also recovered from the disastrous results inflicted on them by the other nations they had mistakenly turned to for help. "I will heal their faithlessness; I will love them freely . . ." (Hosea 14:4 AMPC).

". . . And they will bring your sons in the bosom of their garments, and your daughters will be carried upon their shoulders. And kings shall be your foster fathers and guardians, and their queens your nursing mothers" (Isaiah 49:22-23 AMPC). In this instance, the nations will cooperate and assist in the ultimate return or regathering of Israel from other nations. They will actively participate in the restoration of Israel from the four corners of the earth back to their own homeland, the land of promise.

"Rejoice with Jerusalem and be glad for her, all you who love her; rejoice for joy with her . . . That you may nurse and be satisfied from her consoling breasts, that you may drink deeply and be delighted . . . Then you will be nursed, you will be carried on her hip and trotted (lovingly bounced up and down) on her (God's maternal) knees. As one who her mother comforts, so I will comfort you" (Isaiah 66:10-13 AMPC). Here and throughout the Scriptures, various situations and events are described in terms of loving maternal care. In this example, the prophet Isaiah pictures Jerusalem, the capital city of Israel, as a nurturing mother, nourishing and caring for her child. He lists various ways that natural mothers bear and support their children, and he also depicts a mother playfully amusing and delighting her beloved child.

- CHAPTER 1 -

REVEALED THROUGH: GOD'S WRITTEN WORD, THE BIBLE, GOD'S LOVE LETTER TO MANKIND

> *"There are things about God that people cannot see—his eternal power and all that makes him God . . ." (Romans 1:20 ERV).*

There are many who are secure in the belief that they know of God or that they possess some vague knowledge about God. This supposed knowledge is usually based on totally unreliable sources including current religious practices, traditional denominational belief systems, or accepted customs passed down from one generation to another.

These widely held practices and doctrines are often given a far greater importance than the Bible, God's reliable unchanging Word to mankind. As a result, the truth of the Scriptures becomes of little consequence or effect compared to the uncertainty of man's religious traditions or mindsets.

"Thus says the Lord, 'Let not the wise and skillful person glory and boast in his wisdom and skill; let not the mighty and powerful person glory and boast in his strength and power; let not the person who is rich (in physical gratification and earthly wealth) glory and boast in his (temporal satisfaction and earthly) riches; But let him who glories glory in this: that he understands and knows Me (personally and practically, discerning and recognizing My character), that I am the Lord, Who practices loving-kindness, judgment, and righteousness in the earth, for in these things I delight,' says the Lord" (Jeremiah 9:23-24 AMPC).

God does not ask you to do anything that He does not enable you to do. He sincerely longs for you to know and understand Him, His motives, His character, His conduct and ways, His works, and the thoughts and purposes of His heart. Therefore, He uses universally familiar and easily recognized things in this temporary physical world we live in to explain clearly the operation of the invisible, eternal spiritual realm. Through this, he is ever and always revealing Himself to you, because it gives Him great pleasure when you experience and know Him personally.

In the very first words of Genesis in the Bible, God's written revelation to man, He begins to unfold the wonder of His essential nature and character, His attributes and distinguishing qualities. His ultimate aim is that you know Him, the desires of His heart, His thoughts toward you, the good pleasure of His will, and His ways as He works out His ultimate, eternal, redemptive plan and purpose to do you good, to benefit and bless you. You were created for fellowship and close communion with a living God. His desire is that you walk together in union, in agreement, in a loving personal relationship.

God reveals Himself to mankind through His written word, the Bible. It is not necessary for Him to prove or explain the reality of His existence either by argument or human reasoning. The Scriptures absolutely declare His eternal existence as Supreme Being of the universe. "Every Scripture is God-breathed (given by His inspiration) and profitable for instruction, for reproof and conviction of sin, for correction of error and discipline in obedience, (and) for training in righteousness (in holy living, in conformity to God's will in thought, purpose, and action)" (2 Timothy 3:16 AMPC).

God, the source of divine revelation, spoke first through

humans. These holy men were influenced, directed, and divinely inspired by the Holy Spirit, the Spirit of Truth, as they participated by documenting the Word of God. The Bible discloses God's absolute truth about Himself and His plans for His created universe and mankind—and for you individually. He reveals His divine purpose for His chosen people and for His church, those called out to be His family. Through His Word, God speaks directly and personally to you. The Bible tells of God's redeeming love for His people and family, and His ultimate plan to restore all things back to a rightful relationship with Him.

God is! He was, He is, He always will be.

The very first verse of the Bible tells us that God existed "in the beginning" (Genesis 1:1 KJV)—God, the self-existent, eternal one, independent of any other being, who always was and always will be God. God, who has no beginning, will also have no ending. He always was, He always is, and He will forever be. God, who exists from eternity past unto eternity future, is the only true, living, wise God. It is He who can tell both the former things and the outcome of things to come, including those things in the heavens, on the earth, and under the earth. He has designed a divine master plan for all creation, for mankind, and especially for you.

". . . Understand that I am he: before me there was no God formed, neither shall there be after me . . . Before the day was I am he" (Isaiah 43:10, 13 KJV). In eternity past, nothing existed other than the only true, living God. There was nothing or no one that God, the only living, eternal, self-existent One, depended on for His existence other than Himself. He has always been God and will always be God. He is not merely a result of man's imagination or some private, personal revelation through human dreams or visions. Neither is He a "god" fashioned of silver or gold or the work of men's hands. Those figures or idols are incapable of having a loving, personal relationship with those who serve or worship them.

There are many other "gods" and rulers in people's lives, but there is only one true, living God. He is the personal God who seeks you out individually for Himself. He desires close fellowship and communication in a loving relationship as He acts and intervenes on your behalf. Those who worship numerous "gods" must appeal to each one for a specific problem or purpose, but the all-sufficient God will graciously and freely provide for your every need. "The God Who produced and formed the world and all things in it, being Lord of heaven and earth, does not dwell in handmade shrines. Neither is He served by human hands, as though He lacked anything, for it is He Himself Who gives life and breath and all things to all people" (Acts 17:24-26 AMPC).

There is a God in heaven who rules in the affairs of men. He is a real Person, a Spirit Being who is a personal God, capable of relating closely and directly to you as an individual and to all mankind. He has a personality; therefore, He possesses a mind, will, and emotions. He is an intelligent Being who thinks, feels, plans, and purposes. He speaks, decrees, and commands, and because He is God, His words have creative power to bring into existence whatever He has spoken. In spite of resistance, opposition to His purposes, or circumstances that delay or hinder His Divine plan, God shall eventually work out His perfect will.

Unity in Plurality

> "... *The Lord is our God, the Lord is One!"*
> *(Deuteronomy 6:4 KJV).*

The Bible speaks of one God in three Persons, a Divine Trinity, three separate Individuals or distinct persons in the godhead: God the Father, God the Son—the Word made flesh—and God the Holy Spirit. Three in one. One in three, one God who manifests Himself in three different ways. Each One is called God, and the three together can be called one God because of the perfect harmony, unity, and oneness each has with the others. All three are equal, essential, and eternal, working together in perfect oneness, but they each have differing roles, positions, offices, work, and responsibilities in creation, as well as in the lives of all mankind. Each person of the Trinity has a personal spirit body housing the personal soul (mind, will, and emotions) and personal spirit. One God who manifests or shows Himself in three different ways.

"And God said, 'Let us make man in our image, after our likeness . . .'" (Genesis 1:26 KJV). As a result of mutual consideration and consulting together, God the Father, God the Word (Who later became flesh as the Son Jesus) and God the Holy Spirit deliberated together before this very important divine decision. The Father decrees, declares, and commands. The Son accomplishes or does the work decreed or commanded. And the Holy Spirit applies, manifests, or makes known the accomplished work. Most importantly, all cooperate together for your ultimate good. "The grace (favor and spiritual blessing) of the Lord Jesus Christ and the love of God and the presence and fellowship (the communion and sharing together, and participation) in the Holy Spirit be with you all. Amen (so be it)" (2 Corinthians 13:14 AMPC).

Revealed Through: God's Desire for a Family

> *"In Christ, he chose us before the world was made. He chose us in love to be his holy people—people who could stand before him without fault. And before the world was made, God decided to make us his own children through Jesus Christ. This was what God wanted, and it pleased him to do it" (Ephesians 1:4-5 ERV).*

The Loving Heart of Father God

From all eternity past, even before God created the heavens and the earth and all its inhabitants, before he created the entire universe, God's thoughts were on you and His plans for you to become His beloved child. He especially marked you out beforehand to be an object of His grace, His undeserved favor. He personally set you apart to be dedicated to Him, without blame and flawless, because He chose to do so, and this gave Him great satisfaction and pleasure. Since you were made in His unique image and likeness, you also possess a soul, mind, and will, and you are capable of making your own decision to respond, accept, and "choose to be chosen." Each person must personally accept God's invitation.

The God who desires to adopt a family would most certainly and clearly disclose both the paternal (fatherly) as well as the maternal (motherly) aspects of His character. God is pictured as the producer of life, a loving Father who is the head or guardian of His family. He willingly accepts responsibility for providing leadership and direction to those in His household. In His paternal role, like a good Father, He is a generous provider for all the wants and needs that you, His child, may have. He gives you the desires of your heart because He Himself put those deep longings inside you. He sincerely wants the very best for you in every aspect of your life, spirit, soul, and body. His faithful, abiding presence and unfailing love provide complete assurance and strength for the present and hope for the future.

In His maternal role, He births and brings into manifestation, clearly revealing the invisible or unseen. The greatness of His loving kindness and tender mercies is communicated and revealed to the physical senses. He compassionately nourishes and nurtures His family, those who look to Him for comfort and consolation at all times and in difficult or stressful situations. He is responsible for your ease, well-being, and relief from pain and hurt caused by physical, mental, and emotional distress.

There are numerous references in the Bible to children and to the human birth and delivery process. It compares and contrasts these human processes with God's creative works as He brings forth life in various situations and circumstances, including the birth and re-creation of the natural universe, the earth, and the heavens, as well as the birth of a nation. Most importantly, the Bible describes the plan for the spiritual rebirth and restoration of mankind.

The Scriptures reveal God's divine care for all His creation, including animal and plant life, and especially for man, who was created to be a reflection of Him. For you who are in the household of faith, He supernaturally provides for your ultimate eternal welfare. Families, generations, and lineages are faithfully noted and recorded as He rules in the affairs of individuals, people groups, cities, and nations. His loving maternal care extends throughout the earth He prepared and equipped for man's habitation. The entire universe, the heavens, and heavenly host are also ordered and sustained by Him for a purpose. There is no one, no thing, no place beyond His far-reaching, all-encompassing, tender loving care and concern.

Revealed Through Creation:
Look Up—Look All Around You

God reveals Himself in His created universe. "The heavens tell about the glory of God. The skies announce what his hands have made. Each new day tells more of the story, and each night reveals more and more about God's power . . . They don't make any sound we can hear. But their message goes throughout the world. Their teaching reaches the end of the earth" (Psalm 19:1-4 ERV).

Consider the heavens! You need only to look up and search the night sky, where God communicates and confirms His existence and the awesome splendor of His creative powers. He clearly demonstrates His great faithfulness in every place when He maintains and holds the heavenly bodies in their courses as they travel in their divinely ordained paths throughout space. All creation reflects His goodness and the glory of His presence.

Allow God to order and direct your steps on the right path He has set before you. He has established a plan determined even before your earthly existence. The invisible things of a supernatural God are communicated and understood by those things that are visible. As a result, the things you see or have knowledge of by your natural senses are an unveiling or disclosure of the unseen and eternal. One example of this is the revelation of Himself through creation, the created universe in its vastness and in His divine order and arrangement.

It is important that you are able to determine those things that are temporary or passing, as opposed to those things that are permanent and eternal, which are of greater importance. The eternal, spiritual, unseen realm consists of those things not seen or perceived by the natural senses. They are, however, more real than the physical things that are seen or easily perceived, which last only for a limited period of time. The unseen realm has a greater impact on your life and is superior to that of the physical, visible world.

"Faith helps us understand that God created the whole world by his command. This means that the things we see were made by something that cannot be seen" (Hebrews 11:3 ERV). Throughout the ages, the visible world was not made of physical or natural materials already in existence, but were made by the unfailing Word of God. His glory, greatness, and majestic power are obvious to anyone who will look up and observe.

His heart's desire for you, as His child, would assuredly be that His divine purpose for your eternal destiny would come to pass. Since He can order and sustain the universe by the word of His power, He can certainly maintain and bring order to your life and keep you safely in His care.

"Look up to the skies. Who created all those stars? Who created all those 'armies' in the sky? Who knows every star by name? He is very strong and powerful, so not one of these stars is lost" (Isaiah 40:26 ERV). The heavenly hosts clearly proclaim God's existence. They show forth His divine design for the heavens and the earth. His purposes will be fully realized in all creation, including the great starry spaces. He counts and calls those numberless stars by name individually. Surely, He will take account of you, His acknowledged crowning creation. He knows all about you and calls you by name.

He has also planned ahead for your ultimate good, so that you might not be lost spiritually or separated from His glorious presence forever. He knows your name, speaks it softly, and calls you His beloved. Seek His face as a child searches for and focuses on the familiar and comforting face of its mother. Know that His adoring eyes are always on you and that His face is always turned toward you.

When you sleep, you know that He watches attentively and protectively over you. He is the One who never sleeps or slumbers. When He awakens you in the morning, He desires that the first words you hear are from Him and that the first words you speak are to Him, your loving Father. His arms reach out to draw you to Him, and He desires that you respond to the warmth of His loving touch. Everything that God does is motivated by His divine loving-kindness.

Look All Around You

"There are things about God that people cannot see—his eternal power and all that makes him God. But since the beginning of the world, those things have been easy for people to understand. They are made clear in what God has made" (Romans 1:20 ERV). Seeing, sensing, and understanding the physical, natural, visible world assists you in discerning the even greater reality of the spiritual, invisible realm or dimension. For example, man was created by God to be His image bearer, a reflection of Himself.

The things you cannot see about the qualities of God—His eternal power, His divine nature and authority—are revealed by the world He created and by His works. By these He is seen and understood. Therefore, no one has an excuse or defense when they dishonor Him. God's entire orderly creation reveals the truth about His majestic glory, as well as His loving work of restoration and redemption.

The Offspring of the Earth, Vegetation: Everything Produced by the Earth

> *"Thus says God the Lord, who created the heavens and stretched them out, who spread out the earth and its offspring, who gives breath to the people on it and spirit to those who walk in it . . ." (Isaiah 42:5 NASB).*

Vegetation, that which comes out of the earth, was given for the nourishment of all God's created beings. Plant life, as all other life, was to reproduce after its own kind. God's all-encompassing, loving care is expressed as He provides bountifully for all life. "To Him Who gives food to all flesh, for His mercy and loving-kindness endure forever" (Psalm 136:25 AMPC).

The Animal Kingdom and its Offspring

God first provided everything and every element needed to sustain life before He created living beings. Only then did He create fish, fowl, animals, beasts and cattle and moving creatures who were to multiply and fill the earth, the air, and the seas.

In the Gospel of Matthew, Jesus says: "Look at the birds. They don't plant, harvest, or save food in barns, but your heavenly Father feeds them. Don't you know you are worth much more than they are?" (Matthew 6:26 ERV). "When birds are sold, two small birds cost only a penny. But not even one of those little birds can die without your Father knowing it. God even knows how many hairs are on your head. So don't be afraid. You are worth more than a whole flock of birds" (Matthew 10:29-30 ERV).

The passage refers to the common house or English sparrow. Large flocks of these ordinary birds are inhabitants of many cities and countries. Although they are numerous, plain, and not worth much in man's estimation, Creator God is aware of every aspect of their lives and deaths. Every element of His created universe is ordered and sustained by Him.

His Providential Care for All His Creation is Clearly Unfolded

"Lord, you cause water to flow from springs into the streams . . . The streams provide water for all the wild animals . . . Wild birds come to live by the pools; they sing in the branches of nearby trees. You send rain down on the mountains. The earth gets everything it needs from what you have made. You make the grass grow to feed the animals. You provide plants for the crops we grow—the plants that give us food from the earth. You give us . . . the oil that makes our skin soft, and the food that makes us strong. The great cedar trees of Lebanon belong to the Lord. He planted them and gives them the water they need. That's where the birds make their nests, and the storks live in the fir trees. The high mountains are a home for wild goats. The large rocks are hiding places for rock badgers . . .

The earth is full of the living things you made. Look at the ocean, so big and wide! It is filled with all kinds of sea life. There are creatures large and small . . . Lord, all living things depend on you. You give them food at the right time. You give it, and they eat it. They are filled with good food from your open hands." (Psalm 104:10-18, 24-25, 27-28 ERV).

> *"All living things look to you for their food, and you give them their food at the right time. You open your hands and give every living thing all that it needs" (Psalm 145:15-16 ERV).*
>
> *"You take care of the land. You water it and make it fertile. Your streams are always filled with water. That's how you make the crops grow. You pour rain on the plowed fields; you soak the fields with water. You make the ground soft with rain, and you make the young plants grow. You start the new year with a good harvest. You end the year with many crops. The desert and hills are covered with grass. The pastures are covered with sheep. The valleys are filled with grain" (Psalm 65:9-13 ERV).*

There is no area of care for the animal world that God has not planned. He has provided them with protective bodily covering suitable for life and survival in specific climates, including extreme temperatures or harsh conditions. Feathers, fur, hard shells, hair, thick skin, scales, and layers of fat are examples representing God's intelligent design. In many instances, protective coloration, camouflage, and deceptive coverings allow animals to blend in with their natural habitat in order to provide additional security against predators.

God skillfully arranged body parts for protection, self-preservation, freedom, and ease of movement. Animals were equipped for hunting, fishing, gathering, and acquiring the food and water necessary for survival. Horns, claws, beaks, tusks, talons, fangs, wings, and a varied number of appendages offer offensive and defensive support. Inborn survival skills for teaching and training the young are passed on to future generations.

God has placed in all living creatures the maternal instinct to care for and protect offspring. But above all is His divine, loving, providential care for all His created beings. All are dependent upon Him to be the ultimate supplier of all life's necessities.

In animals, the natural inclination is to produce after their own kind and to nurture those offspring conceived and delivered. But first, they prepare for them appropriate, easily accessible homes with locally available materials. These habitations can be in, on, under, or above the earth or water. Holes, webs, caves, nests, hills, burrows, lairs, coral reefs, and dens ensure comfortable places for birth, growth, and the maturation of the young. These homes are usually concealed and conveniently located close to adequate food supply and water sources.

Scripture gives the example of two completely different kinds of birds. Each possesses the God-given natural instinct to nurture, teach, train, provide for, and protect their young, but in different ways. The powerful, swift eagle soars aloft on high, catching the wind under its huge wingspan. A mother hen, however, remains grounded in a very small area. She walks about, head lowered, as she pecks and scratches for food.

"He surrounded them and watched over them . . . like an eagle when she makes her young leave the nest to fly. She stays close to them, ready to help. She spreads her wings to catch them when they fall and carries them to a safe place" (Deuteronomy 32:10-11 ERV). At the appropriate time of life, when the young eaglet develops the feathers necessary for flight, the adult actively encourages it to leave the comfort of the nest high above the ground. The fledgling's first attempts to fly may be hesitant or unsuccessful, but if it begins to fall, it is not unprotected. Suddenly, the adult bird swoops down powerfully under its offspring and skillfully and lovingly catches and supports the young bird safely on its outstretched wings.

"The eternal God is your refuge, and underneath are the everlasting arms" (Deuteronomy 33:27 NIV). God motivates and encourages those who are His own by allowing you to be tested and tried, in order for you to develop the strength to grow and mature spiritually. Throughout this process, God is ever near to guide and protect you throughout your life. ". . . I carried you on eagles' wings and brought you to myself" (Exodus 19:4 NIV).

God Himself desires to bring you out of your current situation in which you are headed toward destruction apart from Him. He plans to bring you into a right relationship of safety and security with Him. He uses the picture of the strength of eagle's wings to provide a medium of safety and security.

In another instance, a mother hen is alerted when an enemy approaches from the air, or if she senses impending danger from the immediate surrounding territory. Also, if storm clouds gather, she spreads out her short wings and quickly gathers her brood under her feathers to cover them and keep them safe and secure. ". . . How often I have desired and yearned to gather your children together (around Me), as a hen (gathers) her young under her wings . . ." (Luke 13:34 AMPC).

You were created with a mind, a will, and emotions. You have the ability to make choices. Any divine offer requires a personal response. Remember, "to believe" is an action word. Run to Him who is able to save you and keep you safe from the attacks of the enemy. "He who dwells in the shelter of the Most High will rest in the shadow of the Almighty. I will say of the Lord, 'He is my refuge and my fortress, my God, in whom I trust' . . . He will cover you with his feathers, and under his wings you will find refuge" (Psalm 91:1, 4 NIV).

You can be confidently assured that your Father desires to shield and protect you from exposure to any hurt, harm, or danger. He draws you close to Him into a secret place of security and safety that only He can provide. Those who put their continual and complete trust in God are secure and safe in His care. You can trust that He is reliable and dependable to protect, guard, and keep you. You can rest assured as you settle down in the secret place of His presence. There you are hidden away from the problems and distractions of the outside world.

You can be in need in any area of life, as when the powerful eagle's wings are placed underneath the falling eaglet, or in such times when the mother hen needs to draw her young close to her, spreading her wings over and around her chicks. God's unfailing love, mercy, and grace will cover, surround, encompass, and undergird you when you come into the circle of His divine protective care.

The Family History of God's Creative Universe: All Things Are Under His Headship

"These are the generations of the heavens and the earth when they were created, in the day that the Lord God made the earth and the heavens" (Genesis 2:4 KJV). This refers to God's original creation with Earth's perfect and ideal state, and the process of rebirth and restoration when the earth was again made perfect for life.

The book of Isaiah also tells us of God's creation of all things: ". . . I, the Lord, am the maker of all things, stretching out the heavens by Myself and spreading out the earth all alone" (Isaiah 44:24 NASB). "I made the earth and created man upon it. I, with My hands, stretched out the heavens, and I commanded all their host" (Isaiah 45:12 AMPC).

God's Creative Plan for the Ages: The Earth—from Perfection to Chaos

"In the beginning God created the heavens and the earth" (Genesis 1:1 NASB). In the beginning, Creator God made all things perfect. "Before the mountains were brought forth or ever You had formed and given birth to the earth and the world, even from everlasting to everlasting You are God" (Psalm 90:2 AMPC). "At the beginning You existed and laid the foundations of the earth; the heavens are the work of Your hands" (Psalm 102:25 AMPC).

"He has made everything beautiful in its time . . ." (Ecclesiastes 3:11 AMPC). Just at the right time, God made all things appropriate, especially suitable and proper for His divine purposes. He could do nothing more, nor was anything more needed to make His work complete.

Angelic Allies, Sons of God

Both the starry host and the angelic host had been created before the original, perfect creation of the earth and were witnesses to God's majestic power. The planetary host of heaven and the angelic host observed in awesome wonder and jubilantly rejoiced at the completed and finished work of the Godhead in the original, perfect creation.

In the book of Job, God calls Job to account when he questions God's infinite wisdom and His power and authority over the affairs of man. The Lord speaks to Job and reveals His supreme power and authority over the heavens and the earth: "Where wast thou when I laid the foundations of the earth? Declare, if thou hast understanding. Who hath laid the measures thereof, if thou knowest? Or who hath stretched the line upon it? Whereupon are the foundations thereof fastened? Or who laid the cornerstone thereof; when the morning stars sang together, and all the sons of God shouted for joy?" (Job 38:4-7 KJV).

The Healing Bible (ERV) translates these same verses: "Where were you when I made the earth? If you are so smart, answer me. And who decided how big the earth should be? Who measured it with a measuring line? What is the earth resting on? Who put the first stone in its place when the morning stars sang together and the angels shouted for joy?" (Job 38:4-7 ERV). A footnote explains that "angels" can be literally translated as "sons of God."

Before the creation of the earth as the habitation for mankind, and before the creation of human life, angelic life existed. God had created a heavenly host of angelic beings called "sons of God." These magnificent creatures joyously glorify God in celebration of His marvelous works as He unfolds His divine plan for you and for all mankind.

These "sons" are unlike Jesus, the eternal Son of the Most High God, the only begotten Son, fully God and fully man. Therefore, He is not a created being, but was with the Father from the beginning. He came down from heaven to Earth, born of a woman and conceived by the Holy Spirit.

Neither are they sons of God, believers, redeemed and born from above, born again by the shed blood of Jesus and adopted into the family of God the Father. These sons by faith are new creations and joint heirs with Jesus Christ. Sons of God, members of the household of faith, are called and chosen from the human race, created by a personal God who continually reveals Himself in your every life situation or need as you develop in your intimate relationship with Him.

Angelic sons of God were created as God revealed His attributes and characteristics as Creator God, the Powerful, Glorious, Majestic Source of Life. They cannot, therefore, be considered as "blood brothers" or "blood kin" or "blood relatives" of Jesus Christ, Son of God, or as born-again sons of God who are recipients of God's great grace as heirs of salvation. These sons of God or angelic beings could only observe joyously as God created an incredibly perfect habitation for mankind. They were onlookers at the birth of the earth prepared particularly as a home for human beings. They continue to watch and witness the amazing revelation of His predetermined intent.

They are too numerous to count, an indefinitely large number of allied angelic host. The Apostle John, in a vision of heaven, said, "Then I looked and I heard the voice of many angels, numbering thousands upon thousands, and ten thousand times ten thousand" (Revelation 5:11 NIV). They differ in rank, status, order, and authority. There are several types or divisions of angels with various roles and responsibilities including those who minister and serve in heaven as they worship and glorify God. They also differ in appearance and form.

As they surround God's throne in heaven, angelic worship never ceases. There, sons of God also worship the Son of God, Jesus, the perfect sacrifice. "And they were calling to one another: 'Holy, holy, holy is the Lord Almighty; the whole earth is full of his glory'" (Isaiah 6:3 NIV). "Day and night they never stop saying: 'Holy, holy, holy is the Lord God Almighty, who was, and is, and is to come" (Revelation 4:8 NIV).

John recorded again in this vision: "They encircled the throne ... In a loud voice they were saying, 'Worthy is the Lamb, who was slain, to receive power and wealth and wisdom and strength and honor and glory and praise!'" (Revelation 5:11-12 NIV). All of their jubilant, joyful praise and worship is directed only to God and to Jesus, the Lamb of God.

God Supernaturally Cares for His Family

"All the angels are spirits who serve God and are sent to help those who will receive salvation" (Hebrews 1:14 ERV). There are those whose specific function is to serve believers on earth. They are activated or stirred into action when God's voice is heard or when the Word of God is released out of the mouths of His called-out ones, the church. God's Word is so creatively powerful that His Word, when spoken in faith by a believer, is as effective as if God Himself had released it.

"Praise the Lord, you his angels, you mighty ones who do his bidding, who obey his word. Praise the Lord, all his heavenly hosts, you his servants who do His will" (Psalm 103:20-21 NIV). God's angels, His mighty ones, excel in strength; they are superhuman in power. They are not, as often pictured, adorable, cuddly, helpless babies with useless tiny wings sprouting out of chubby shoulders. Nor are their days occupied frolicking playfully together on fluffy clouds as they blissfully make heavenly music on harps of gold.

In many works of art, they are pictured as elegant, feminine, winged creatures with shining halos encircling their heads. On the contrary, the Bible gives an accurate description of an imposing, supernatural army under the supreme command of God who serves on your behalf. "The Lord's angel builds a camp around his followers, and he protects them. Give the Lord a chance to show you how good he is. Great blessings belong to those who depend on him!" (Psalm 34:7-8 ERV).

You are not alone in this immense universe. There are more invisible allies with you, working for you and on your behalf, than those unseen evil adversaries warring against you. "For he will command his angels concerning you to guard you in all your ways" (Psalm 91:11 NIV).

Even when they are unrecognizable or we are unaware of their presence, they are all around us and with us to accomplish God's purposes. They are always available to comfort, encourage, watch over, protect, guard, aid and assist, strengthen, rescue or deliver and defend, direct, lead and guide, bring heavenly messages, communicate, proclaim and announce, escort and accompany, and celebrate the miraculous works of God.

In the Gospel of Luke, Jesus tells the parable of the woman and the lost coin: "Or suppose a woman has ten silver coins and loses one. Doesn't she light a lamp, sweep the house and search carefully until she finds it? And when she finds it, she calls her friends and neighbors together and says, 'Rejoice with me; I have found my lost coin.' In the same way, I tell you, there is rejoicing in the presence of the angels of God over one sinner who repents" (Luke 15:8-10 NIV). God expresses overwhelming joy over the salvation, and as a result, the return to right standing after a lost sinner's separation from Him. He shares that great joy with His heavenly family, the angelic host who rejoice with Him at the rebirth of one believer.

The Apostle Peter writes to the recipients of God's grace and peace received through salvation unavailable to others: ". . . You heard them from those who told you the Good News with the help of the Holy Spirit sent from heaven. Even the angels would very much like to know more about these things you were told" (1 Peter 1:12 ERV).

The prophets of old foretold the coming of a Savior born in human flesh who, by His sacrificial death, would bring man back into a right relationship with a loving Father. They wonder at God's willingness to forgive and to bless a rebellious and disobedient people.

Angels can only observe God's evolving plan for His crowning creation. They desire to understand the message of the good news of the gospel of Jesus Christ. They can never enjoy the same intimacy or fellowship with their Creator.

Not only do the angelic host ponder over the mercy and grace available only to man, but David, God's chosen king on earth, also voices his amazement at the extent of mankind's value above His creation. Why is man, who appears so weak and insignificant in comparison to the splendor of the vast universe, afforded such glory and authority?

God in His infinite wisdom created a detailed, orderly, harmonious space, but focused His attentions on one small planet, Earth, as a perfect environment especially prepared for His family. "I look at the heavens you made with your hands. I see the moon and the stars you created. And I wonder, 'Why are people so important to you? Why do you even think about them? Why do you care so much about humans? Why do you even notice them?'" (Psalm 8:3-4 ERV).

The angelic host are called "sons of God." This expression is used in several instances in the Scriptures. It expresses the relationship of angelic beings who are subject to God. They rejoice in perfect harmony and agreement with His perfect work in creation. "He has made everything beautiful in its time. He also has planted eternity in men's hearts and minds (a divinely implanted sense of a purpose working through the ages which nothing under the sun but God alone can satisfy) . . ." (Ecclesiastes 3:11 AMPC).

A perfect God perfectly created His original creation for a specific purpose. Before He created the heaven and earth or laid the foundation of the world, He had a personal plan for you. You are created for intimacy. Even before Creator God laid the foundation of the earth, He chose you to be His very own. He specifically picked you out for Himself. His eternal vision for your destiny was being unfolded and worked out before you were conceived in your mother's womb. You are forever in His thoughts, on His mind, and in His loving heart.

But first, by intelligent design and divine purpose, God planned for the welfare and care for you and for all mankind. He created a home, the earth, a dwelling place capable of sustaining life to the fullest.

From Perfection to Chaos

> *"And the earth was formless and void, and darkness was over the surface of the deep . . ." (Genesis 1:2 NASB).*

A defiant, high-ranking angel, Lucifer, later called Satan (adversary) or the devil (slanderer, accuser) attempted to and continues to obstruct and hinder God's eternal purposes. A perfect creation had become imperfect because of opposition and rebellion by a created being, an enemy of God who would suffer as a consequence of his choices and actions. The darkness covering a flooded earth indicated God's divine judgment and the removal of his presence from the scene.

"For thus says the Lord—Who created the heavens, God Himself, Who formed the earth and made it, Who established it and did not create it to be a worthless waste; He formed it to be inhabited . . ." (Isaiah 45:18 AMPC). God's original plan was to prepare and establish a home for mankind as a habitation during his natural life. Eventually, man was to receive the earth as his inheritance for eternity. "But the meek (in the end) shall inherit the earth and shall delight themselves in the abundance of peace" (Psalm 37:11 AMPC).

A good parent leaves an inheritance for his or her natural children. God desires the very best for His spiritual family, those who live by faith in Jesus Christ and who are in total and complete dependence on His loving care, mercy, and grace. "The heaven, even the heavens, are the Lord's; but the earth He has given to the children of men" (Psalm 115:16 NKJV).

"The earth is the Lord's, and everything in it, the world, and all who live in it" (Psalm 24:1 NIV). God is the creator of the earth. He brought it into being by His great supernatural power. Therefore, He is possessor and owner of everything in it and is ultimately responsible for sustaining, keeping, maintaining, and holding up all that is in His care, but He has assigned the earth to mankind.

His divine design for all that is His is for the total restoration of a world in rebellion against Him and His original purpose. His plan, arranged before His creative work, includes all nations, cities, people of every ethnic group and language, and each individual. Those who accept, believe, receive, and avail themselves of His great loving-kindness will benefit and enjoy renewal, revival, and redemption.

God, who is morally perfect in every aspect of His being, would not and could not create an unproductive, formless, chaotic, wasted, empty Earth. Rather, the earth became vain, dark, and confused as a result of the actions of one of His created beings.

Since He formed the earth to be inhabited, God's divine purpose and will eventually comes to pass, as the Bible indicates that He is a God of restoration and order. Although His divine plan would be opposed, He is a God whose will and good pleasure is the eventual achievement of a harmonious relationship between Himself, man, and all creation, and additionally for harmonious relationships between all men, and between mankind and the created world.

God prepared an earth home to be inhabited by intelligent beings with free will and the ability to make right choices: mankind, a reflection of God Himself, people who would be able to receive His essential character and nature and would be recipients of His divine love, His amazing grace, favor, and supernatural blessings. God created the heavens and the earth and all its vast resources for the benefit of the children of men. He not only supplies all your need and gives you the desires of your heart, but He is also the one ". . . who richly supplies us with all things to enjoy" (1 Timothy 6:17 NASB).

From Chaos to Re-Creation

> *"In the beginning God created the heavens and the earth . . . and the Spirit of God was hovering over the waters. And God said, 'Let there be light,' and there was light" (Genesis 1:1-3 NIV).*

All three divine members of the Godhead were involved in the re-creation of the heavens and earth. The first member of the Godhead is God, later revealed as Father. He is the head, and it is He who imagines purposes and plans. He is a person who wills and speaks unseen things (His Word) into existence.

". . . The Spirit of God was moving over the surface of the waters" (Genesis 1:2 NASB). The third member of the Godhead, God the Holy Spirit, is also involved in this creative process. He does so in a similar manner as a mother hen brings forth life as she incubates her eggs by hovering over them, brooding, and fluttering her wings to prepare and maintain conditions favorable for reproduction. God the Holy Spirit reveals and brings into manifestation the will and work of the other two Persons in the Trinity.

The Holy Spirit hovers, awaiting the spoken Word communicating God's thoughts. Immediately, as the Word and the Spirit come together to reproduce, the created power of God's Word is released. God's specific intent and purpose is made visible and comes into manifestation, evident to the physical senses. ". . . Yea, I have spoken it, I will also bring it to pass; I have purposed it, I will also do it" (Isaiah 46:11 KJV).

"And God said, 'Let there be light': and there was light" (Genesis 1:3 KJV). God sent His Word, pregnant with inherent creative power, to bring forth light and life into a dark, chaotic, lifeless, desolate situation. Immediately, the presence of God, the second member of the Godhead, the Word—later made flesh in Jesus Christ, the light of the world, the Son of God—went forth. The light was the visible presence of God Himself coming into a hopeless situation, bringing His life and love into a wasted earth.

Only God, through Christ Jesus, can fill the void and emptiness of your own life. Only God can restore your wasted years. Only He can bring order into your disorganized, unproductive, or chaotic life. Only God's presence can complete and make productive a disorderly and confused existence without purpose. Only He can come in to fill that God-shaped empty place. Only through Him can you achieve the ultimate satisfaction for that internal desire and longing of your heart and soul.

The Earth Birthed out of Water

> "And God said, 'Let the waters under the heaven be gathered together unto one place, and let the dry land appear': and it was so. And God called the dry land Earth; and the gathering together of the waters called he Seas" (Genesis 1:9-10 KJV).

The earth was birthed out of water. The dry land, the restored earth, immediately appeared out of the waters under the heavens as they were gathered together at the word of Creator God. The earth was birthed out of the water and chaotic darkness by the will of God, the word of God, and the work of the Holy Spirit.

In the divine manner of operation, God, the first Person of the

Godhead, the Headship, commanded and declared it. The Word of God, the second Person, carried out or executed the plan. The Holy Spirit, the third Person, made the plan visible or manifested it to the senses. All three cooperated in creation, just as they will cooperate on every plan for your life to restore and reconnect you back to a right relationship with God.

". . . By God's word the heavens existed and the earth was formed out of water and by water" (2 Peter 3:5 NIV). He called forth a fully formed Earth out of the water and into His marvelous light. He brought forth and birthed it to newness of life. The earth broke through, appearing into view after concealment in the depth of the water. "Before the mountains were born, or Thou didst give birth to the earth and the world, even from everlasting to everlasting, Thou art God" (Psalm 90:2 NASB).

Everything Created with Purpose

"And God said, 'Let there be light': and there was light. And God saw the light, that it was good: and God divided the light from the darkness. And God called the light Day, and the darkness he called Night . . . And God said, 'Let there be a firmament in the midst of the waters, and let it divide the waters from the waters.' And God made the firmament, and divided the waters which were under the firmament from the waters which were above the firmament: and it was so. And God called the firmament Heaven . . . And God called the dry land Earth; and the gathering together of the waters called he Seas: and God saw that it was good. And God said, 'Let the earth bring forth grass . . . the herb . . . the fruit tree . . . upon the earth': and it was so . . . And God saw that it was good . . . And God said, 'Let there be lights in the firmament of the heaven to divide the day from the night; and let them be for signs, and for seasons, and for days, and years; and let them be for lights in the firmament of the heaven to give light upon the earth': and it was so. And God made two great lights; the greater light to rule the day, and the lesser light to rule the night: he made the stars also. And God set them in the firmament of the heaven to give light upon the earth. And to rule over the day and over the night, and to divide the light from the darkness: and God saw that it was good . . . And God said, 'Let the waters bring forth abundantly the moving creature that hath life, and fowl that may fly above the earth in the open firmament of heaven. And God created great whales, and every living creature that moveth, which the waters brought forth abundantly . . . and every winged fowl . . . and God saw that it was good. And God blessed them, saying, 'Be fruitful, and multiply, and fill the waters in the seas, and let fowl multiply in the earth' . . . and it was so. And God made the beast of the earth . . . and cattle . . . and every thing that creepeth upon the earth . . . and God saw that it was good" (Genesis 1:3-25 KJV).

- CHAPTER 2 -

THE EXCITING CLIMAX OF GOD'S CREATIVE ACTIVITY

In the beginning, Genesis 1:1, the eternal God of power, majesty, and authority, all that God is, Creator God established the heavens and the earth. Genesis 1:27 shows another aspect of His nature and character: God, a Person, created another person, the first man Adam, specifically for close personal relationship and fellowship. "God said, 'Let Us (Father, Son, and Holy Spirit) make mankind in Our image, after Our likeness'" (Genesis 1:26 AMPC).

The Triune God: one God in three Persons, each separate, distinct, each one God, singular yet more than one, plural. God the Father, God the Son, God the Holy Spirit. All are divine with differing roles, and all work together harmoniously for your ultimate good. All have personality; all are eternal Spirit beings with personal Spirit bodies and souls. Therefore, all three possess minds, intellects, wills, and emotions. All are capable of making choices and have decision-making ability. "God is Spirit (a spiritual Being) and those who worship Him must worship Him in spirit and in truth (reality)" (John 4:24 AMPC).

"So God created man in His own image, in the image and likeness of God He created him; male and female He created them" (Genesis 1:27 AMPC). Man is also an eternal spirit being who temporarily inhabits a physical body necessary for life on this earth. Man has a soul and is capable of thinking, feeling, and making choices. Man was created to be a reflection of God and to be a recipient of all that is good that comes from Him. God created man to be like Himself, a reflected image of Him, a spirit being to live in a body, an earth suit, to be sheathed by a physical body suitable for existing and flourishing on the earth. Man was to resemble Him in outward form, but also as a three-part being: spirit, soul, and body.

Man, an intelligent being with the ability to make free-will choices, would be capable of responding to and returning the love awakened in him by God's boundless unconditional love. God created man to be a person like Himself, with whom he could have a relationship, close fellowship, and communion.

Man was given the responsibility as God's agent or steward to have dominion over the earth and all that is on it. "Then the Lord God took the man and put him into the garden of Eden to cultivate it and keep it" (Genesis 2:15 NASB) Man was to care for the earth, to manage it, to stand guard and watch over it, to keep all intruders from having access.

At His word, His very presence brought the light of His Glory to the earth. He placed a protective canopy or tent, the firmament, over the earth. He established two lights and all of the heavenly host to illuminate the earth and to fix and distinguish days, seasons, and years. Each was sustained and held together in its predictable course by the power of the Word of God, indicating God's unfailing guiding care and provision.

He created a supportive environment, a climate-controlled atmosphere, and an effective water supply and irrigation system. Vegetation, grass, herbs, and trees supplied food for man and animals. A great variety of inhabitants of sea, field, and sky all lived in harmony with one another. He also placed treasures to be discovered, hidden in, on, and underneath the earth's surface. Every essential detail necessary to support life was completed before any plant or animal life was placed in its natural habitat on the earth.

God climaxed his creative work when He made man in His own image and likeness. "Male and female created he them" (Genesis 5:2 KJV). He wanted a people to whom He could reveal His nature and character, those who could experience His boundless blessings and infinite goodness. Man was to be a reflection of Himself with whom He could commune and fellowship with in an intimate personal relationship. His ultimate desire was to have a family, sons and daughters on whom He could lavish His unfailing love and who would respond and return that love.

In conclusion, the Lord God gave his approval on His work and saw that "it was good." Men's earthly home was pleasant, suitable, beautiful, and filled with God's bountiful abundance.

But as for man, God's crowning achievement, when He surveyed all He had done, He pronounced it not just as good, but as "very good" (Genesis 1:31 KJV). Strong's Concordance states: "approved in the widest sense, exceedingly, wholly, especially, and utterly good."

At that time, man received his spoken words of blessing, commitment, and divine benefits. "And God blessed them and said to them, 'Be fruitful, multiply, and fill the earth, and subdue it (using all its vast resources in the service of God and man); and have dominion over the fish of the sea, the birds of the air, and over every living creature that moves upon the earth'" (Genesis 1:28 AMPC).

"So I tell you, don't worry about the things you need to live— what you will eat, drink, or wear. Life is more important than food, and the body is more important than what you put on it. Look at the birds. They don't plant, harvest, or save food in barns, but your heavenly Father feeds them. Don't you know you are worth much more than they are? . . . Don't worry and say, 'What will we eat?' or 'What will we drink?' or 'What will we wear?' That's what those people who don't know God are always thinking about. Don't worry because your Father in heaven knows that you need all these things. What you should want most is God's kingdom and doing what he wants you to do. Then he will give you all these other things you need" (Matthew 6:25-26, 31-33 ERV).

Your heavenly Father will provide for your every need. He anticipates and supplies whatever you require to live an overcoming life. He will freely, abundantly, and continually pour out His blessings on you. He is able to maintain and support you in spirit, soul, and body.

Revealed by His Love and His Goodness Toward All Mankind, the Just and the Unjust

"God is love" (1 John 4:8 and 4:16 KJV)! His essential character is love. It is who He is, not only what He does. Love is initiated by God, for all love ultimately comes from Him and flows out from Him. Love results from a conscious decision or choice, and it is not based merely on an emotional response or feeling. God's kind of love seeks only for the good and well-being of another and is the incentive for someone to move supernaturally for the benefit of those other than himself.

Love is the truth that motivates all that He does, because it is His essential nature to do so, for He is love. God's kind of love is sacrificial: the love that gives up or surrenders its most precious and desirable things for the benefit of others. God's love initiates because of the good pleasure of His will, and that love desires a similar response by the receiver. It is a love that is unconditional and not based on your actions, conduct, or manner of life. It is not dependent on who you are, where you are, what you are, or what you have or have not done.

No matter what, God loves you! This is not restricted or reserved for a precious few.

The God-Kind of Love: Divine Love

Love gives sacrificially and is concerned about the welfare of others. It motivates, provokes, arouses someone to action. It stimulates one person on behalf of someone else and provides insight to bring about a specific, desirable result for the well-being of another. "Love is patient and kind. Love is not jealous, it does not brag, and it is not proud. Love is not rude, it is not selfish, and it cannot be made angry easily. Love does not remember wrongs done against it. Love is never happy when others do wrong, but it is always happy with the truth. Love never gives up on people. It never stops trusting, never loses hope, and never quits. Love will never end. . ." (1 Corinthians 13:4-8 ERV).

"But God, who is rich in mercy, for his great love wherewith he loved us . . ." (Ephesians 2:4 KJV). God is love, and because of the motivation of unconditional love, He had already determined and purposed His redemptive plan of salvation for you. "For the Lord is good; His mercy and loving-kindness are everlasting, His faithfulness and truth endure to all generations" (Psalm 100:5 AMPC).

". . . The Lord is a kind and merciful God. He is slow to become angry. He is full of great love. He can be trusted. He shows his faithful love to thousands of people. He forgives people for the wrong things they do, but he does not forget to punish guilty people . . . (Exodus 34:6-7 ERV). Because of God's great love, He is concerned for your ultimate good. When you rely on Him to do as He has promised, you will be rewarded for your faith. But when you are in a state of unbelief, you will receive the consequences of trusting in your own ability and self-efforts.

All that God does or allows in your life is intended to bring you closer to Him so that He might prove to you His loving-kindness and faithfulness. But all mankind has the God-given ability to make choices, and those choices and the resulting behaviors have consequences, whether for good or for condemnation. Overall, it is only by the mercies of God that you who chose life are kept and will be able to endure with patience until the end, when God's family will be gathered together.

"For God so greatly loved and dearly prized the world . . ." (John 3:16 AMPC). God's unfailing love extends throughout this world's social system, a system defined by moral, political, and economic principles operating in direct opposition to His predetermined, eternal plan. God's loving, far-reaching embrace extends and is available, without exception, to all people. You who desire to respond to His gracious offer will be welcomed into His family circle. As a beloved child, you will be assured and secure in His protective care. Surrender in total dependence, relying solely on His provision for your entire well-being.

He died not only for the whole world, for mankind, but He made the ultimate sacrifice especially for you, individually and personally. He is "the Son of God, Who loved me and gave Himself for me" (Galatians 2:20 AMPC).

> *"Christ died for us when we were unable to help ourselves. We were living against God, but at just the right time Christ died for us. Very few people will die to save the life of someone else, even if it is for a good person. Someone might be willing to die for an especially good person. But Christ died for us while we were still sinners" (Romans 5:6-8 ERV).*

God's love is not based on your actions, conduct, or manner of life; therefore, while you were—or are—still a sinner, Christ died for you. You were powerless to help yourself by your own efforts. While you were far away from a relationship with God, He in His loving-kindness was concerned about your well-being. Motivated by love, He had already given His very best, His precious Son Jesus. Jesus Christ willingly and obediently gave His life specifically for you. In His love for you, He gave His all. "And before the world was made, God decided to make us his own children through Jesus Christ. This is what God wanted, and it pleased him to do it" (Ephesians 1:5-6 ERV).

Because God so greatly loved and cared for you and for mankind, before He created life, He intelligently and divinely designed and created a perfect environment as a home for His family. This earth was a perfect place to bring up children.

> *"Even as (in His love) He chose us (actually picked us out for Himself as His own) in Christ before the foundation of the world, that we should be holy (consecrated and set apart for Him) and blameless in His sight, even above reproach, before Him in love. For He foreordained us (destined us, planned in love for us) to be adopted (revealed) as His own children through Jesus Christ, in accordance with the purpose of His will (because it pleased Him and was His kind intent) . . . His glorious grace (favor and mercy), which He so freely bestowed on us in the Beloved. In Him we have redemption (deliverance and salvation) through His blood, the remission (forgiveness) of our offenses (shortcomings and trespasses), in accordance with the riches and the generosity of His gracious favor, which He lavished upon us . . . (Ephesians 1:4-8 AMPC).*

"For God so loved the world, that he gave his only begotten Son, that whosoever believeth in him should not perish, but have everlasting life" (John 3:16 KJV). Love is the motivation. He who loves much gives much. God's love is limitless, boundless, and unconditional; therefore, He gave His most precious, His best, His own Son begotten of Him. God loved the entire world system and its people. However, His plan for the restoration of His original created universe was disrupted by the rebellion and sin of His crowning achievement, the first man Adam.

The maternal heart of God yearns for all to be adopted into His family. That free choice is up to you as an individual. It is your decision to accept or reject this free gift. "Whosoever" means whatsoever person; therefore, not one person is excluded from God's desire to bring you into a loving family relationship with Him. No one is beyond the reach of His outstretched arms as He desires to draw you near to Himself. Absolutely no one is unloved, and no one is unredeemable or past redemption.

"Whosoever" means that absolutely no one is exempt from God's love and saving grace. Without exception, no matter who you are, your condition, or what you have done or left undone, all are invited personally and welcomed without reservation to become a partaker of His loving-kindness.

To believe on Jesus as Savior is to trust in and rely on His atoning death as your substitute to settle the question of sin and its consequences. Believing in His resurrection identifies you as also being raised to newness of life. To believe—that is, to come into agreement—is to trust in and adhere to God's word, resulting in a change of mind and behavior. It involves action and a commitment of complete reliance in the name of Jesus, on who He is and all that He has accomplished on your behalf. You must not only know who He is, but also know who you are in Christ Jesus.

". . . If any man be in Christ, he is a new creature: old things are passed away; behold, all things are become new" (2 Corinthians 5:17 KJV). To be saved is to be "in Christ" or "united in Christ," and the result is an intimate personal relationship with the one who you trusted to reconcile you back to God. Before His crucifixion, Jesus prayed: ". . . Father, just as You are in Me and I am in You, may they [believers] also be in Us . . ." (John 17:21 NIV).

"For God did not send the Son into the world in order to judge (to reject, to condemn, to pass sentence on) the world, but that the world might find salvation and be made safe and sound thru Him" (John 3:17 AMPC). "Salvation" means to be made sound, to be rescued from sin and its consequences. It includes deliverance, health, welfare, safety, provision, defense, and victory in all areas or aspects of life: spirit, soul, and body.

Salvation involves a one-time event of conversion: your change of belief from trusting in your own self-efforts to complete trust in the finished work of Jesus on the cross. "And this is eternal life: (it means) to know (to perceive, recognize, become acquainted with, and understand) You, the only true and real God, and (likewise) to know Him, Jesus (as the) Christ (the Anointed One, the Messiah), Whom You have sent" (John 17:3 AMPC). To know, in this instance, does not mean just having head knowledge or mental assent or agreement. It is that personal relationship that comes through loving fellowship and communication and the direct familiar experience resulting from that shared time together.

"Then the Lord God formed man out of the dust of the ground and breathed into his nostrils the breath or spirit of life, and man became a living being" (Genesis 2:7 AMPC). God has marked out man as His focal point of creation, separate and distinct from all other beings. First, He personally shaped and formed man's body with His own hands. Then He lovingly stooped down, and by a creative act, He breathed the breath of life into Adam's lifeless body, and man became a living, breathing, spirit being with a mind, will, and emotions.

God created mankind to be relational beings, people made in His image and likeness. He desired a people made like Him, capable of personal fellowship and communication with Him, human beings who would receive His unconditional love and who would love Him, and others, in return.

God created man as a three-part spirit being, with souls (minds, wills, and emotions) like Himself, but also with physical bodies capable of life on the earth, the ideal home prepared for them. You are a spirit being: you have a soul, living or encased in a physical body. It is that eternal spirit being or inner man that will continue to live forever, either in an eternal relationship with Him or separated from His presence.

New Creation

With your spirit, you touch or have contact with the eternal, unseen spiritual world. With your soul, you contact the intellectual realm. With your natural body, you touch the physical world perceived by the senses. It is only the eternal spirit man, the inner man, that eternal part, the real you, that is re-created or made new when you become saved. The inner man becomes an entirely new creation, one never before in existence.

It is that newly created inner man, perfect, righteous, and holy, who is capable of affecting and taking complete control over your spiritually unborn physical body and unrenewed soul. Surrender, submit, and commit to God, in obedience to His word of truth. That new life on the inside should be worked out by discipline and training so that it is visible, available, and evident to others.

". . . All of God lives in Christ fully, even in his life on Earth. And because you belong to Christ you are complete, having everything you need" (Colossians 2:9-10 ERV). Because you are in Christ, a child of God, His divine nature continually dwells in you as it does in Jesus. You are fulfilled and satisfied in all that is necessary as you mature in your Christian walk. The Holy Spirit lives and dwells in you when you become a child of God. Therefore, all that God is, is also in you. So, experience Him; enjoy His presence as you spend quiet, quality time communicating with Him on a personal level.

> ". . . If God is for us, no one can stand against us. And God is with us. He even let his own Son suffer for us. God gave his Son for all of us. So now with Jesus, God will surely give us all things. Who can accuse the people God has chosen? No one! God is the one who makes them right. Who can say that God's people are guilty? No one! Christ Jesus died for us, but that is not all. He was also raised from death . . . Can anything separate us from Christ's love? Can trouble or problems or persecution separate us from his love? . . . But in all these troubles we have complete victory through God, who has shown his love for us. Yes, I am sure that nothing can separate us from God's love—not death, life, angels, or ruling spirits. I am sure that nothing now, nothing in the future, no powers, nothing above us or nothing below us— nothing in the whole created world—will ever be able to separate us from the love God has shown us in Christ Jesus our Lord" (Romans 8:31-35, 37 ERV).

The completeness of His love for you, His child, covers all things, in all places; from the accusations of all beings, physical and spiritual; during all events, situations, and experiences;

and for all times, past, present, and future. His love never fails. You cannot escape from so great a love. Neither can you nor anyone else do anything to prevent Him from loving you or cause Him to love you any more or less then He does at this present moment.

The Father's Love

A parable—a story for the illustration of divine truth—found in Luke 15:11-24. A certain man had two sons; the younger one took his inheritance and left for a distant country, away from his loving father. While there, he recklessly wasted his fortune, seeking pleasure in wild, loose living and conduct with no restraint. His destructive habits and excessive spending led to ruin. After all his money was gone, he was without friends, destitute, hopeless, and perishing. In order to survive, he accepted degrading work.

He finally came to his senses. Realizing he was without hope in his present condition, he humbly repented and said, "'I will get up and go to my father, and I will say to him, "Father, I have sinned against heaven and in your sight. I am no longer worthy to be called your son; (just) make me like one of your hired servants."' So he got up and came to his (own) father. But while he was still a long way off, his father saw him and was moved with pity and tenderness (for him); and he ran and embraced him and kissed him (fervently). And the son said to him, 'Father, I have sinned against heaven and in your sight; I am no longer worthy to be called your son (I no longer deserved to be recognized as a son of yours)!'" (Luke 15:18-21 AMPC).

When the son came to his senses, he humbly made an inward decision. He had a change of mind resulting in a change of actions—to turn away from his current way of living and to seek a new relationship with his father.

His father, who was intensely, passionately longing for his lost son, waited and watched diligently for his return. For this reason, he saw him while he was still a long way away, and he ran toward him to draw him mercifully into his arms of forgiving love, kissing him warmly and repeatedly and fervently. The father received him just as he was, disgusting in his own sight, destitute, degraded, dirty, depressed, downcast, despised, and dead in his trespasses and sins. The son was accepted and forgiven, restored by his father with all rights and privileges as a son, in right standing, just as if nothing had happened.

> *"'. . . Let us revel and feast and be happy and make merry, because this my son was dead and is alive again; he was lost and is found!' And they began to revel and feast and make merry" (Luke 15:23-24 AMPC).*

Paul the Apostle writes on the love of Christ: "I pray that your life will be strong in love and be built on love. And I pray that you and God's holy people will have the power to understand the greatness of Christ's love—how wide, how long, how high, and how deep that love is" (Ephesians 2:17-18 ERV). Christ's love is greater than anyone can ever know, but I pray that you will be able to experience that love. Then, you can be filled with everything God has for you.

> *"So Jesus answered them. . . 'No one is able to come to Me unless the Father Who sent Me attracts and draws him and gives him the desire to come to Me, and (then) I will raise him up (from the dead) at the last day" (John 6:43-44 AMPC).*

God's Word draws and attracts you to Him because, at some time, you heard or are hearing the word of truth. But the Holy Spirit is continually hovering over you, patiently waiting for the Word (God's seed) to fall on a heart ready and prepared to receive the good news of the gospel of Jesus Christ, God's Son, and receive the light of God's presence into a dark place.

God, the Father, loves you so much that He gave His most precious heavenly gift, His only begotten Son Jesus Christ. Jesus Christ, the Son, loves you so much that He paid the ultimate price of a sacrificial death on the cross to bring you into a right relationship with the Father. God the Holy Spirit loves you so much that He has hovered over you and wooed you during all of your dark times of rebellion against God. At that time of your complete rejection of the truth of His word and His way of doing what is good and right, it was the Holy Spirit who convinced you of your unbelief about sin and the price Jesus paid to restore you to favor with God.

- CHAPTER 3 -

ISRAEL, GOD'S FIRSTBORN: THE BIRTH OF A NEW NATION

God reveals His pre-determined intent to bless the nations of the Earth initially through one man and one family, then down through generations and, in the course of time, through one seed, one man, Jesus. He initiated His plan by birthing a new nation, one never before in existence, through Abraham, in naturally impossible, hopeless circumstances. God formed this nation (Israel) to become His people, God's special possession.

Israel (The Nation) is My Son

> ". . . Thus saith the Lord, 'Israel is My son, even my firstborn'" (Exodus 4:22 KJV).

> ". . . For I am a father to Israel" (Jeremiah 31:9 KJV).

The nation of Israel was conceived in the heart of God. It is the firstborn nation admitted to sonship by adoption; therefore, Israel has a special relationship with God their Father. They are His chosen people, with the responsibility of being an example to the nations of the world. When they are faithful and obedient to God, they are privileged to be blessed above all other nations.

> ". . . My servant, Israel, whom I have chosen. This is what the Lord says—he who made you,

who formed you in the womb, and will help you: 'Do not be afraid' . . ." (Isaiah 44:1-2 NIV).

Abram and Sarai Called to be Father and Mother to Birth a Nation

". . . You should look at Abraham your father . . . Abraham is your father, so look at him. Look at Sarah, who gave birth to you. Abraham was alone when I called him. Then I blessed him, and he began a great family with many descendants" (Isaiah 51:1-2 ERV). The nation of Israel was the first to be admitted to sonship by adoption. God birthed a newly created nation through Abraham, the father of nations, and Sarah, his wife, the mother of nations.

Under the terms of the everlasting covenantal agreement, Abraham and his descendants were to be blessed and were also to be a blessing to all the families or nations of the Earth. They were specifically chosen or set apart by God to be an example by their obedience to God's word, so that others could witness the resulting blessings and favor freely bestowed by the only true God. Ultimately, through one seed or descendant, Jesus, all nations could experience His saving grace.

The Revelation of God the Father by Jesus, Abraham's Seed

"All things have been committed to me by my Father. No one knows the Son except the Father, and no one knows the Father except the Son and those to whom the Son chooses to reveal him" (Matthew 11:27 NIV). Jesus came to Earth to communicate the fullness of the Father. He became man so that others like Him could identify with Him as He revealed His Father who was in Heaven.

". . . Then Jesus would be the firstborn of many brothers and sisters. God planned for them to be like his Son . . ." (Romans

8:29-30 ERV). God's firstborn Son Jesus came into this earth to fully reveal the Father and to bring back to Him a people separated from Him by sin. Jesus, the expressed image of His Father, is the standard, ideal, or role model for those who came after Him and are adopted into God's family.

> ". . . God is love. Everyone who lives in love lives in God, and God lives in them. If God's love is made perfect in us, we can be without fear . . . because in this world we are like Jesus" (1 John 4:16-17 ERV).

So, like Father, like Son—and like the Son Jesus, so also should be the other children in the household of faith. "Jesus gave this answer: 'I tell you the truth, the Son can do nothing by himself; he can only do what he sees his Father doing, because whatever the Father does the Son also does. For the Father loves the Son and shows him all he does . . .'" (John 5:19-20 NIV).

"He is also head of the body, the church; and He is the beginning, the firstborn from the dead, so that He Himself will come to have first place in everything" (Colossians 1:18 NASB). The Apostle Paul in his first letter to the church at Thessalonica writes, "We believe that Jesus died, but we also believe that he rose again. So we believe that God will raise to life through Jesus any who have died and bring them together with him when he comes" (1 Thessalonians 4:14 ERV).

According to God's eternal plan, Jesus was born to die! Neither His supernatural birth nor His sinless life could redeem man back to a holy God. This could only be accomplished by His sacrificial death as a substitute for sinful man. He paid the ultimate price—death on the cross. The debt owed was paid in full. His resurrection from the dead proved His divinity, for He was not only fully man, but also fully God.

He is the first to be raised from the dead, never to experience death again. Believers will see Him as He is and will be like Him, raised up in glorified, immortal, indestructible bodies. Together, they will return to earth with Him at His second coming.

". . . Joseph and Mary . . . returned to Galilee to their own town of Nazareth . . . Then he [Jesus] went down to Nazareth with them and was obedient to them . . . And Jesus grew in wisdom and stature, and in favor with God and men" (Luke 2:39-40, 51-52 NIV). Here Jesus was taught the family trade by Joseph who was His mother's husband, although not His biological father, and who worked as a carpenter.

However, His true heavenly Father God had revealed His own predetermined plan to benefit and bless mankind through His Son Jesus Christ, who said, "Did you not know that I must be about My Father's business?" (Luke 2:49 NKJV). Because He was the Son of man on earth, He grew physically, mentally, emotionally, and spiritually as He matured while walking in obedience to the godly teaching and training of His parents.

Jesus Returns with His Family

Jesus was born to an earthly mother, Mary, and was conceived by the Holy Spirit, with God as His Father. Mary and her husband Joseph had other children after the birth of Mary's firstborn, Jesus. They continued to live in Nazareth.

During His earthly ministry, Jesus returned to His hometown where He grew up with His family. When he taught in the synagogue there, the people said, "Isn't he just the carpenter we know—Mary's son, the brother of James, Joses, Judas, and Simon? And don't his sisters still live here in town?" (Mark 6:3 ERV).

> *"While Jesus was talking to the people, his mother and brothers stood outside. They wanted to talk to him. Someone told him, 'Your mother and brothers are waiting for you outside. They want to talk to you.' Jesus answered, 'Who is my mother? Who are my brothers?' Then he pointed to his followers and said, 'See! These people are my mother and my brothers. Yes, anyone who does what my Father in heaven wants is my true brother and sister and mother"* (Matthew 12:46-50 ERV).

Only believers who are registered in the Lamb's Book of Life are the true family of Jesus. This record in heaven documents and certifies each person's rebirth into God's family. It therefore authorizes all legal rights and privileges, as well as obligations and responsibilities, as a result of becoming joint heirs with Jesus.

Jesus went about doing His Father's business. "I will build my church" (Matthew 16:18 KJV). The church is a spiritual building or house, the church of the firstborn, called-out ones with power and authority as God's representatives and legislative body on earth. Mary's husband Joseph taught Him His trade or business as a carpenter, building with natural, wooden, temporary material. He was trained in occupational job skills by the man who was accepted as His earthly father. Hard work and self-effort were necessary to achieve proficiency.

The supernatural gifts and callings from above are unlearned and unearned, but they require action and stirring up by use, in faith and motivated by love. They are to be received, never to be neglected, considered of little value, or treated with disregard. These gifts and callings are necessary so that believers will exercise their God-given gifts mutually and cooperatively to encourage, edify, comfort, and build each other up.

In this way, they are equipped to work the works of Jesus and do the heavenly Father's business.

> *"I finished the work you gave me to do . . . You gave me some people from the world. I have shown them what you are like . . . Now they know that everything I have came from you"* (John 17:4, 6-7 ERV).

Jesus came in the flesh to reveal the unseen Father to a people separated from a loving, compassionate God who greatly desired a relationship of intimacy and fellowship. As a Father who dotes on His children, He desires the very best for them. Jesus went about demonstrating the tender loving-kindness, the mercies and goodness of a just God. His authority and power over the works of the enemy were evident when He walked on this earth.

Christ the Anointed One

Anointing can be either physical or spiritual. Physical anointing is "to pour a special oil on people or things to show that they have been chosen by God and set apart for a special work or purpose" (ERV glossary, "Anoint"). Spiritual anointing is described in the book of Acts: "How God anointed Jesus of Nazareth with the Holy Spirit and power, and how he went around doing good and healing all who were under the power of the devil, because God was with him" (Acts 10:38 NIV).

". . . In Christ Jesus, God made us new people so that we would spend our lives doing the good things he had already planned for us to do" (Ephesians 2:10 ERV). Having put aside His divinity, Jesus Himself, as fully man, needed supernatural power through His Spirit to do the work He could not do by His own natural ability. So we, following His example as anointed ones on earth, must also have this same extraordinary power working in us to do the good works we were created to do. Whatever God has asked of you, He will surely equip you to do. God, the Holy Spirit working in you through Jesus Christ, enables you to do much greater works beyond your limited human capability or imagination.

Angels participated in each event in the life and ministry of Jesus, and they will continue to do so in the future. They communicated with His mother Mary and her husband Joseph prior to His birth. They proclaimed the good tidings of His birth. They were involved in and announced His resurrection after His death and burial. They were present at the time He ascended into Heaven. They will accompany Him when He returns to Earth with His family of believers. "... When God brings his firstborn into the world, he says, 'Let all God's angels worship him'" (Hebrews 1:6 NIV).

The angels jubilantly rejoiced as they announced and celebrated the birth of the Savior, Jesus, Son of God and Son of man, Immanuel, God with us. The birth announcement included the date and place of birth as well as the purpose for His coming to earth. "And there were shepherds living out in the fields nearby, keeping watch over their flocks at night. An angel of the Lord appeared to them, and the glory of the Lord shown around them, and they were terrified. But the angel said to them, 'Do not be afraid. I bring you good news that will cause great joy for all the people. Today in the town of David a Savior has been born to you; he is the Messiah, the Lord . . .' Suddenly a great company of the heavenly host appeared with the angel, praising God and saying, 'Glory to God in the highest heaven, and on earth peace to those on whom his favor rests.' When the angels had left them and gone into heaven, the shepherds said to one another, 'Let's go to Bethlehem and see this thing that has happened, which the Lord has told us about'" (Luke 2:8-15 NIV).

Angels were involved in and announced the resurrection of Jesus. In the days of Jesus' death and burial, a cave or an opening cut out of a rocky cliff typically served as a tomb or a burial site. Burial usually took place on the day of death. In preparation, after the body was washed and anointed with spices, it was wrapped in a shroud. A huge, round stone was rolled into place over the opening of the tomb.

The women went to anoint Jesus' body, as was the custom, because there had been no time or occasion to do so prior to burial. "On the first day of the week, very early in the morning, the women took the spices they had prepared and went to the tomb" (Luke 24:1 NIV). "And they asked each other, 'Who will roll the stone away from the entrance of the tomb?'" (Mark 16:3 NIV).

> *"There was a violent earthquake, for an angel of the Lord came down from heaven and, going to the tomb, rolled back the stone and sat on it. His appearance was like lightning, and his clothes were white as snow" (Matthew 28:2-3 NIV).*
>
> *"They found the stone rolled away from the tomb, but when they entered, they did not find the body of the Lord Jesus. While they were wondering about this, suddenly two men in clothes that gleamed like lightning stood beside them. In their fright the women bowed down with their faces to the ground, but the men said to them, 'Why do you look for the living among the dead? He is not here; he has risen!'" (Luke 24:2-6 NIV).*

Angels brought an encouraging message when Jesus ascended to heaven after His death, burial, and resurrection. They foretold His return again, accompanied by angelic host. ". . . He was lifted up into the sky. While they were watching, he went into a cloud, and they could not see him. They were staring into the sky where he had gone. Suddenly two men wearing white clothes were standing beside them. They said, 'Men from Galilee, why are you standing here looking into the sky? You saw Jesus carried away from you into heaven. He will come back in the same way you saw him go" (Acts 1:9-11 ERV).

When Jesus Christ comes again to Earth a second time, He will return in power and glory. "The Son of Man will come again with his Father's glory and with his angels" (Matthew 16:27 ERV). "When the Son of Man comes in his glory, and all the angels with him, he will sit on his glorious throne" (Matthew 25:31 NIV). At His first coming, He was born and destined to be a suffering servant to take the punishment you deserved. At His second coming, He will return triumphantly as a conquering King to rule and reign.

Abram, Specifically Chosen by God to be a Father

There was a man named Abram, an idol worshiper, who lived comfortably and prosperously in an ancient Middle Eastern empire. He and his wife Sarai made their home in an ungodly, pagan environment in one of the wealthiest cities in the world. In the Hebrew Scriptures, personal names expressed an individual's identifying characteristics. The name Abram means "high, exalted father," while Sarai means "my lady, my princess." At the time that the historical events unfold, they were a childless couple, without offspring or descendants.

> *"Now the Lord had said to Abram: 'Get out of your country, from your family and from your father's house, to a land that I will show you. I will make you a great nation; I will bless you and make your name great; and you shall be a blessing. I will bless those who bless you, and I will curse him who curses you; and in you all the families of the earth shall be blessed'" (Genesis 12:1-3 NKJV).*

Abram, an idolater, bowed down and worshipped lifeless, powerless images made by men's hands, yet he heard the voice of the only true living God who communicates, instructs you of His will, and leads you in the pathway to receive His very best for your life. As an idolater, Abram had neither earned nor merited God's favor; nevertheless, he was specifically singled out of all the inhabitants of the earth to fulfill God's sovereign plan for the nations, or families, of the earth.

Perhaps on one clear, starry night, he had marveled at the precise order of the movements of the planets and constellations. Who held them in their place in the heavens? Was it possible that some unseen higher power, an intellectual being, controlled and sustained the vast universe? Or had he observed the animal kingdom, male and female, as they lovingly nurtured, trained, and protected their young? Who taught them these skills? Or who formed the remarkable human body and made it live, unlike wood, clay, or stone, a lifeless image that had to be moved from place to place? Or who designed all of the parts and systems working so wonderfully together to perform the tasks of daily living? But of this truth, you can be assured that he was the sovereign choice of God, who said,

> *"For I have chosen him, so that he will direct his children and his household after him to keep the way of the Lord by doing what is right and just, so that the Lord will bring about for Abraham what he has promised him" (Genesis 18:19 NIV).*

When Abram was ninety-nine years old, God changed his name to Abraham, "father of a multitude," and the name of his wife Sarai to Sarah, "mother of nations." God established their new identities to reflect His divine purpose and destiny for them. The name changes communicate to them and to others His prophetic intent.

"By faith Abraham, when called to go to a place he would later receive as his inheritance, obeyed and went, even though he did not know where he was going" (Hebrews 11:8 NIV). In expectant faith, Abraham trusted in and acted on God's word, having confidence that God would do as He promised. Abraham, at age seventy-five, left his family, his home, his country, and his pagan life, all that was familiar, to begin his journey to an unknown destination. With each step, Abraham was directed and guided by God's providential care as He continually revealed His sovereign character.

"I will make you into a great nation" (Genesis 12:2 NIV). "For you are a people holy to the Lord your God. The Lord your God has chosen you out of all the peoples on the face of the earth to be his people, his treasured possession. The Lord did not set his affection on you and choose you because you were more numerous than other peoples, for you were the fewest of all peoples. But it was because the Lord loved you and kept the oath he swore to your ancestors . . ." (Deuteronomy 7:6-8 NIV).

Despite human faults, failures, or shortcomings, it is not impossible for God to work out all that He has decided in advance for the good of nations or families, people groups, or for you as an individual. The God who is in control of all things dedicates and sets apart those He chooses for His special service and particular purpose.

> *"It is not because of your righteousness or your integrity that you are going to take possession of their land; but on account of the wickedness of these nations, the Lord your God will drive them out before you, to accomplish what he swore to your fathers, to Abraham, Isaac and Jacob. Understand, then, that it is not because of your righteousness that the Lord your God is giving you this good land to possess, for you are a stiff-*

necked people" (Deuteronomy 9:5-6 NIV).

They were not deserving or worthy, nor did they merit or were they entitled to receive God's favor; in fact, God knew that they would become stubborn, proud, disobedient, and willful. He was aware that the nation and its people would require discipline and training, and to suffer the consequences for their actions, before they could become an example to the nations of God's unfailing love and goodness to His chosen.

The Word of the Lord came to the prophet Ezekiel with these instructions: ". . . I am sending you to the Israelites, to a rebellious nation that has rebelled against me; they and their ancestors have been in revolt against me to this very day. The people to whom I am sending you are obstinate and stubborn. Say to them, 'This is what the Sovereign Lord says.' And whether they listen or fail to listen—for they are a rebellious people—they will know that a prophet has been among them" (Ezekiel 2:3-5 NIV).

The Lord, speaking through another prophet, asks His faithless people to return to Him: "I myself said, 'How gladly would I treat you like my children and give you a pleasant land, the most beautiful inheritance of any nation.' I thought you would call me 'Father' and not turn away from following me" (Jeremiah 3:19 NIV).

God desired and expected obedience from His chosen ones. He sent His special messengers, prophets such as Isaiah, Jeremiah, and Ezekiel, to speak His inspired word about current and future events. They gave correction, edification, comfort, and encouragement to the people as they warned them of the consequences of unrepentant disobedience and rebellion. "And the Lord God of their fathers sent to them by his messengers . . . because he had compassion on his people, and on his dwelling place" (2 Chronicles 36:15 KJV).

God's motivation is always love; even when He chastises or disciplines us, it is to keep us on the right path. The people of Israel were to be an example and a witness to all other nations, who would see how God blessed and demonstrated His tender loving-kindness to those who received and obeyed Him, as well as the effects of disobedience and the rejection of the true God.

> *"But now, this is what the Lord says—he who created you, Jacob, he who formed you, Israel: 'Do not fear, for I have redeemed you; I have summoned you by name; you are mine.' . . . 'You are my witnesses,' declares the Lord, 'and my servant whom I have chosen, so that you may know and believe me and understand that I am he. Before me no god was formed, nor will there be one after me'"* (Isaiah 43:1, 10 NIV).

". . . For he is faithful that promised" (Hebrews 10:23 KJV). God is faithful to keep His word—if He spoke about it, He will do it. He made a promise to Abraham and to his seed or descendants, to Isaac his son and to Jacob his grandson, whose name He changed to Israel. God singled them out as a nation when as yet, they were but one family. He gave them a homeland when there were other highly populated nations and very powerful kingdoms already existing on the earth.

This promise was given to a childless couple when Abraham was seventy-five and Sarah was sixty-five. After that, God caused them both to wait until they were long past childbearing age, Abraham at one hundred years old and Sarah at ninety, for the promise to be fulfilled. God does the impossible: as He promised to Abraham, Sarah his wife conceived and gave birth to a son, Isaac.

> *"And by faith even Sarah, who was past childbearing age, was enabled to bear children*

> *because she considered him faithful who had made the promise. And so from this one man, and he as good as dead, came descendants . . ."* (Hebrews 11:11-12 NIV).
>
> *"Without weakening in his faith, he faced the fact that his body was as good as dead—since he was about a hundred years old—and that Sarah's womb was also dead. Yet he did not waver through unbelief regarding the promise of God, but was strengthened in his faith and gave glory to God, being fully persuaded that God had power to do what he had promised"* (Romans 4:19-21 NIV).

Later, after his son's birth, Abraham continued to walk by faith through tests and trials, believing with great anticipation and taking God at His word. He believed without wavering that his lineage would continue for generations.

The Scriptures specifically state that that Abraham's offspring or seed would be the source of blessing to all nations: "And through your offspring all nations on earth will be blessed, because you have obeyed me" (Genesis 22:18 NIV).

"Now the promises were spoken to Abraham and to his seed. He does not say 'And to seeds,' as referring to many, but rather to one, 'And to your seed,' that is, Christ" (Galatians 3:16 NASB). In Christ, God's chosen One, He focuses and concentrates on one seed, one singled-out offspring. The eventual fulfillment of the promise is accomplished through Jesus Christ descending from the line of Abraham through David the King.

> *"This is the genealogy of Jesus the Messiah the son of David, the son of Abraham: Abraham was the father of Isaac, Isaac the father of Jacob,*

*Jacob the father of Judah and his brothers . . ."
(Matthew 1:1-2 NIV).*

Judah was the fourth of the twelve sons of Jacob, the head of the tribe of Judah. The word "Jew," or "Yehudi" in Hebrew, is from the original source, Judah.

These verses give a precise and detailed account of the generations leading to Jesus from Abraham. They provide a careful and thorough lineage of the literal and physical family and national heritage of Jesus. He is a descendant of David, the founder of the kingly royal branch of the family tree. He is also a descendant of Abraham, man of faith, who was head of the nation of Israel. ". . . I have not chosen a city in any tribe of Israel . . . nor have I chosen anyone to be ruler over my people Israel. But now I have chosen Jerusalem for my Name to be there, and I have chosen David to rule my people Israel" (2 Chronicles 6:5-6 NIV).

Just as God provided a special home, the earth, for Adam and his descendants, for Israel, He provided a strategically placed location for a homeland. It was centrally located, where their godly influence could be experienced by others and affect other nations or families throughout the earth. "The Lord said to Abram . . . 'Look around from where you are, to the north and south, to the east and west. All the land that you see I will give to you and your offspring forever . . . Go, walk through the length and breadth of the land, for I am giving it to you'" (Genesis 13:14-15,17 NIV). After Abraham reached the land of promise, he stood on a high mountain with an extended view in all directions to see the land only visible before with the eyes of faith.

". . . For I am a Father to Israel . . ." (Jeremiah 31:9 AMPC). God declares that He is a Father to the nation of Israel and that, as head of a family, He has the authority and responsibility for guidance and provision for His children. He is accountable for all things needed or required for their well-being and has the responsibility to adequately supply all needs of the spirit, soul, and body. He provides direction, instruction, and training to ensure growth and maturity to achieve an expected end or future. His role and function is to support and protect those under His charge so they are secure and confident in His loving care. He diligently trains and disciplines, with love, to restore erring children back on the right path and in right relationship to Him.

A son is obligated to respect and honor his father in obedience to his way, his will, and his word. He should receive correction and discipline, knowing that his father wants only the best for him. Therefore, it is required that he have a teachable spirit in order to grow in wisdom and in favor with his father and with others.

"... Thus says the Lord, 'Israel is My son, even My firstborn'" (Exodus 4:22 AMPC). God had birthed a new nation, the first to be adopted to sonship: the nation and people of Israel, the Israelites, the Jewish people. The firstborn, biblically, enjoyed a special favored position in the family structure, a greater inheritance and duty to carry on the family legacy.

> *"So I bow in prayer before the Father. Every family in heaven and on earth gets its true name from him" (Ephesians 3:14-15 ERV).*

Before there were families on Earth, there was a family in the heavens: angelic beings called sons of God. Therefore, every fatherhood, whether existing in the unseen realm or on the physical, visible Earth, derives its name from one source: that is, from God the Father. He is an inspiration for all who follow Him; He functions by example as the ideal pattern.

In ancient Middle Eastern culture, the birth of a firstborn son was a significantly important occasion, as it often still is today.

The firstborn son, or heir, has the unique advantage of a distinctly favorable relationship with his father. He additionally enjoys a prominent status in the family. Because he will eventually assume his father's role as head of the family, his inheritance may be greater that that of other members of the family. With leadership comes the additional charge of responsibility of obedience to the Father's will.

Jesus was the only begotten Son of God, physically born on Earth to a natural mother and a heavenly Father. Born again spiritually, believers are adopted into the family of God by faith in Jesus Christ. Israel, however, was adopted, chosen out as a son from among all other nations to a distinct relationship with God. They enjoyed a unique status with privileges and favor, as well as the responsibilities and duties required to attain their God-given destiny and realize their full potential.

". . . The people of Israel. Theirs is the adoption to sonship . . ." (Romans 9:4 NIV). "I will bless those who bless you, and I will curse him who curses you" (Genesis 12:3 NKJV). Those who bless Abraham's descendants, God will reward by doing good to benefit them. Those who cause them to prosper, be successful, and enjoy happiness will receive from God the same benefits. But those who despise, scorn, or have contempt for Abraham's descendants will be subject to God's judgment and punishment and experience His indignation and wrath.

As people respond to or treat God's chosen ones, they can expect like treatment from God in return. He will deal harshly with those who are against His family, nation, or children, and will bestow His loving-kindness on those whose dealings are right toward them. God Himself will repay in justice.

> ". . . The Lord had said . . . 'In Jerusalem, which I have chosen out of all the tribes of Israel, I will put my Name forever" (2 Kings 21:7 NIV). "This is what the Sovereign Lord says: 'This is

> *Jerusalem, which I have set in the center of the nations, with countries all around her'" (Ezekiel 5:5 NIV).*

The earthly Jerusalem, the capital or chief city of Israel, is centrally and strategically located geographically in the midst of three continents: Europe to the west, Asia to the east, and Africa to the south. It was surrounded by prosperous neighboring kingdoms.

The capital city, Jerusalem, was once an enemy fortress called Mountain of Zion. It was captured by King David, Israel's greatest ruler. He built and called it, at that time, the City of David. He later renamed it Jerusalem, meaning "foundation of peace."

Many important historical events have occurred in Jerusalem. Jesus ministered there; He was crucified, died, buried, and was resurrected in that city. But none will compare to those events at His second coming, when He will dwell there and rule eternally with His family. God Himself will come to live there, and it will be established forever as the world's capital city.

"Daughter of Jerusalem . . . the city that men call 'The perfection of beauty, the joy of the whole earth'" (Lamentations 2:15 KJV). Out of God's maternal heart flows His unconditional, eternal love for all people. But to His family, He is a devoted Father who patiently and tenderly nurtures and cares for the total welfare of those who are His own. He is a source of affirmation and encouragement when appropriate, but He also provides comfort and protection in times of disappointment, weakness, or fear.

He forgives and forgets the mistakes of those who change their minds and ways in sincere repentance for disobedience and failure to conform to the Father's will. His ultimate desire is to draw all back to restored fellowship and a right relationship with Him. He takes pleasure in expressing His loving-kindness to His children. He is a doting, adoring Father who has a divine plan for each one in order for their full potential to be realized.

". . . Rejoice greatly, O daughter of Zion! Shout, O daughter of Jerusalem!" (Zechariah 9:9 NKJV). "Daughter of Jerusalem" is symbolic of the people of Israel and their relationship with a compassionate Father. They can celebrate and be glad that He can and will do even more than they can think, imagine, or dream to cause them to triumph over their enemies. Those nations with more physical strength and military force will not prevail over the power and might of God and will eventually assist in that nation's restoration and return. The divine deliverance and protection of the heavenly Father will be evident to those who rise up against her to destroy.

Spiritual Descendants of Abraham

> "... Abraham believed God, and because of this faith he was accepted as one who is right with God. So you should know that the true children of Abraham are those who have faith . . . Abraham believed . . . and because he believed, he was blessed. All people who believe are blessed the same as Abraham was . . . Because of what Jesus Christ did, the blessing God promised to Abraham was given to all people. Christ died so that by believing in him we could have the Spirit that God promised . . . You are all children of God through faith in Christ Jesus . . . You belong to Christ, so you are Abraham's descendants. You get all of God's blessings because of the promise that God made to Abraham" (Galatians 3:6-7, 9, 14, 27, 29 ERV).

- CHAPTER 4 -

GOD IS GOOD

"For the Lord is good; His mercy and loving-kindness are everlasting, His faithfulness and truth endure to all generations" (Psalm 100:5 AMPC). Because of God's great love for you, He has plans for your well-being in every area of your life. He has no desire to afflict you or cause you distress or adversity, but rather to bless you and to bring you his peace and joy now and forevermore.

It is God's goodness that draws men, personally and individually, to Himself so that they can become full beneficiaries of His promise for His own family. And the attraction of God's unconditional and everlasting love, His mercy and His goodness, is expressed perfectly in the good news of the gospel of Jesus Christ. It becomes satisfactory and gratifying to those who are separated by unbelief from a long-suffering God. The gospel accomplishes its purpose to bring you into His family.

"Everything good comes from God. Every perfect gift is from him . . ." (James 1:17 ERV).He is a personal, loving God who will meet your needs right here, right now, and in every area of your life. "The Lord is gracious and full of compassion, slow to anger and abounding in mercy and loving-kindness. The Lord is good to all, and His tender mercies are over all His works (the entirety of things created)" (Psalm 145:8-9 AMPC). There is an overflow of His goodness to all creation and especially to man. Therefore, even those who do not respond to His gracious invitation to come to Him will receive some of the benefits of His loving-kindness. But to His own, all things are possible because He works out everything for your ultimate good.

Revealed through His Names and Titles

Every person is known, identified, and addressed by different names and titles depending on relationships, times and seasons, and specific life situations. A title may be determined by position, status, role, or responsibility. What someone is called in informal, casual circles often differs from how he is addressed in formal or official gatherings. His first (given) name and last (family) name written on legal documents may not be the same ones used by personal friends and acquaintances. They may greet him by given name only or by a nickname. The nickname may be a shortened form of his name or one derived from physical appearance, attributes, characteristics, or reputation. Family members, children, spouses, grandchildren, and relatives all use differing terms of endearment reflecting affection and love.

In social situations, designated names vary from those in the workplace, corporate offices, or other professional environments. A person may also be identified by an individual number assigned officially by those in authority.

Some people, individually or collectively, are labeled in derogatory terms by others who are ignorant or indifferent to their value as those equally made in God's image and likeness. God, King of the Universe, is a personal God, One who is not distant, indifferent, remote or far away. His utmost desire is that you get to know Him in the most intimate of relationships.

Throughout the Bible, God's written Word, He is described by many different names and titles as He orchestrates the affairs of men. Each name or title reveals an aspect of His divine character, personality, and work as He unfolds His plans and purposes for all creation and for mankind, His highest creation. Each of these names expresses an aspect of His infinite and magnificent majesty. Some reveal His awesome power and might. Others, however, point toward His maternal care and concern for creation, mankind, and especially His own family.

When God called Moses to deliver the people of Israel from bondage in Egypt, Moses said, "'. . . [If] they ask me, "What is his name?" Then what shall I tell them?' God said to Moses, 'I AM WHO I AM. This is what you are to say to the Israelites: "I AM has sent me to you" . . . This is my name forever, the name you shall call me from generation to generation'" Exodus 3:13-15 NIV).

Therefore, as God introduces and identifies Himself as "I AM," you can assuredly say of Him that "HE IS" all that you need Him to be in every area of life. He introduces and pronounces His divine name to be "I AM" and "I Will Be"—I am, and I will be for you in any situation—indicating His steadfast love and faithfulness in the past, present, and future. He is dependable, reliable, and completely trustworthy to be all that He has promised to be. He is and will be all that He has proclaimed Himself to be. He is the only Eternal One, Who will fulfill and confirm His promises and binding agreements or covenants.

Revealed through His Covenants and Agreements

God is the One who is continually revealing Himself. "In the beginning God created the heavens and the earth" (Genesis 1:1 KJV). He first reveals Himself as the God of creation, God who brought into being the heavens and the earth and all that is in the universe. In Genesis 2:4, God discloses Himself as Lord God, the eternal, never-changing One who was, is, and is to come. He is the One who can be depended on to be the same yesterday, today, and forever, the One who made a solemn, binding agreement with and on behalf of those who are His.

He pledges His loving-kindness and faithfulness to be who He says He is and to do what He says He will do. In return, He expects complete submission of all you are and have, and reliance on His unearned, unmerited grace to fulfill His promised word. He is a merciful God, and in His unfailing love, He keeps His word and honors His covenants, His person-to-person agreements.

"God made a promise to Abraham. And there is no one greater than God, so he made the promise with an oath in his own name—an oath that he would do what he promised" (Hebrews 6:13 ERV). God's agreement or covenant with Abraham promised that He would be a father to the great nation whose descendants would be given a land to inhabit. God promised to bless him and to make his name great so that all the other people on earth would be blessed through Abraham and his children. This refers both to his natural or physical children and to his spiritual offspring through his one descendant or seed, Christ. Believers are in the family of God and are blessed also, as was faithful Abraham. You are heirs to God's promises when you put your complete trust in Him and His word.

> *". . . I swear by myself, declares the Lord . . ." (Genesis 22:16 NIV). ". . . Since He could swear by no one greater, He swore by Himself" (Hebrews 6:13 NASB). Because there is no one greater then God to swear by or take an oath, He swore by Himself, as He did when He made an agreement or covenant with Abraham that "Every nation on the earth will be blessed through your descendants. I will do this because you obeyed me" (Genesis 22:18 ERV).*

> *". . . I will bless you . . . And so you shall be a blessing; and I will bless those who bless you . . ." (Genesis 12:2-3 NASB).* God's blessings are gifts that cause you to prosper, benefit, and be happy and joyous. You, in turn, can become a channel to bless other people.

In this mutual pledge, God promises that whatever is His is yours when you agree to give and submit all that you are and have to Him with love, and to prove that love in unreserved obedience. You, therefore, are privileged to be the recipient of all that God has to offer: provision for salvation, wholeness, healing, deliverance, protection, security, and everything that you need for a godly life here on this earth.

God is always fully committed to do what He says He will do, to act on your behalf, and He will never go back on His word. Those who are His own have a responsibility, in return, to commit to trust and give themselves totally and completely over to Him in covenant relationship.

Expressions of God's maternal care are revealed in these covenant names and titles:

> **"Provider"**: "The Lord provides . . . he will give us what we need" (Genesis 22:14 ERV). He is the God who sees ahead and makes preparation to satisfy your every need. He graciously supplies all that is required.

> **"Peace"**: ". . . The Lord is Peace" (Judges 6:24 ERV). Peace is the Person Christ Jesus. He is the One who brings contentment, satisfaction, stability, tranquility, and completeness for your total well-being, spirit, soul, and body. There will be nothing missing or lacking in any area of your life as God brings all things together in orderly arrangement.

"Shepherd": "The Lord is my shepherd . . ." (Psalm 23:1 KJV) Just as the shepherd cares for the sheep in his charge, God is your constant companion. He watches over you to defend and protect you. He meets your every need as He leads and guides you. He keeps you from going astray and wandering heedlessly and carelessly down the wrong path. He cares for you in every challenging situation. Because they spend so much time together, the sheep know His voice and follow Him.

"There": ". . . The Lord is there" (Ezekiel 48:35 KJV). He is right here, right now, at this very moment and at any time. He is forever, permanently present and abundantly available. Wherever you are, He is there. He is currently residing in your heart and will be forever present with you when He makes His eternal habitation here on Earth.

"Healer": ". . . I, the Lord, am your healer" (Exodus 15:26 NASB). He makes you whole and sound again. He cures and restores you to health, wellness, and wholeness, physically, mentally, and emotionally.

"Banner": ". . . The Lord is my Banner" (Exodus 17:15 AMPC). In times of tests and trials, the opposing spiritual forces attempt to prevent you from reaching your God-given destiny. The name of the Lord is your banner in the time of war or conflict. You need to rally around the name of Jesus, for you know that God is forever faithful to stand with you in your battle. He is more than able to bring you through victoriously, for He has already triumphed.

"Righteousness": ". . . This is His name by which He will be called: The Lord Our Righteousness" (Jeremiah 23:6 NKJV). Righteousness is in the Person of Jesus

Christ, and it is through faith in Him that you will have right standing with God. Jesus Christ became sin with your sinfulness and paid the penalty of death that He did not owe. You, in turn, became the righteousness of God in Christ Jesus.

Self-Revelation of God Himself

There is no better way to understand the different aspects of His inherent nature than to find out what God says about Himself. He opens up Himself to view by disclosing and manifesting His character as revealed by His name and all the implications of His name to bring confident expectations for good.

God Himself announces and makes known His essential qualities and character to Moses, proclaiming His name: "The Lord, the Lord, the compassionate and gracious God, slow to anger, abounding in love and faithfulness . . . and forgiving wickedness, rebellion and sin. Yet he does not leave the guilty unpunished . . ." (Exodus 34:6-7 NIV).

He is a compassionate, tenderhearted, merciful God who is sympathetic to your personal problems and life situations. He is a God who is gracious, willing to bend down and stoop low in kindness and to grant you His favor, His unearned, unmerited, and undeserved blessings.

He is long-suffering, slow to anger, patient, and not easily irritated. He is willing to forgive and forget when you turn to Him and repent, changing your mind and your ways. He carries away and does not hold your offenses against you. He is full of loving-kindness, overflowing in goodness, kindness, and tender regard for you.

He is faithful and true. He can be relied on and trusted in any situation or need. You can be certain that He will never leave you alone and forsaken. You can depend on His eternal word to be right and sure. He will do what He promises. He is a just God. In His judgments, He administers that which is right with merited reward or allows appropriate consequences for continued and intentional disobedience. He takes no pleasure in wicked behavior.

It is in response, by faith, to God's goodness that leads unbelievers to repentance, a change of mind and manner of life. His loving offer of grace, unmerited favor, is available to all who would desire to be in right relationship to Him.

God announces His own name, expressing the nurturing attributes of His essential character. He declares a fuller definition and explanation of His merciful grace and compassionate care; He reveals His willingness to forgive and to extend His grace, unearned, undeserved favor to all who desire to come to Him and receive the benefit of a right relationship.

Revealed to You When you Seek Him with All your Heart

God desires to give you a greater revelation of Himself as a Person. God mercifully reveals Himself to anyone who seeks Him. Come to Him just as you are, no matter your current present state or past condition. When you are sincere in your effort to seek God, you will not be disappointed, for He is committed to bless you. Seek Him with all your heart. Pursue Him with a passion. Silently wait on Him, intently listening for His voice.

"In my distress I called upon the Lord and cried unto my God; He heard my voice . . . and my cry came before Him, even unto His ears" (Psalm 18:6 KJ21). God assures you that He is approachable, accessible, available, and not distant, uncaring, or unfeeling. "This message is from the Lord. 'I am God, and I am always near. I am not far away" (Jeremiah 23:23 ERV).

"The Lord is near to all those who call upon Him, to all who call upon Him in truth" (Psalm 145:18 One New Man). No one is excluded who comes to God with a genuine, heartfelt, and honest intent. ". . . In him we live, and move, and have our being . . . For we are also his offspring (Acts 17:28 KJV). The Apostle Paul, while in Athens, Greece, wrote: ". . . You worship a god that you don't know. This is the God I want to tell you about. He is the God who made the whole world and everything in it. He is the Lord of the land and the sky. He does not live in temples built by human hands. He is the one who gives people life, breath, and everything else they need. He does not need any help from them. He has everything he needs. God began by making one man, and from him he made all the different people who live everywhere in the world. He decided exactly when and where they would live. God wanted people to look for him, and perhaps in searching all around for him, they would find him. But he is not far from any of us. It is through him that we are able to live, to do what we do, and to be who we are . . . We all come from him" (Acts 17:23-28 ERV).

God rules in the affairs of men. He is in control of all historical events. Now is the time in your life to seek Him with all your heart, and you will find Him because he is as close as the mention of His name. Choose to allow Him to be in control of your personal life.

Since God desires that you seek Him and find Him, you must realize that He is much nearer to you than you can imagine. He is actively pursuing you in order that you might perhaps stop, turn toward him, and run into His loving maternal arms. "'And you will seek Me and find Me when you search for Me with your heart. And I shall reach for you,' says the Lord . . ." (Jeremiah 29:13-14 One New Man).

He is not an angry "god" who must be appeased by your own efforts, an elusive one who is distant and far away. But rather,

His Word indicates that He is available, approachable, and accessible as well as accepting to all who sincerely look to Him. He will assuredly, in return, draw you close in His divine arms of love and compassionate care.

"But without faith it is impossible to please and be satisfactory to Him. For whoever would come near to God must (necessarily) believe that God exists and that He is the rewarder of those who earnestly and diligently seek Him (out)" (Hebrews 11:6 AMPC). You cannot approach God unless you believe that He exists; however, because He is a hearing God and One who communicates, even to those who are unsure of His existence, call out to Him in sincerity, and He will surely answer you and make known His presence.

Faith

Faith is a supernatural spiritual force that pulls the promises of God from the invisible, unseen realm into the physical, visible, observable, tangible, realm of the senses. "Faith is what makes real the things we hope for. It is proof of what we cannot see . . . Faith helps us understand that God created the world by his command. This means that the things we see were made by something that cannot be seen" (Hebrews 11:1, 3 ERV). Faith or confidence gives reality—right now, at this present time—to the things we are hoping for. You are convinced of them as real facts even though they are not perceived by the senses.

"For You, O Lord, are good, and ready to forgive (our trespasses, sending them away, letting them go completely and forever); and You are abundant in mercy and loving-kindness to all those who call upon You" (Psalm 86:5 AMPC). "Come near to God and he will come near to you . . ." (James 4:8 ERV).

Recognize that you are in need of help to change your life. You are incapable of helping yourself by your own efforts or initiatives. God stoops down as a mother does when she picks up her child. He will graciously raise you up out of your present condition when you call out to Him and lift up your arms in submission to His perfect will.

Reach out to Him if you are dissatisfied with continued striving to fill a void in your existence that only God can fill. In the security of His presence, there is no longer any need for striving and struggling to achieve acceptance. He welcomes you unconditionally, for He is not a "god" to be appeased by your performance or by good works completed before He can be approached. So, lift up your arms in total surrender to be received by Him just as you are, just as a child desires to be drawn up into the security of its mother's welcoming embrace.

"Many people are suffering— crushed by the weight of their troubles. But the Lord is a refuge for them, a safe place they can run to. Lord, those who know your name come to you for protection. And when they come, you do not leave them without help" (Psalm 9:9-10 ERV).

> *"Come to Me, all you who labor and are heavy-laden and overburdened, and I will cause you to rest (I will ease and relieve and refresh your souls) . . . You will find rest (relief and ease and refreshment and recreation and blessed quiet) for your souls" (Matthew 11:28-29 AMPC).*

God's unfailing promise is for all who will reach out to draw near to Him, trusting in His word. He will gather you to Himself to comfort and cherish you as His own beloved child. He will hold you close to His heart, a place of refuge and safety. No matter your past experiences or present circumstances, your future is assured. He will accept you unconditionally, just as you are, when you totally rely on Him. He invites you into His family so that He can tenderly care for you and provide for your every need. The desire of His maternal heart is to protect and nurture you with the compassion and loving-kindness that only He can supply.

It does not matter how others perceive you or how you see yourself. You can confidently expect to enjoy all rights and privileges of a member of God's divine family, as well as the responsibilities. He will always be there to guide and encourage you in every step of your spiritual growth and development while you are securely in His care. His thoughts toward you are forever for your welfare and for your ultimate good as you mature in agreement with His word and His predetermined plan and purpose for your life.

". . . The one who comes to Me I will most certainly not cast out (I will never, no never, reject one of them who come to Me)" (John 6:37 AMPC). ". . . 'I will receive you kindly and treat you with favor, and I will be a Father to you, and you shall be My sons and daughters,' says the Lord Almighty" (2 Corinthians 6:17-18 AMPC).

He is stretching out to you right now. Reach out to Him in return to accept His offer for you to become a child of the living God. And like a mother who delights in her child, it is His good pleasure to do you good and to wonderfully bless you.

Very importantly, God is revealed as Father through Jesus, the only born or begotten Son of God. He came to earth in human flesh, conceived by the Holy Spirit. He was born of a woman and came to show the true revelation of God the Father. The Father desired a family; so, to fulfill God's eternal plan, Jesus became the first born among many others. Many other brethren or spiritual children would be adopted into the family by God as joint heirs with Jesus and legally His own beloved children.

A Divine Conception, Jesus Christ, the Son of God

"Before the world began, the Word was there. The Word was with God, and the Word was God. He was there with God in the beginning" (John 1:1-2 ERV). The Word is Christ, the Divine Expression, how God communicated to the world an understanding about Himself and what He is like. He is The Message, the demonstration of God's love for humankind.

"No one has ever seen God. The only Son is the one who has shown us what God is like. He is himself God and is very close to the Father" (John 1:18 ERV). ". . . No one fully knows and accurately understands the Son except the Father, and no one fully understands the Father except the Son and any one to whom the Son deliberately wills to make Him known" (Matthew 11:27 AMPC).

". . . He is a perfect copy of God's nature. . ." (Hebrews 1:3 ERV). Jesus, God the Son, was with God the Father from the beginning, before the creation of the universe. They enjoyed the closest of fellowship and relationship with each other.

Jesus, the only begotten, unique Son of God, declared what God is like when He came to live on Earth as a human. ". . . Who is in the bosom (in the intimate presence) of the Father, He has declared Him (He has revealed Him and brought Him out where He can be seen; He has interpreted Him and He has made Him known)" (John 1:18 AMPC).

Jesus, God the Son, is the one closest to the Father. He has shown and demonstrated what the Father is like. "So when Christ came into the world he said . . . 'You [God] have prepared a body for me . . . Then I said, "Here I am, God . . . I have come to do what you want."' . . . Jesus Christ did what God wanted him to. Because of that, we are made holy through the sacrifice of Christ's body. Christ made that sacrifice one time—enough for all time" (Hebrews 10:5, 7, 10 ERV).

"(Now) He is the exact likeness of the unseen God (the visible representation of the invisible); He is that Firstborn of all creation" (Colossians 1:15 AMPC). God the Father, in order to fulfill His pre-ordained plan and purpose to redeem man back to intimacy and fellowship with Himself, a holy God, needed a perfect human, born on earth in a physical body. God needed a baby as an agent to do His divine will. Jesus, God the Son, willingly made Himself available to leave the glories of heaven to come to earth as a child born of a natural mother.

"He was like God in every way, but he did not think that his being equal with God was something to use for his own benefit. Instead, he gave up everything, even his place with God. He accepted the role of a servant, appearing in human form. During his life as a man, he humbled himself by being fully obedient to God, even when that caused his death—death on a cross" (Philippians 2:6-8 ERV).

Jesus Christ, the Son of God, revealed God as Father to all who put their trust in Him as Savior and Lord. Therefore, when you are accepted as a child of God, you are adopted into His family by God the Holy Spirit. You are no longer alienated and standing alone, afar off in fear, trembling, separated from His tender, loving care. Gone is the old spirit of bondage and slavery to sin, rejection, guilt, shame, and condemnation. Instead, you have received the Spirit of sonship with the freedom to call God your Father by a very intimate, familiar. affectionate name as used by Jesus and also by Hebrew children: "Abba," meaning "Father."

"The Spirit that we received is not a spirit that makes us slaves again and causes us to fear. The Spirit that we have makes us God's chosen children. And with that Spirit we cry out, 'Abba, Father.' And the Spirit himself speaks to our spirits and makes us sure that we are God's children. If we are God's children, we will get the blessings God has for his people. He will give us all that he has given Christ . . ." (Romans 8:15-17 ERV).

Not only are you His legitimate heir as Jesus is, but you are also loved by God the Father, just the same and just as passionately as He loves His only unique Son Jesus.

Just before His arrest to be tried and crucified, Jesus, His mission completed on this earth, prayed to His Father for Himself and for His followers. "Neither for these alone do I pray . . . but also for all those who will ever come to believe in (trust in, cling to, rely on) Me through their word and teaching. That they all may be one, (just) as You, Father, are in Me and I in You, that they also may be one in Us, so that the world may believe and be convinced that You have sent Me . . . I have made Your name known to them and revealed Your character and Your very Self, and I will continue to make (You) known, that the love which You bestowed on Me may be in them (felt in their hearts) and that I (Myself) may be in them" (John 17:20-21, 26 AMPC).

- Chapter 5 -

The Miracle of Physical Conception Revealed from Conception to Delivery

To produce new human physical life, the sperm or seed of the male must be alive, active, and powerful in order to initiate the process of conception. It takes the union of the male sperm and the female egg to result in this new life when the male's living and active sperm penetrates the female egg cell. If the sperm is successfully implanted into the fertile egg of the female, conception, or pregnancy, occurs.

The implanting of the sperm can be compared to the process of sowing or planting seed in the fertile ground of the natural earth. Both seed and egg must contain the inherent, God-given, creative power and capability for breeding and reproduction. The female is then considered to be "with child."

The Bible often refers to the offspring or descendants in a family as "the seed." "And God said unto Abraham, 'Thou shalt keep my covenant therefore, thou, and thy seed after thee in their generations'" (Genesis 17:9 KJV). When no seed is planted, there will be no reproduction or harvest, no resulting benefit or compensation. God is the source of all life, and His natural laws go into effect no matter the circumstances of the union.

". . . Children are a heritage from the Lord, the fruit of the womb a reward" (Psalm 127:3 AMPC). All life is precious in

God's sight. There are no mistakes, no unplanned, unwelcome, or illegitimate children from His point of view. Natural children are a gift of God and are produced when His universal physical laws of reproduction are set in motion. He directed your formation and surrounded you with His loving compassion while you were yet in your mother's womb. You are, therefore, not merely the result of a physical union between your natural parents.

> *". . . You put me together in my mother's womb. I praise you because you made me in such a wonderful way. I know how amazing that was! You could see my bones grow as my body took shape, hidden in my mother's womb. You could see my body grow each passing day. You listed all my parts, and not one of them was missing"* (Psalm 139:13-16 ERV).

No miracle of a child's natural birth is an error in God's eyes. Whatever the circumstances or conditions of your birth, they will not result in your being unloved, unwanted, or undesired in His sight. There is nothing about you that God does not know. He has the utmost concern and care for your well-being because He Himself put you together in your mother's womb and brought you forth to deliver you so that you could begin a new life.

God's wonder-working miracle power is awe-inspiring. "You have beset me and shut me in—behind and before, and You have laid Your hand upon me" (Psalm 139:5 AMPC). God has touched you tenderly. He has completely enclosed you with His loving kindness and surrounded you protectively with His divine compassion.

You are of great value to God. Even before you were born, He had already planned for your destiny to do good things for you, to you, and through you. He knows your potential and capability because He is your source. He knows you better than you know yourself because you were designed by Him. God's great grace is demonstrated by His ability and desire to be personally involved in all phases of your life.

No Unexpected Physical Births

With God there are no mistakes, accidents, or unexpected pregnancies, for according to His natural laws of reproduction, specific physical actions produce probable or likely results. Therefore, there are no surprise children in God's eyes. All are divinely appointed.

After your conception, God put together your inner parts as He shaped you in your mother's womb. He is intimately acquainted with all that you are. While you were yet unformed, He fashioned your physical organs. He continued weaving them together while you were not yet fully developed until the time when your body was capable of living independently outside the womb.

"I will confess and praise You for You are fearful and wonderful and for the awful wonder of my birth! Wonderful are Your works . . ." (Psalm 139:14 AMPC). His works, as He put you together in your mother's womb, are awe-inspiring and wonderfully impressive, as are all His creative designs.

After that, God Himself also supervised and directed your physical birth into your natural family. The All-Knowing, All Powerful, Everywhere Present God knows your every thought, word, and deed. He lovingly expressed His thoughtful care and concern for you in every phase of your conception, development, and delivery.

". . . The Lord God formed the man from the dust of the ground and breathed into his nostrils the breath of life, and the man became a living being" (Genesis 2:7 NIV). Therefore, man became a three-part spirit being like God, who is Spirit. The man, however, lives in a physical body, an earth suit, suitable for life on the wonderful habitation prepared for him. Like God, he has a mind, will, and emotions. He is capable of receiving and returning God's love because he was especially created for relationship and intimacy.

God Reproduces Himself Physically

"So God created man in his own image, in the image of God He created him . . ." (Genesis 1:27 NIV). God's crowning creative work was the reproduction of Himself in human form. To man, He delegated dominion and authority over the earth especially prepared for him. He created a thinking, speaking being with feelings, passions, and emotions: someone like Himself for a personal relationship as they fellowship and have close communion together in love, unity, and agreement.

"And God blessed them and said to them, 'Be fruitful, multiply, and fill the earth, and subdue it (using all its vast resources in the service of God and man); and have dominion over the fish of the sea, the birds of the air, and over every living creature that moves upon the earth" (Genesis 1:28 AMPC).

To Adam, the first man, God delegated authority as His representative on earth, and with that authority came responsibility: guard, keep the garden, replenish and multiply, be productive, preserve and bring forth God's purposes and plans for the earth and its inhabitants. Use the vast God-given resources on the earth for the glory of God and for the service of man. In giving mankind dominion and authority over the created earth, God imparted to man the divine creative power of words, as He had demonstrated effectively through His own words. The earth's dwellers, therefore, are to order their own world or sphere of influence by speaking or decreeing God's creative word over and into every situation.

After God created male and female, "God blessed them and said to them, 'Have many children. Fill the earth . . .'" (Genesis 1:28 ERV). "God began by making one man, and from him he made all the different people who live everywhere in the world" (Acts 17:26 ERV).

The Miracle of Physical Birth

The Father heart of God conceived and decreed that by physical and natural reproduction, the whole earth was to be replenished and populated with eternal generations of the descendants of Adam, the first man. These children of future generations would be empowered to fulfill and accomplish God's plan and purpose for His created universe. They would also, as a result, inherit His wonderful promises throughout eternity.

God, whose internal character is good, when He restored the earth, declared everything and everyone good or very good. Man, therefore, as a reflection of God, would also desire a loving, intimate relationship with another person like himself. God always executes and sets in motion a plan to bring all things and all people back into harmony and agreement with His divine nature.

"The Lord God said, 'It is not good for the man to be alone. I will make a helper suitable for him'" (Genesis 2:18 NIV). So the Lord God made or skillfully formed "woman," taken from one of Adam's ribs, and brought her to him. Man could not reproduce, be fruitful, or multiply alone, without a suitable partner, a counterpoint, a helper compatible, a good fit in all areas: physically, emotionally, mentally, and spiritually.

Because woman was taken out of physical man, the two were to come together and live as one, in a harmonious union with one another. "For this cause a man shall leave his father and his mother, and shall cleave to his wife; and they shall become one flesh" (Genesis 2:24 NASB). The human family unit and the covenant of marriage between a man and a woman were ordained and established by God Himself.

". . . And did not God make (you and your wife) one (flesh)? . . . And why (did God make you two) one? Because He sought a godly offspring (from your union) . . ." (Malachi 2:15 AMPC). Adam was to reproduce children in his likeness and after his image, as he had been created in the likeness of God. All in the human family have descended physically from the same original parents. God gave Adam and Eve the power to reproduce after their kind. God sought godly children through Adam because He desired a family.

God's Laws of Reproduction

> *"As you know not what is the way of the wind, or how the spirit comes to the bones in the womb of a pregnant woman, even so you know not the work of God, Who does all" (Ecclesiastes 11:5 AMPC).*

"And the Lord God formed man of the dust of the ground, and breathed into his nostrils the breath of life; and man became a living soul" (Genesis 2:7 KJV). God had formed and molded Adam out of the earth, but He created his inner man, his eternal being, by the breath of His mouth. For Adam's natural descendants, during the early development period in the womb, the eternal spirit comes into the body of the child by the supernatural miracle work of God, the Father of spirits.

For the born-again believers, the children of God, that physical body will return to the earth, while the eternal spirit will return to God, the heavenly Father who made it. The various processes of physical birth often mirror a corresponding reality of spiritual rebirth and the born-again experience.

Born into a Family: Natural Bloodline and Direct Descent

God created man in His own image, as we know from Genesis 1:27. "Then the Lord God said, 'I see that it is not good for the man to be alone. I will make the companion he needs, one just right for him'" (Genesis 2:18 ERV). "Adam named his wife Eve. He gave her this name because Eve would be the mother of everyone who ever lived" (Genesis 3:20 ERV).

Eve means "life-giver," and the resulting history of Adam's family is listed in Genesis 5. Here, the book of the generations of Adam is traced up to Noah and his three sons. "This is the history of Adam's family. When God created people, he made them like himself. He created them male and female . . ." (Genesis 5:1-2 ERV).

When Adam had sons and family, he fathered them also in his image and likeness. Children were born to Adam and Eve by God's eternal law of natural reproduction. Since God is the ultimate life-giver, children are a gift from God; therefore, Eve became the first physical life-giver.

". . . For it is He Himself Who gives life and breath and all things to all (people)" (Acts 17:25 AMPC). God is the source of all life, the first cause of everything. All mankind, therefore, is a result of God's creative purpose. Every human springs from Him as physical descendants of Adam, the first man. All men originally are from one family with one common natural ancestor.

The Family History of Adam

> *"This is the written account of Adam's line. When God created man, he made him in the likeness of God. He created them male and female and blessed them. And when they were created, he called them 'man.' When Adam had*

> *lived 130 years, he had a son in his own likeness, in his own image; and he named him Seth . . . and had other sons and daughters"* (Genesis 5:1-4 NIV).

The history of Adam's family is listed in Genesis 5, tracing his lineage forward to Noah and his sons, Shem, Ham, and Japheth. All people on earth are natural descendants of Noah's three sons, whose families, generations, and nations are listed in Genesis 10:1-3. "These three were the sons of Noah, and from these the whole earth was populated" (Genesis 9:19 NASB). "These are the families of the sons of Noah, according to their genealogies, by their nations; and out of these the nations were separated on the earth . . ." (Genesis 10:32 NASB).

God's Word, the Scriptures, notes the importance of family histories. It documents detailed accounts of natural bloodlines, offspring, and descendants. He has determined, in advance, specific time periods and the exact places and geographical boundaries of habitation for every nation and people.

God, the Creator of heaven and earth, rules over the affairs of men, the nations, and historical events. He determines times, places, and circumstances affecting the people of the earth. Yet His ultimate aim is that they reach out to Him to receive the love that He so freely offers to all. ". . . For we are also His offspring. Since then we are God's offspring, we ought not to suppose that Deity (the Godhead) is like gold or silver or stone, (of the nature of) a representation by human art and imagination, or anything constructed or invented" (Acts 17:28-29 AMPC).

Adam's Rebellion and God's Response

When Adam and Eve rebelled by disobeying God's specific instructions, they attempted to make things right by their own performance and efforts. They lost their child-like trusting innocence and dependence on God, who had made them and blessed them. They made a conscious choice to live independently of God's divine plan and purpose. The consequence of sin and unbelief was separation from a holy God. They lost the personal communication and intimate fellowship they once enjoyed with a personal God.

After Adam's sin, God graciously revealed His redemptive plan to reconcile men in right relationship back to Himself. "'For I know the thoughts and plans that I have for you,' says the Lord, 'thoughts and plans for welfare and peace and not for evil, to give you hope in your final outcome'" (Jeremiah 29:11 AMPC). You were always in His heart of love and in His divine thoughts. It pleased Him to prepare a plan for your welfare, to bless you even before He created the heavens and the earth.

"Then the man and his wife heard the sound of the Lord God as he was walking in the garden in the cool of the day . . ." (Genesis 3:8 NIV). Adam was created for intimacy and a loving personal relationship with the God who came down to walk and talk with him in close communion and fellowship. After Adam and Eve disobeyed God's word, they no longer were sinless and innocent. They immediately felt the sense of guilt and shame resulting from their failure to obey. So instead of running to God in joyful anticipation of face-to-face sharing together, they ". . . hid themselves from the presence of the Lord God amongst the trees of the garden" (Genesis 3:8 KJV).

When man has sinned and feels he is not acceptable or pleasing to God, his natural tendency is to run from God. But because the Lord is long-suffering and slow to anger, and His mercy is everlasting, He will reach out to draw you to Him. When He calls out to Adam, "Where are you?" He is not asking about Adam's physical location but the state of his spiritual relationship with God.

"As for me, all I need is to be close to God. I have made the Lord God my place of safety . . ." (Psalm 73:28 ERV). Despite having to suffer the consequences of disobedience, Adam and his descendants, all mankind, are offered by God a plan and provision for redemption and restoration back to favor with Him. God's divine purpose is to bring or restore to completion whatever is missing, needed, or lacking in all areas of existence.

In Genesis, an empty, dark, lifeless, void earth was restored and supplied with all that was needed to nourish, sustain, and support life for mankind. The first man, Adam, as a male, was incapable of filling again the earth with people on his own, so God provided a female to supply and fill that void in Adam's life. Eve was a suitable mate, compatible with Adam and able to complement or complete a harmonious arrangement and relationship.

After the birth of children, Adam, in his paternal role as the father, was to fulfill his designated duties of bringing order, structure, and discipline to the family. Eve, in the mother's maternal role, was responsible for nurturing, nourishing, supporting, and sustaining family life.

God fills the empty places, those unfilled or unfulfilled spaces which are unproductive according to His eternal plan. From the formless, empty earth and the empty place in Adam's existence to a God-shaped void in your own life, God has a plan for restoration. He is more than able to lovingly supply what is needed in any area, whether spiritually, physically, emotionally, or relationally.

> *"A father of the fatherless and a judge and protector of the widows . . . God places the solitary in families and gives the desolate a home in which to dwell . . ." (Psalm 68:5-6 AMPC).*

God provides places of rest for those who are forsaken or deserted. He invites and welcomes into His own spiritual family those who are lonely or solitary and all who put their trust in Him. When you are accepted into God the Father's loving family, you join with many others, the multitudes of brothers and sisters worldwide, and the firstborn Jesus Christ, your older brother.

Rebirth and Adoption into God's Family, Your Heritage and Spiritual Bloodline

Since Eve is the mother of all who live or have ever lived, you can follow your own physical lineage back to Adam and Eve, as does Jesus, Son of Man. When you accept Jesus as your Savior and Lord, you can also trace your spiritual lineage back to Abraham, as Jesus did, as a son by promise.

". . . That the promise by faith of Jesus Christ might be given to them that believe" (Galatians 3:22 KJV). To Abraham, a great man of faith, God said, "And I will make you a great nation, and I will bless you, and make your name great; and so you shall be a blessing . . . And in you all the families of the earth shall be blessed" (Genesis 12:2-3 NASB). ". . . For I will make you the father of a multitude of nations. I will make you exceedingly fruitful, and I will make nations of you . . ." (Genesis 17:5-6 NASB).

Those who are Christians, spiritual children of God, are also directly descended from Abraham and are blessed as he is. ". . . You are all children of God through faith in Jesus Christ" (Galatians 3:26 ERV). "And if you belong to Christ, then you are Abraham's offspring, heirs according to promise" (Galatians 3:29 NASB).

Revealed Through Spiritual Rebirth

"As you know not what is in the way of the wind, or how the spirit comes to the bones in the womb of a pregnant woman, even so you know not the work of God, Who does all" (Ecclesiastes 11:5 AMPC). God is an all-knowing, supernatural God. He allows you to understand some things now through the revealed Word of God, the Bible. By this, you are able to know His will for your life.

Jesus explains: "The wind blows (breathes) where it wills; and though you hear its sound, yet you neither know where it comes from nor where it is going. So it is with everyone who is born of the Spirit" (John 3:8 AMPC). The natural man cannot discern the mystery of the intimate union resulting in the physical or spiritual rebirth. He hears only the sound of the wind, but the born-again man hears the voice of the Spirit.

"The secret things belong to the Lord our God, but the things revealed belong to us and to our children forever . . ." (Deuteronomy 29:29 NIV). You can trust that God will allow you to hear and to know all that is necessary for you to be an overcomer and to triumph in this life as God's beloved child.

The Plan of Salvation was Conceived in the Heart of God

The perfect plan for your restoration and redemption was conceived in the heart of a loving God. ". . . All things work together and are (fitting into a plan) for good to and for those who love God and are called according to (His) design and purpose" (Romans 8:28 AMPC). Before He laid the foundation of the earth, God foreknew—He knew in advance—determined, and planned the restoration of mankind back to Himself through the shed blood, death, and resurrection of Jesus, God the Son. This was determined when Jesus, the Word, the second member of the Godhead, existed in His pre-human form, before He took on human flesh.

Even before the first man Adam's rebellion and separation from a holy God, God had predetermined that Jesus would receive the judgment and penalty due to sinful mankind. ". . . But (you were purchased) with the precious blood of Christ (the Messiah), like that of a (sacrificial) lamb . . . It is true that He was chosen and foreordained (destined and foreknown for it) before the foundation of the world . . ." (1 Peter 1:19-20 AMPC).

Although all mankind are offspring of God as descendants from the first man Adam, God has already called you, individually, to have an especially intimate, personal, eternal relationship with Him as your Father. He desires that you experience a spiritual rebirth, to be fathered from above, to be born again with a new identity, the Spirit and nature of God Himself. You, by faith, can become a child of the living God, a new legal heir, adopted into His family with all rights, privileges, provisions, and responsibilities.

No Unplanned New Births

> *"We know that in everything God works for the good of those who love him. These are the people God chose, because that was his plan. God knew them before he made the world. And he decided that they would be like His Son. Then Jesus would be the firstborn of many brothers and sisters. God planned for them to be like his Son. He chose them and made them right with him. And after he made them right, he gave them his glory" (Romans 8:28-30 ERV).*

God, who is all-knowing, left nothing to chance when He planned in advance for your eternal good. He has determined before, conceived, and brought forth His divine purpose when He chose you to be His own. To accomplish His will, God has called you, personally and individually, for a specific purpose.

Your response and acceptance to that invitation will result in your adoption into His family. You will be received and accepted in right standing with the Father. You will be welcomed into the household of faith without bringing with you any guilt, shame, or condemnation from the past. His love is unconditional, and He lavishes everlasting love on you.

God also gives you His divine permission to love yourself, despite your concerns about your past history or your current condition. See yourself as He sees you and your glorious future in Christ, beginning at the moment of new birth and throughout eternity.

"And before the world was made, God decided to make us his own children through Jesus Christ. This is what God wanted, and it pleased him to do it" (Ephesians 1:5 ERV). So God in His infinite wisdom covered you in your mother's womb as you were formed. He was overseer at your physical birth. He also preplanned the divine conception and birth of His Son Jesus, the Savior of the world. And, ultimately, He conceived the plan for your spiritual rebirth into His family.

Conception of God's Plans and Purposes for You

> *"'For I know the thoughts and plans that I have for you,' says the Lord, 'thoughts and plans for your welfare and peace and not for evil, to give you hope in your final outcome'" (Jeremiah 29:11 AMPC).*

> *"How precious and weighty also are Your thoughts to me, O God! How vast is the sum of them!" (Psalm 139:17 AMPC).*

His thoughts were and are and always will be towards you. He thinks about you individually and personally. He is continually, earnestly desiring that you reach out to Him to accept His gracious offer for your ultimate eternal good.

"Many, O Lord my God, are the wonderful works which You have done, and Your thoughts towards us; no one can compare with You! If I should declare and speak of them, they are too many to be numbered" (Psalm 40:5 AMPC). His plan for your life was conceived before He laid the foundation of the world. His desire is to work out all things until your preplanned destiny is fulfilled. "God wants everyone to be saved and to fully understand the truth" (1 Timothy 2:4 ERV).

In the view of the Almighty, All-Knowing God, these future events have already been predetermined and assured. He leaves nothing to chance to fulfill His intents and purposes. "For He foreordained us (destined us, planned in love for us) to be adopted (revealed) as His own children through Jesus Christ, in accordance with the purpose of His will (because it pleased Him and was His kind intent)" (Ephesians 1:5 AMPC). ". . . When the set time had fully come, God sent his Son, born of a woman . . . that we might receive adoption to sonship" (Galatians 4:4-5 NIV).

His perfect plan will be accomplished in the fullness of time, at the appropriate time. At the decisive exact moment, God brings to a climactic end each phase, season, or era necessary for His Sovereign purpose to be finalized.

The divine plan is conceived in God's maternal heart. It is tenderly incubated in the thoughts and womb of His mind. He orchestrates, shifts, orders, arranges, and aligns opportunities, encounters, events, circumstances, people, places, and things. Then, according to His timing, His spoken words, pregnant with creative power and life, bring forth and birth His program for the ages.

"Christ had no sin, but God made him become sin so that in Christ we could be right with God . . . Don't let the grace that you received from God be for nothing. God says, 'I heard you at the right time, and I gave you help on the day of salvation.' I tell you that the 'right time' is now. The 'day of salvation' is now" (2 Corinthians 5:21; 6:1-2 ERV).

Christ Jesus has completed the work He came to Earth to do. When in His suffering on the cross, He cried out, "It is finished," reconciliation back to God was made available to mankind. So, from that past event until the future occasion of His second coming as a conquering King, you are in the opportune or appropriate time to accept the free, gracious gift of salvation. God's loving arms are open wide to accept you unconditionally into His family. Therefore, today, now, this very moment, is the right time for you to ask Jesus Christ to come and rule and reign in your heart.

"God's goal was to finish his plan when the right time came. He planned that all things in heaven and on earth be joined together with Christ as the head" (Ephesians 1:10 ERV). Heaven and earth will be gathered together and united again in peace when He comes again to earth. God will restore all things in harmonious relationships when the old ways are gone and a new order is instituted.

In eternity past and before time began, God designed a plan and set it in motion. He finished His work to bring you into His family and back to a restoration of intimate fellowship with Him. The choice is yours. Accept or reject His generous offer.

Spiritual Rebirth: Birth From Above

Jesus explained to Nicodemus, an important religious leader: "'I assure you, everyone must be born again. Anyone who is not born again cannot be in God's kingdom.' Nicodemus said, 'How can a man who is already old be born again? Can he go back into his mother's womb and be born a second time?'

Jesus answered, 'Believe me when I say that everyone must be born from water and the Spirit. Anyone who is not born from water and the Spirit cannot enter God's kingdom. The only life people get from their human parents is physical. But the new life that the Spirit gives a person is spiritual" (John 3:3-6 ERV). Water, in this instance, is used to indicate the good news of the gospel, the Word of God. You are born from above, born again by the Word of God and the Spirit of God.

". . . The seed is the word of God . . ." (Luke 8:11 KJV). The Word of God is the seed which produces new spiritual life, rebirth from above. "For the Word that God speaks is alive and full of power (making it active, operative, energizing, and effective) . . ." (Hebrews 4:12 AMPC).

God, Holy Spirit implanted the seed of God's Word, the good news of Jesus Christ, within willing, fertile hearts, making possible the miracle of spiritual conception to produce bornagain believers. The seed was from heaven above. ". . . As for that (seed) in the good soil, these are (the people) who, hearing the Word, hold it fast . . ." (Luke 8:15 AMPC).

"You have been regenerated (born again), not from a mortal origin (seed, sperm), but from one that is immortal by the ever living and lasting Word of God" (1 Peter 1:23 AMPC). It is the ultimate oneness and union of the Word of God and God the Holy Spirit that results in the miracle of life.

God's Word, His seed, is implanted into receptive hearts to create and produce new spiritual life. It is able to penetrate and pierce deeply into the place of the joining of the soul and the eternal spirit. "God's word is alive and working. It is sharper than the sharpest sword and cuts all the way into us. It cuts deep to the place where the soul and spirit are joined . . . It judges the thoughts and feelings in our hearts" (Hebrews 4:12 ERV).

- CHAPTER 6 -

SPIRITUAL CONCEPTION

This is what God's Word, the Bible, says about being made right, in right standing with God. "This is what the Scripture says: 'God's teaching is near you; it is in your mouth and in your heart.' It is the teaching of faith . . . If you openly say, 'Jesus is Lord' and believe in your heart that God raised him from death, you will be saved . . . and so we are made right with God. And we openly say that we believe in him, and so we are saved" (Romans 10:8-10 ERV).

You are in need of the Deliverer and Savior. Acknowledge and openly say, "Jesus is Lord," which means you submit to the Lordship of Jesus; you make Him a master and ruler of your life, the one you place in charge, actively trusting in Him as your Savior, the one who saves. You will be welcomed joyfully into God's family, receiving all its benefits and blessings.

". . . This is what the Lord God says . . . 'I will also put a new spirit in you to change your way of thinking. I will take out the heart of stone from your body and give you a tender, human heart. I will put my Spirit inside you and change you . . .'" (Ezekiel 36:21, 26-27 ERV). Your heart is the core or innermost part of your life or entire being. It is the center of everything you are: your feelings, your will, and your understanding. When you give your heart, or all that you are, to God, He gives you a new heart, His heart of love. Then, you will be able to respond to that lavish love and express your

The Loving Heart of Father God

love to Him and to others.

The Word of God reveals to all His unchanging heart of loving-kindness and compassion. He diligently watches over you, His attention is fixed, His mind is certain. All the while, He yearns for your heart's desire to be at one with His for eternity. There is absolutely no person, not one unbeliever, who is out of the reach of God's expansive, loving heart. He desires to draw you close to Him. All believers, who are children of the living God, are assured by the dependability and faithfulness of His steadfast mercy and grace.

"Behold, the Lord's eye is upon those who fear Him (who revere and worship Him with awe), who wait for Him and hope in His mercy and loving-kindness . . . Our inner selves wait (earnestly) for the Lord; He is our Help and our Shield. For in Him does our heart rejoice, because we have trusted (relied on and been confident) in His holy name. Let Your mercy and loving-kindness, O Lord, be upon us . . ." (Psalm 33:18, 20-22 AMPC).

When your hearts beat as one, you will trust in Him to give you all that He has promised you. In return, in humble submission, you will do only what pleases Him to bring joy to His maternal heart.

"Or are you (so blind as to) trifle with and presume upon and despise and underestimate the wealth of His kindness and forbearance and long-suffering patience? Are you unmindful or actually ignorant (of the fact) that God's kindness is intended to lead you to repent (to change your mind and inner man to accept God's will)?" (Romans 2:4 AMPC). Do not make the yearning of God's heart, revealed through His unchanging Word, to be of little value or importance. Do not continue in unbelief and refuse to respond to God's gracious offer of the free gift of eternal fellowship and communion with Him as your Father.

The time is now; this is the right time for celebration. Everyone is redeemable for "whosoever will" let Him come (Revelation 22:17 KJV). Get your heart in tune with God's heart. Believe the truth of God's Word in your own heart, then speak out confidently and boldly what is in your heart. ". . . What people say with their mouths comes from what fills their hearts . . ." (Luke 6:45 ERV).

Since God is not subject to time in the human sense, some might not understand His long and enduring patience towards unbelievers. It is not His will or heart's desire to be eternally separated from anyone. His eternal plan is for everyone to be saved and joined together with Him in a loving family relationship.

All mankind, beginning with Adam, was created in God's image with the ability to make choices by an act of his own will. God waits with extraordinary patience and with a loving expectation for your response to the good news, the gospel of Jesus Christ. ". . . To the Lord a day is like a thousand years, and a thousand years is like a day. The Lord is not being slow in doing what he promised—the way some people understand slowness. But God is being patient with you. He doesn't want anyone to be lost . . ." (2 Peter 3:8-9 ERV).

". . . Receive and welcome the Word which implanted and rooted (in your hearts) contains the power to save your souls" (James 1:21 AMPC). When you accept the truth of God's Word planted deeply in you, it will germinate, grow, and develop. It will spring up and produce eternal life.

The Specific Work of God the Holy Spirit in the New Birth

God the Holy Spirit proves beyond doubt that unbelief or lack of trust in Jesus as Savior will result in eternal separation from a loving God. He exposes ignorance, rejection, and rebellion against the Word of truth that leads to a personal relationship with the only true God.

God the Holy Spirit is sent by both God the Father and God the Son in order that you might make the right choice to become a beloved child of God. All members of the Godhead, the Divine Trinity, actively initiate and are involved in every aspect of your life, even when you are without faith and your thoughts are far from the things of God.

The Holy Spirit broods or hovers over an unbeliever while He awaits God the Father's life-giving Word, preparing to penetrate willing hearts made ready to receive the good news of the gospel. Just as a mother hen broods and flutters over her nest when she awaits the hatching of eggs and the birth of her young, the Holy Spirit broods over nonbelievers, awaiting and anticipating the rebirth of those outside the household of faith. And as an eagle protectively sweeps down and flies over her nest to cover and guard her brood, so the Holy Spirit zealously pursues unbelievers to draw them to the truth of God's Word.

"And it was of His own (free) will that He gave us birth (as sons) by (His) Word of Truth . . ." (James 1:18 AMPC). A natural new birth is produced from mortal seed or natural sperm that dies or perishes, but a born-again believer is produced from God's spiritual seed or immortal divine sperm. The ever-living ". . . word of our God stands forever" (Isaiah 40:8 NIV). "For you have been born again, not of perishable seed, but of imperishable, through the living and enduring word of God" (1 Peter 1:23 NIV).

> *"Yes, the Scriptures say, 'Anyone who trusts in him will never be disappointed.' It says this because there is no difference . . . The same Lord is the Lord of all people. And he richly blesses everyone who looks to him for help. Yes, everyone who trusts in the Lord will be saved" (Romans 10:11-13 ERV).*

Expecting Expectancy: Confident Expectation

The expectant mother eagerly and confidently anticipates the birth of her child. She willingly accepts responsibility for the welfare of the innocent newborn infant entrusted to her care. She looks forward with pleasure to the tender, intimate moments that only the two of them can share together. She will pour out her love and give sacrificially and, as a result, will awaken love in her child's heart. Her maternal arms will become a secure place, a restful peace for a fretting or uncomfortable baby. She will also be assured and content in her ability to nurture and provide for its every need.

> *"My soul, wait only upon God and silently submit to Him; for my hope and expectation are from Him. He only is my Rock and my Salvation; He is my Defense and my Fortress, I shall not be moved" (Psalm 62:5-6 AMPC).*

God ultimately is the only hope for your total well-being: spirit, soul, and body. He is your strength, a safe place of refuge in times of need. In God alone can you trust and confide. You can utterly depend on Him for victory, deliverance, health, prosperity, and preservation. He is everything you need Him to be in every area of your life. You can expect God's best as His beloved child. You can expect to be secure in that sure and safe place of His loving-kindness and tender mercies.

"'For I know the thoughts and plans that I have for you,' says the Lord, 'thoughts and plans for welfare and peace and not for evil, to give you hope in your final outcome'" (Jeremiah 29:11 AMPC).

You can anticipate and have great expectation that God's promises extend far past your brief lifespan here on this earth. You can also, with great hope, look forward to and prepare for an eternity with God, your heavenly Father. Your future was determined in the past and is ever being revealed to you daily by His Word. His compassionate plan for you as His child is unfolding as you believe and walk in faith. You can be absolutely sure of this; it is a divine certainty that He will do exactly as He promised He will do. "(Resting) in the hope of eternal life, (life) which the ever truthful God Who cannot deceive promised before the world or the ages of time began" (Titus 1:2 AMPC).

"Now faith is being sure of what we hope for and certain of what we do not see" (Hebrews 11:1 NIV). You can have complete confidence and absolute assurance in God the Father's ability to make real those promises yet to be manifested and made real to the senses.

The child, from birth, can grasp the finger of its mother. It holds on tightly to the only one who has been its nurturing comfort in the womb. Likewise, cling to Him, hold fast to His comforting hand of mercy, and you will not waver or fall or be moved from your steadfast faith and expectation of His faithfulness. He will never let you go or fail you.

"God raised the Lord Jesus from death, and we know that he will also raise us with Jesus . . . Our physical body is becoming older and weaker, but our spirit inside us is made new every day. We have small troubles for a while now, but these troubles are helping us gain an eternal glory. That eternal glory is much greater than our troubles. So we think about what we cannot see, not what we see. What we see lasts only a short time, and what we cannot see will last forever" (2 Corinthians 4:14, 16-18 ERV).

You can be assured that the Spirit, through the power of God, will raise you up, resurrect you as He did Jesus. Although you cannot see it now, know that all resurrected bodies will last throughout eternity. Those who all are God's own children by faith will also be resurrected to live forever with Him.

> "... We are waiting for our Savior, the Lord Jesus Christ ... He will change our humble bodies and make them like his own glorious body. Christ can do this by his power, with which he is able to rule everything" (Philippians 3:20-21 ERV).

He will meet His spiritual family as they are caught up together in the air with Him, never to be separated, to be forever together. Later, He will return from heaven to earth in His glorified body with His family who are just like Him. All will live together in peace and righteousness throughout eternity. With the resurrection of the body, the spirit, soul, and body are reunited forever.

Others will live eternally separated from the Father's loving favor and blessing. Since He is long-suffering, patient, and kind, it is not His desire that any perish. However, His Word positively declares that only those who avail themselves of God's great grace will be privileged to become God's children.

It was God's predetermined plan for all to be adopted into His family. He has already called and chosen you for Himself. By an act of your will, it is now up to you to make a decision to respond to that call. The choice is yours. He patiently waits in expectation for your answer to His generous plan to receive you as His own child through Jesus Christ. He continues to reveal His loving-kindness and goodness to draw you to Him. The perfect day of acceptance for you is today! The right time is right now!

Rapture, The Catching Away

Jesus prays to His Father: "Father, I desire that they also whom You have entrusted to Me (as Your gift to Me) may be with Me where I am, so that they may see My glory ..." (John 17:24 AMPC). Here Jesus prays specifically for born-again believers,

His brethren. He desires that all will be reunited together with Him in glorious, resurrected bodies.

Before His return to His Father in heaven and after His resurrection, Jesus promised never to leave His brethren again. He will return in the air for His own. He will later return to the earth with His family. Be confident that when we first see Him, we will see Him as He is and be like Him.

You can be assured that "the good work God began in you will continue until he completes it on the day when Jesus Christ comes again" (Philippians 1:6 ERV). Born-again believers, God's children, can know without any doubt that their heavenly Father will keep His word. He sent His Son Jesus to die for you, so live a life pleasing to Him and not for yourself.

God's plan for you and His work in you is so complete that He also sent the Holy Spirit to live in you, to be your teacher of His truth. He will lead you and guide you and empower you in your Christian walk. Expectantly listen to His voice.

". . . You are looking forward to the coming of God's Son from heaven—Jesus, whom God raised from the dead. He is the one who has rescued us from the terrors of the coming judgment" (1 Thessalonians 1:10 NLT). There is no need for hopelessness in your life, but only the certainty of God's unfailing love.

Whole Creation in Expectancy

"For (even the whole) creation (all nature) waits expectantly and longs earnestly for God's sons to be made known (waits for the revealing, the disclosure of their sonship) . . . That nature (creation) itself will be set free from its bondage to decay and corruption (and gain an entrance) into the glorious freedom of God's children (Romans 8:19, 21 AMPC).

Until that time, all creation is waiting and writhing in pain as a mother ready to give birth. Creation awaits to be made free from ruinous natural disasters, ecological and global neglect, and events such as droughts, paralyzing blizzards and snow storms, earthquakes, hurricanes, mudslides, typhoons, tornadoes, tidal waves, tsunamis, forest fires, floods, and heat waves. Medically, devastating plagues and viruses spread throughout various populations.

Everything that God created, all nature has been waiting with excitement for the time He will reveal to the world those who are His children. They long to see those resurrected believers who will enjoy the glory of His inheritance. All creation anticipates God's promise of a new heaven and a new earth to fulfill its purposes with the glory and freedom belonging to God's children.

All creation is in decline; it is deteriorating and decaying from the perfection of the Genesis 1:31 account when God saw everything He had made and said that it was very good. As a result of the first man Adam's rebellion and disobedience, the entire created world awaits in anticipation for a release from bondage and corruption. This will occur at the time when God's children are revealed to the created universe. After that, the restoration and renovation of the heavens and earth will complete God's plan as a new home for His family.

"Then I saw a new heaven and a new earth. The first heaven and the first earth had disappeared . . . And I saw the holy city, the New Jerusalem, coming down out of heaven from God . . . I heard a loud voice from the throne. It said, 'Now God's home is with people. He will live with them. They will be his people. God himself will be with them and will be their God. He will wipe away every tear from their eyes. There will be no more death, sadness, crying, or pain. All the old ways are gone . . . 'All those who win the victory will receive all this. And I will be their God, and they will be my children'" (Revelation 21:1-4, 7 ERV).

Be encouraged and receive strength to be an overcomer in Christ Jesus. The battle has already been won, and you can have the victory. Know for certainty that your loving Father desires to be with you forever and ever.

- CHAPTER 7 -

BLESSINGS FROM THE WOMB

Paul said regarding his gospel and ministry: "But when it pleased God, who separated me from my mother's **womb**, and called me by his grace" (Galatians 1:15 KJV). The word translated as *womb* is defined in Strong's Concordance (Greek 2836) as "a cavity, the abdomen, by implication, the matrix; figuratively, the heart—belly, womb." Using Webster's definition of a matrix, the womb is "a place or enveloping element within which something originates, takes form or develops" after conception.

The womb or uterus is the female organ for containing and nourishing the young during all of the phases and stages of pregnancy prior to the birth and delivery of the child. It is the place of protection, a place of refuge and safety where the child is nourished and flourishes because all that is necessary for growth and development is provided.

"Because of the Lord's great love, we are not consumed, for His **compassions** never fail. They are new every morning; great is your faithfulness" (Lamentations 3:22-23 NIV). The word for compassion comes from the Hebrew word for womb, *racham*. Strong's Exhaustive Concordance of the Bible defines *racham* (7356) as "compassion . . . by extension, the womb (as cherishing the unborn child) . . . tender love, (great, tender) mercy, pity." As a loving mother cherishes her unborn child, God cherishes the unborn child, forming its body tenderly and compassionately as it is developed, protected and carried in the mother's womb.

As God prepared the earth as a perfect habitat for mankind, so is the womb a perfect habitat prepared for the process of the unborn child to come to full development. The developing child is enclosed and nurtured in the warm, protective comfort of the mother's womb. It is its first home, especially prepared by God to meet its every need. It floats in a sea of amniotic fluid. The umbilical cord connects the child with the placenta, which connects mother and child. The placenta is the structure by which the unborn baby is nurtured in the uterus. It is a suitable habitat to maintain favorable conditions, the perfect climate and atmosphere, protected, secure, nourished by a food source, and cleansed by a waste removal system.

The unconditional love of God, His compassion and tender mercy for His own, is more of a reality than that tender love of a mother for the unborn child in her womb. The compassion that comes from God's heart holds you in the highest esteem. He treasures and values you. He treats you with tender, loving, nurturing care and affection.

DNA: Divine Nature and Ability

Genes determine and transfer hereditary characteristics from one generation to another. DNA is your unique physical genetic makeup or fingerprint. It is genetic material, a complex combination of amino acids that are essential components of all living cells. They regulate how specific hereditary character traits and distinguishing qualities are passed on generationally to biological descendants.

You inherited the physical DNA of your parents, which therefore determines without doubt who you are and whose you are! DNA is the interaction of genetic instructions from your father and mother. This process results in the development of the very special individual that you are. At conception, the egg cell of the mother is penetrated by the father's sperm or seed. As a result, a new physical life is produced. Each parent's genetic traits interact together to bring forth a child, a special, unique individual, the person you are, with specific individual traits or characteristics.

Ancestral lineage may include positive or negative inclinations in intellectual, physical, mental, and emotional areas, and DNA is responsible for passing down these hereditary distinctions. Specific strengths and weaknesses can be transmitted down through family lines, since natural DNA carries biological and physical genetic information and instructions to regulate a child's legacy. Inherited from parents and from past generations may be recognizable facial features, general physical appearance, or body structure. Also, there may be tendencies toward specific problem areas such as infirmities, weaknesses, or diseases. Medical personnel routinely document family health histories in order to effectively diagnose and treat their patients. Additionally, other areas of life are affected genetically, including personal identity and social and behavioral tendencies. However, all these specific traits combined create unique individuals and personalities.

Born-again children have the spiritual genetic makeup of their spiritual Father, God. You possess the DNA of your heavenly Father; therefore, you have an entirely new genetic code inherited from Him. You have a shared life source from the life giver.

"No one born (begotten) of God (deliberately, knowingly, and habitually) practices sin, for God's nature abides in him (His principle of life, the divine sperm, remains permanently within him); and he cannot practice sinning because he is born (begotten) of God. By this it is made clear who take their nature from God and are His children . . ." (1 John 3:9-10 AMPC).

At the new birth, God supernaturally and miraculously imparts His Divine Nature and Ability—His DNA—into your human spirit. You receive the unseen, the real unchanging life of God in your inner, hidden man of the heart, your internal spirit.

God, a loving Father, supplies His children with everything they need to lead an overcoming life. His exceedingly precious promises allow those who are His by faith to become partakers or sharers of His divine nature in spite of natural DNA and human characteristics. All that you need to live a God kind of life has already been provided through Christ Jesus, so those positive aspects or strengths not inherited through natural foreparents are available through your spiritual DNA, God's Divine Nature and Ability.

As a true believer, you will receive a new identity with the sameness of your Father's essential character and His attributes. You will possess His life, His nature and ability.

You will share His nature by your new birth as you are fathered from above. At that moment, you are indwelt by God through His Holy Spirit. Your heavenly Father's DNA communicates with you, His child, His supernatural design or appointment for your life. The Holy Spirit helps and empowers you to be conformed to the image of Jesus, the only begotten Son of God the Father.

"Jesus, the one who makes people holy, and those who are made holy are from the same family. So he is not ashamed to call them his brothers and sisters" (Hebrews 2:11 ERV). All believers, children of God, are members of the same family, the household of God. All, with Jesus Christ, God the Son, are related through the same heavenly Father's DNA. Jesus Christ was the only sinless, perfect human; therefore, He is your example and ideal of faithfulness and obedience.

Once you are born again and in union with Christ Jesus, you

become a new creature with a brand-new identity. That old nature that once controlled your life has passed away and is no more. It is past history, so a decision to continually and repeatedly be disobedient to your Father's word and will is not pleasing nor acceptable to Him.

Follow the standard of the life of Jesus, God's unique Son, His firstborn, your elder brother. He walked on this earth as a man. He was subject to all the temptations, tests, and trials common to all humans. He was affected by the same passions, feelings, and emotions. He experienced similar physical and mental issues to those confronting you in your daily life. Yet He led an overcoming life without sin and in perfect obedience to His Father and yours.

Announce and Acknowledge Publicly—Physical Birth

"I'm pregnant!"

"There is a new life within me!"

That which has been accomplished miraculously inwardly is confessed openly, publicly, and joyously by the expectant mother. Afterwards, when she begins to "show," the outward transformation and manifestation is the proof or confirmation of the announcement or confession.

When a child is born, the proud parents joyously announce and acknowledge the physical birth of the newborn. They make a public announcement to family and friends about the new member welcomed into the family.

Mary, the mother of Jesus, and Joseph came to Joseph's hometown, where there was no place for them in the inn. They settled in a stable for the night, "And she gave birth to her Son, her Firstborn . . . And in that vicinity there were shepherds living (out under the open sky) in the field, watching (in shifts) over their flock by night. And behold, an angel of the Lord stood by them, and the glory of the Lord flashed and shone all about them, and they were terribly frightened. But the angel said to them, 'Do not be afraid; for behold, I bring you good news of a great joy which will come to all the people. For to you is born this day in the town of David a Savior, Who is Christ (the Messiah) the Lord" (Luke 2:7-11 AMPC).

The birth of Jesus, God's Son, is announced by an angel from heaven to shepherds on Earth. The good news is to all people of the world. All are welcome to hear, receive, and believe with great joy the message of the birth of a person, a Savior, a Deliverer who will bring peace and God's favor to mankind. Christianity is a relationship to a personal God through His Son Jesus.

"Then suddenly there appeared with the angel an army of the troops of heaven . . . praising God and saying, 'Glory to God in the highest (heaven) and on earth peace among men with whom He is well pleased (man of goodwill, of His favor)" (Luke 2:13-14 AMPC). Good news is to be shared, so the shepherds searched for the child in order to see and confirm what the Lord had made known to them. "And when they saw it, they made known what had been told them concerning this Child, and all who heard it were astounded and marveled at what the shepherds told them . . . And the shepherds returned, glorifying and praising God for all the things they had heard and seen, just as it had been told them" (Luke 2:17-18, 20 AMPC).

God acknowledged and publicly introduced Jesus as His Son immediately after He was prepared for His earthly ministry. At that time, God, His Father, expressed great delight and pleasure in His beloved Son Jesus before He ever completed successfully the work He was sent to accomplish. "And behold, a voice from heaven said, 'This is My Son, My Beloved, in Whom I delight!'" (Matthew 3:17 AMPC).

To be welcomed into the family of God, you must also acknowledge and confess your belief in that finished work of Jesus on the cross. You must sincerely and wholeheartedly believe and confess that He is who the Father says He is. You must agree with God's Word that He accomplished what He was sent to Earth to do according to His Father's eternal purpose and plan.

Repent! Turn away and change your mind and attitude toward sin and unbelief, its causes, and the resulting consequences. Turn toward the outstretched arms of the forgiving God of love who has already provided for you a substitute to pay the ultimate price, Jesus Christ, His Son. Realize that you are not capable of changing yourself or your lifestyle by self-effort and that you are in need of a Savior. Allow the Holy Spirit to birth a new nature in you, one that is in right standing with God the Father.

"Because if you acknowledge and confess with your lips that Jesus is Lord and in your heart believe (adhere to, trust in, and rely on the truth) that God raised Him from the dead, you will be saved. For with the heart a person believes (adheres to, trusts in, and relies on Christ) and so is justified (declared righteous, acceptable to God), and with the mouth he confesses (declares openly and speaks out freely his faith) and confirms (his) salvation" (Romans 10:9-10 AMPC).

I Have the Life of God Inside!

As a child of the living God, your life is not your own anymore: you have been bought with a price. Allow Jesus to be the One in complete control of your life as you follow His example and do only what pleases your Father. By your change of mind and lifestyle, you will acknowledge and confirm to others that you know whose you are and that you are what your Father says you are.

Your words and actions publicly and openly announce your change of heart. ". . . Live in a way that gives meaning to your salvation. Do this with fear and respect for God. Yes, it is God who is working in you. He helps you want to do what pleases him, and he gives you the power to do it" (Philippians 2:12-13 ERV).

Once you become a born-again believer, you must accomplish or work outwardly that which God has already done inwardly. Do this with reverence and awesome respect, while at the same time realizing your inability to accomplish it through your own strength and willpower. Recognize that it is God who is working in you, giving you both the desire and power to do His will and to satisfy and delight Him.

Submit, dedicate, and offer your physical body completely, and give yourself over to God. Honor God with your body and renew your mind with God's Word in order to have a new way of thinking as well as a new attitude and ideals. ". . . So that you may prove (for yourselves) what is the good and acceptable and perfect will of God" (Romans 12:2 AMPC).

When you put your trust in God's word of truth and make Jesus Lord of your life, make Him the One who is in control, your life will surely show it. "If you stand before others and are willing to say you believe in me, then I will tell my Father in heaven that you belong to me" (Matthew 10:32 ERV).

God's ultimate divine plan is to gather together His family and to live among them in peace and harmony. If you boldly confess that Jesus is your Savior and Lord to others while you live here on earth, Jesus will confess you are His to the Father in heaven. ". . . I will acknowledge him (as Mine) and I will confess his name openly before My Father and before His angels" (Revelation 3:5 AMPC). Jesus Himself will openly accept you are His own, a brother or sister, when you publicly acknowledge Him as your Savior and Lord of your life. When you claim to be His before others on earth, He will declare you to be His before His heavenly Father and the angelic host.

Dramatic Physical and Emotional Changes

Expectant mothers experience some dramatic physical and emotional changes during pregnancy, labor, and delivery. Examples include gain in bodily weight, changes in physical image and form, back pain, varicose veins, swelling in the extremities, difficulty in movement, queasiness, uneasiness, nausea, morning sickness, vomiting, loss of balance, lack of sleep, discomfort, specific food cravings, and a sensitivity to certain everyday aromas and odors. These changes result from internal changes in the body as the unborn child grows and develops in the womb and as the mother-to-be attempts to adjust and compensate for her rapidly changing physical situation. Emotional changes including mood shifts, anxiety, and depression may also occur during pregnancy. At times, severe depression may be experienced after delivery and also during the early months of the child's life. An expectant mother is willing to undergo the discomfort and stress of pregnancy, as well as the pain and travail of delivery. In exchange, the glorious result is the birth of her beloved child.

For the new birth, it was necessary for Jesus Christ, a substitute for sinful man, to endure great indignities and extreme suffering during the entire crucifixion process. As a result, He willingly experienced extreme physical, mental, and emotional changes. "So then Pilate took Jesus and scourged (flogged, whipped) Him" (John 19:1 AMPC). "Then they spat in His face and struck Him with their fists; and some slapped Him in the face" (Matthew 26:67 AMPC). "And, weaving a crown of thorns, they put it on His head and put a reed (staff) in His right hand . . . And they spat on Him, and took the reed (staff) and struck Him on the head" (Matthew 27:29-30 AMPC).

A First-Person Account of Crucifixion

> *"I am poured out like water, and all my bones are out of joint. My heart is like wax; it is softened (with anguish) and melted down within me. My strength is dried up like a fragment of clay pottery; (with thirst) my tongue cleaves to my jaws . . . I can count all my bones..."* (Psalm 22:14-15, 17 AMPC).

The physical appearance of Jesus Christ was dramatically altered and disfigured by the abuse, torture, and inhumane treatment inflicted on Him by others. Throughout His arrest, imprisonment, trial, and conviction, and finally during His crucifixion, He suffered in your place and for all mankind. He was mutilated, pierced, scourged, bruised, beaten, and struck to such an extent that people were amazed and shocked by His outward form.

Additionally, deep emotional wounds severely affected His overall well-being. He was despised, rejected, scorned, and mocked as He was surrounded by enemies, wicked men, probably including some that He had once lovingly blessed and comforted during His earthly ministry.

The ultimate agony resulted when Jesus took in His own body all of your sins and was made sin for you. At that moment, He was forsaken by a holy God who could not look with approval upon sin, even when carried by His own Son. Jesus, the Son, who had been eternally with the Father, coequal with Him, and dearly loved by Him, was rejected when He became your substitute to satisfy the punishment, the penalty of death. All of this was necessary to make you acceptable and to reconcile you back to a loving, forgiving Father.

The prophet Isaiah foretells the suffering of Jesus: "He was despised and rejected and forsaken by men, a Man of sorrows and pains, and acquainted with grief and sickness . . . Surely He has borne our griefs (sicknesses, weaknesses, and distresses) and carried our sorrows and pains (of punishment) . . . But He was wounded for our transgressions, He was bruised for our guilt and iniquities; the chastisement (needed to obtain peace) and well-being for us was upon Him, and with the stripes (that wounded) Him we are healed and made whole" (Isaiah 53:3-5 AMPC).

There was a great exchange at the cross when Jesus was offered up: His total well-being, spirit, soul, and body, for your complete welfare and wholeness, spirit, soul, and body. Your sins, sickness, and diseases all fell on Him and were taken away in an exchange on the cross. He was made sin for you, and you are made His righteousness. He took your sicknesses and diseases in exchange for your healing and health.

"(For many the Servant of God became an object of horror; many were astonished at Him.) His face and His whole appearance were marred more than any man's, and His form beyond that of the sons of men—but just as many were astonished at Him" (Isaiah 52:14 AMPC). Jesus was physically broken, shattered, and weakened so that you by faith may be made whole, delivered, protected, saved, and preserved in spirit, soul, and body.

From Physical Being to Spiritual Being

"When anyone is in Christ, it is a whole new world. The old things are gone; suddenly, everything is new!" (2 Corinthians 5:17 ERV). The new believer is instantly a newly created spiritual being, never before in existence. The old nature is gone, and all things have become new spiritually. What is made new on the inside must be outworked on the outer physical body and in the soulish area of mind, will, and emotion.

The final bodily change occurs at resurrection, when the nature of the physical body will change. ". . . When those who have died are raised to life. The body that is 'planted' in the grave . . . is without honor. But when it is raised, it will be great and glorious. When the body is 'planted,' it is weak. But when it is raised, it will be full of power. The body that is 'planted' is a physical body. When it is raised, it will be a spiritual body . . ." (1 Corinthians 15:42-44 ERV).

Developmental Periods of Life Before Physical Birth

The period of incubation for life in the womb is three trimesters, for a total of nine months:

First Trimester (months 1, 2, and 3): The organs are forming, and blood flows in the child's veins; however, its blood does not mix with the blood of the mother.

Second Trimester (months 4, 5, and 6): The child receives comfort from the sound of its mother's voice. The mother can sense the child moving in womb. The organs, muscles, limbs, and brain continue to grow and develop.

Third Trimester (months 7, 8, and 9): The child grows in height and weight until the womb, its living space, becomes too small and cramped for comfort. The child itself triggers the labor and birth process.

There are also three stages of labor and delivery:

Stage I:
The beginning of mild contractions, which gradually become stronger and begin to occur more regularly.

Stage II:
This stage of labor is very difficult and requires great physical effort by the mother. The actual birth of the baby occurs in

Stage II after it grows too large for its home inside the womb.

Stage III:
This stage includes the expulsion of the placenta, which was necessary during pregnancy to supply nourishment from the mother to her unborn child.

Stage I of labor can be further divided into three phases:

Early:
Mild contractions occur every five to twenty minutes and become more regular and intense.

Active:
Contractions increase and occur about every three minutes.

Transition:
The most difficult and exhausting contractions occur every two to three minutes and each usually continues for about 1 minute.

Babies the world over are born with the God-given capacity to learn and speak any language. This is just one aspect of the miraculous growth and development of a child before birth. God lovingly designed and crafted every part of your total being, and therefore each part functions according to His divine plan. "You formed the way I think and feel. You put me together in my mother's womb. I praise you because you made me in such a wonderful way. I know how amazing that was!" (Psalm 139:13-14 ERV).

At six months, a child is able to distinguish sound. During that same period of pregnancy, the mother can feel the movement of the baby's limbs. The Gospel of Luke records what happened when Mary, who had just learned from the angel Gabriel that she would become the mother of Jesus, visited the home of Zacharias and greeted his wife Elizabeth, who was six months pregnant: "When Elizabeth heard Mary's greeting, the baby leaped in her womb . . . In a loud voice she exclaimed: 'Blessed are you among women, and blessed is the child you will bear! But why am I so favored, that the mother of my Lord should come to me? As soon as the sound of your greeting reached my ears, the baby in my womb leaped for joy. Blessed is she who has believed that what the Lord has said to her will be accomplished!" (Luke 1:41-45 NIV).

The Symbolic Significance of Biblical Numbers

The number three (3) denotes completed testimony. One example of this is the Trinity: God the Father, God the Son, and God the Holy Spirit. God is three persons but one in unity.

"For there are three that bear record in heaven, the Father, the Word, and the Holy Ghost: and these three are one. And there are three that bear witness in earth, the Spirit, and the water, and the blood: and these three agree in one" (1 John 5:7-8 KJV). The three both in heaven and on earth bear witness to the humanity and sonship of Jesus, the first one of many brothers. When Jesus was born to an earthly mother, he was, as all other humans, a whole person, a spiritual being with a soul enclosed in a physical body.

"May God himself, the God of peace, sanctify you through and through. May your whole spirit, soul and body be kept blameless at the coming of our Lord Jesus Christ" (1 Thessalonians 5:23 NIV). Paul writes to the church at Thessalonica and prays that the believers will walk in the hope of Jesus Christ's coming to meet them in the air. The whole person will be caught up at the rapture of the dead in Christ and also of those believers who are alive. The physical body will be reunited with the eternal soul and spirit.

This scripture clearly refers to the three-part being of man: the inner man (or spirit man of the heart) with a soul (mind, will, and emotions) enclosed in a physical body.

The number nine (9) biblically indicates divine judgment, finality in divine things, and fullness, divine completeness. The natural birth of a child is usually accomplished at delivery in nine months, and the completed work of Jesus on the cross was finished at the ninth hour. Through this event, all who choose by faith can become children of God the Father by the new birth.

"He that spared not his own Son, but delivered him up for us all . . ." (Romans 8:32 KJV). God brought forth, gave up, and gave over His Son Jesus, who was delivered in nine months of Mary, His own natural mother. The same child who was destined to be the Deliverer of all mankind gave up His life at the ninth hour on the cross so you could be born again to newness of life.

Physical death is the separation of the spirit and soul from the body. Spiritual death or eternal separation from a loving God is the penalty for sin. At physical death, before the natural body returns to the dust from which it was formed, the soul and spirit continue on in conscious existence: for believers, first in heaven in the presence of the Father, then on the New Earth with Him forevermore, but for unbelievers, in the Lake of Fire, separated from Him.

After the death of Jesus on the cross, He temporarily went down into hell, the place of departed spirits in the heart of the earth, to conquer death, hell, and the grave. He was raised in triumph from the dead by the power of the Holy Spirit. His resurrected spiritual body has returned to His Father in heaven. Jesus is seated at God's right hand, a place symbolic of honor, power, and union with God. He is seated because He has completed His preplanned work on Earth.

In the book of Jonah, the narrative illustrates the mercy of

God, who does not wish that anyone should perish. He charged Jonah to warn a brutal, evil nation of impending destruction if they did not repent of their sinful ways. Jonah wanted that nation to be destroyed because of their cruel deeds of disobedience to a faithful God. Therefore, he traveled by ship in the other direction! While at sea, he was swallowed by a big fish and spent three days and three nights in its belly. He was vomited up and eventually fulfilled God's plan. The nation turned from their wicked ways, and a loving, compassionate God responded by mercifully canceling the threatened punishment.

This story illustrates, or pictures, the death, burial, and resurrection of Jesus Christ. "Jonah was in the stomach of the big fish for three days and three nights. In the same way, the Son of Man will be in the grave for three days and three nights" (Matthew 12:40 ERV). A merciful God will use any part of His created universe, including the plant and animal kingdom, to assist in bringing many people to restored favor and right standing with Him. His favor and tender loving-kindness for the undeserving is clearly pictured here.

When Jonah disobeyed God and ran from Him, going by ship to a faraway city, "the Lord brought a great storm on the sea . . ." (Jonah 1:4 ERV). Jonah knew that the storm was a result of his failure to do God's will, so he asked that he be thrown overboard to save the lives of the others aboard the ship.

"When Jonah fell into the sea, the Lord chose a very big fish to swallow Jonah . . ." (Jonah 1:17 ERV). While in the stomach of the fish, Jonah prayed to the Lord his God. "Then the Lord spoke to the fish, and it vomited Jonah out of its stomach onto the dry land" (Jonah 2:10 ERV).

Then Jonah obeyed and went to the city of Nineveh. He preached to the people, and they repented of their evil deeds and turned to God. However, Jonah became angry because they were not destroyed. In his complaint to God, he said, ". . . I knew that you would forgive the people of this evil city . . . I knew that you are a kind God. I knew that you show mercy and don't want to punish people. I knew that you are kind, and if these people stopped sinning, you would change your plans to destroy them" (Jonah 4:2 ERV).

Then Jonah went out of the city and made a shelter, and he sat in its shade and waited. "The Lord made a gourd plant grow quickly over Jonah. This made a cool place for Jonah to sit and helped him to be more comfortable" (Jonah 4:6-8 ERV). But the next morning, God sent a worm to eat part of the plant, and the plant died. "After the sun was high in the sky, God caused a hot east wind to blow . . ." (Jonah 4:8 ERV). Jonah became very angry because he had grown weak and was about to die. Then the Lord said to him, "If you can get upset over a plant, surely I can feel sorry for a big city like Nineveh . . . There are more than 120,000 people there who did not know they were doing wrong" (Jonah 4:11 ERV). His great concern and desire is that all should be in right standing with Him. His goodness causes men to repent and turn to Him after they hear the word of truth.

Darkness, or the absence of light, is symbolic of God's judgment. The number six (6) is the Biblical number of "mankind." In Genesis 1:27, the creation of man occurred on the sixth day. Jesus, the Son of Man, who was fully God and fully Man, came to earth in the form of human flesh to pay the penalty of death for all sinful man. At the sixth hour, your sin and mine—past, present, and future—was judged after He had suffered on the cross for about six agonizing hours. "And it was the third hour (about nine o'clock in the morning) when they crucified Him . . . And when the sixth hour (about midday) had come, there was darkness over the whole land until the ninth hour (about three o'clock)" (Mark 15:25, 33 AMPC).

After an attempt by one of His disciples to defend Him from the soldiers who came to arrest Him, Jesus said, "Do you suppose that I cannot appeal to my Father, and He will immediately provide Me with more than twelve legions (more than 80,000) of angels? But then how would the Scriptures be fulfilled, that it must come about this way?" (Matthew 26:53-54 AMPC).

The evil schemes and plots of the enemy, Satan, were carried out to influence others as well as Jesus Christ Himself. The enemy attempted to abort or terminate God's original perfect plan to reconcile mankind to Himself, to a right relationship with the Holy God. Satan had hoped to motivate Jesus through His humanity to avoid the suffering and agony of crucifixion. He expected that his continued pressures and attacks would provoke Jesus to seek on His behalf the intervention of the heavenly angelic host. This would, in effect, bring about a miscarriage of God's divine justice plan. Nothing or no one, however, can prevent God's conceived purpose from coming to full term. Jesus knew that He must complete the work for the plan of salvation established by His Father before the foundation of the world. He humbled himself on the cross, despising the shame, yet took control over his mind, will, and emotions despite the ridicule, mockery, scoffing, and sneering.

"Two others also, who were criminals, were led away to be executed with Him. And when they came to the place which is called The Skull (Latin: Calvary; Hebrew: Golgotha), there they crucified Him, and (along with) the criminals, one on the right and one on the left. And Jesus prayed, 'Father, forgive them, for they know not what they do' . . . Now the people stood by (calmly and leisurely) watching, but the rulers scoffed and sneered (turned up their noses) at Him, saying, 'He rescued others (from death); let Him now rescue Himself, if He is the Christ (the Messiah) of God, His Chosen One!' The soldiers also ridiculed and made sport of Him . . . One of the criminals who was suspended kept up a railing at Him, saying,

'Are you not the Christ (the Messiah)? Rescue Yourself and us (from death)!" (Luke 23:32-36, 39 AMPC).

Satan's ultimate aim was to destroy Jesus before He could accomplish the offering up of Himself. Therefore, Satan's attempts to thwart God's loving provision for the redemption of fallen man have been ongoing throughout history, from long before His birth and continuing even as He was hanging on the cross. ". . . The reason the Son of God was made manifest (visible) was to undo (destroy, loosen, and dissolve) the works the devil (has done)" (1 John 3:8 AMPC).

"But when the proper time had fully come, God sent His Son, born of a woman . . . to purchase the freedom of (to ransom, to redeem, to atone for) those who were subject to the Law, that we might be adopted and have sonship conferred upon us (and be recognized as God's sons)" (Galatians 4:4-5 AMPC). In God's plan, there are no premature events, no delayed or overdue occurrences. All will come in the fullness of time, on the due date, as He had willed even before the foundation of the world. When God sent His Son, Jesus, born of a woman, at just the right appointed time and season, no opposing force could hinder the exact moment of His arrival on earth to accomplish the will of His Father on behalf of mankind.

"And at the ninth hour Jesus cried with a loud voice . . . 'My God, My God, why have You forsaken Me (deserting Me and leaving Me helpless and abandoned)?' . . . And Jesus uttered a loud cry, and breathed out His life" (Mark 15:34, 37 AMPC). Not only was the death of Jesus exchanged for your life, He was forsaken at the exchange of His righteousness for your sin. As a result, He was forsaken by a holy God so that in exchange, you might be accepted into His family. God, "having predestined us to adoption as sons by Jesus Christ to Himself, according to the good pleasure of His will, to the praise of the glory of His grace, by which He made us accepted in the Beloved" (Ephesians 1:5-6 NKJV).

You can benefit by God's glorious grace, favor and loving kindness—He freely planned beforehand and willingly granted you this special honor because it pleased Him to do so. The work of Redemption was complete! ". . . Jesus, knowing that all was now finished (ended) . . . He said, 'It is finished!' and He bowed His head and gave up His spirit" (John 19:28, 30 AMPC). It was completely complete and perfectly perfect! Everything has already been done; there is nothing that you by your own effort or accomplishment can avail for salvation.

"And Jesus, crying out with a loud voice, said, 'Father, into Thy hands I commit My Spirit.' And having said this, He breathed His last" (Luke 23:46 NASB). Jesus gave up His life voluntarily. He came to Earth as a man to do His Father's will, to reconcile mankind to a Holy God by paying the ultimate price: His death in exchange for your life. "For Christ (the Messiah Himself) died for sins once for all, the Righteous for the unrighteous (the Just for the unjust, the Innocent for the guilty), that He might bring us to God . . ." (1 Peter 3:18 AMPC).

". . . Thus it is written, that the Christ should suffer and rise again from the dead the third day" (Luke 24:46 NASB). Christ Jesus was resurrected bodily and is now alive and will be forevermore. All others, who are children of the heavenly Father, will also have resurrected bodies to live with Him eternally.

Quickening—Physically Feeling Life

"Quickening" is an old-fashioned term referring to the physical movements of the unborn child in the womb. These movements are felt by the mother, assuring her that the baby is alive and that she is "feeling life." She may experience faint flutters and tickling sensations initially. Feelings of being punched or kicked result from frequent leg and arm movements as the child develops. The baby may turn somersaults and have other periods of violent activity while yet in the womb. The motions are easily discerned, since the child is said to be "alive and kicking."

Long before medical science confirmed it, Biblical truth related this event in Luke 1:39-44. Elizabeth is in the sixth month of her own pregnancy when Mary, pregnant with Jesus, visited her with the good news of the impending birth. When Mary entered Elizabeth's house and greeted her, Elizabeth responded: "For behold, when the sound of your greeting reached my ears, the baby leaped in my womb for joy" (Luke 1:44 NASB).

Spiritual Resurrection or Quickening

"But God—so rich is He in His mercy! Because of and in order to satisfy the great and wonderful and intense love with which He loved us, even when we were dead (slain) by (our own) shortcomings and trespasses, He made us alive together in fellowship and in union with Christ . . ." (Ephesians 2:4-5 AMPC). You are spiritually resurrected from the dead, raised up from the death of your life of sin and made alive by grace through the finished work of Jesus Christ on the cross.

"For Christ also hath once suffered for sins, the just for the unjust, that he might bring us to God, being put to death in the flesh, but quickened by the Spirit" (1 Peter 3:18 KJV). When Christ died in His physical body—the righteous for the unrighteous, the guiltless for you, the guilty one,—He brought you back into fellowship with God, your Father. But He was made alive and given life by the Spirit. He is the first to be resurrected of all His brethren who are believers.

Spiritual Quickening, Spiritual Body

"Your body will always be dead because of sin. But if Christ is in you, then the Spirit gives you life, because Christ made you right with God. God raised Jesus from death. And if God's

Spirit lives in you, he will also give life to your bodies that die. Yes, God is the one who raised Christ from death, and he will raise you to life through his Spirit living in you" (Romans 8:10-11 ERV).

Your physical body is subject to natural death, but those who are children in God's family have the life-giving Spirit indwelling them. This Spirit of life will restore again to life your mortal bodies through resurrection. The indwelling presence of the life-giving Holy Spirit is the guarantee that God is faithful to fulfill His eternal plan for you.

Bodily Resurrection

> *"If we who are (abiding) in Christ have hope only in this life and that is all, then we are of all people most miserable and to be pitied. But the fact is that Christ (the Messiah) has been raised from the dead, and He became the firstfruits of those who have fallen asleep (in death)" (1 Corinthians 15:19-20 AMPC).*

Jesus was the first one of His brethren to be raised from the dead, and we also, a great harvest of believers, will be physically raised from the dead. Our bodies will be quickened or made alive again by God, the Holy Spirit, who lives inside of us.

Birth Pains for Natural Birth

Pain and agonizing effort, stress, and exertion are needed for physical birth. God said to Eve, ". . . with pain you will give birth to children . . ." (Genesis 3:16 NIV). Before a woman brings forth a child physically, she usually goes through an agonizing struggle and experiences extreme anguish as she gives birth. ". . . A woman with child drawing near to the time of her delivery is in pain and writhes and cries out in her pangs" (Isaiah 26:17 AMPC). Her labor pains become increasingly more intense, occur more frequently, and continue for longer periods of time of until the baby is born. Nevertheless, for the mother there is great satisfaction when she has successfully brought forth and given birth to her baby. Stress, striving, and strain are first required before and during the physical delivery process. Only after that ordeal can the mother experience stillness and rest from her labor.

Travail—Birth Pains For Spiritual Rebirth

Jesus, in the garden of Gethsemane, prayed before he was arrested. ". . . He began to show grief and distress of mind and was deeply depressed. Then He said to them [His disciples], 'My soul is very sad and deeply grieved, so that I am almost dying of sorrow' . . . And going a little farther, He threw Himself upon the ground on his face and prayed saying, 'My Father, if it is possible, let this cup pass away from Me; nevertheless, not what I will (not what I desire), but as You will and desire" (Matthew 26:37-39 AMPC).

Jesus Christ Himself experienced travail before spiritual rebirth was possible for you. ". . . Jesus declared, 'I tell you the truth, no one can see the kingdom of God unless he is born again" (John 3:3 NIV). Because the first man, Adam, willingly sinned in the garden of Eden, the perfect last man, Jesus, willingly paid the penalty of death, thereby accepting that punishment to satisfy a just and holy God. He then was satisfied Himself that He had completed the work set before Him by His Father. "But the Lord was pleased with this humble servant who suffered such pain. Even after giving himself as an offering for sin, he will see His descendants and enjoy a long life. He will succeed in doing what the Lord wanted. After his suffering he will see the light, and he will be satisfied with what he experienced" (Isaiah 53:10-11 ERV).

Jesus took the judgment due to sinful man in exchange for

pardon for those who put their trust in Him. Unbelievers need not stress, strain, or strive for the new birth. No self-effort or performance is required, for there is peace, stillness and rest in trusting Jesus by faith in Jesus.

Inner Travail or Birth Pains for a Spiritual Body

We travail in this physical body, but we are spirit beings. We have a soul, and currently we live in a physical body, an earth suit fitted for this present life on this earth. Our eternal home will be with our heavenly Father, so we will no longer need to be ensheathed in a temporary house, tent, or body. God will prepare for His children a heavenly body that is eternal and will continue in existence forever. You will not then be plagued with the burdens of life as you presently know it. So when this earth suit—your physical body—returns to the dust again, your resurrected body will be raised from the dead and made alive to live forever. "For we know that if the tent which is our earthly home is destroyed (dissolved), we have from God a building, a house not made with hands, eternal in the heavens. Here indeed, in this (present abode, body) we sigh and groan inwardly, because we yearn to be clothed over (we yearn to put on our celestial body like a garment, to be fitted out) with our heavenly dwelling" (2 Corinthians 5:1-2 AMPC).

The Creation Travails

God's creation travails, as a woman in labor, waiting longingly for a return to the order and perfection as in the beginning. "Everything that God made is waiting with excitement for the time when he will show the world who his children are. The whole world wants very much for that to happen . . . That the creation would be made free from ruin—that everything God made would have the same freedom and glory that belong to God's children . . . Everything God made has been waiting until now in pain like a woman ready to give birth to a child" (Romans 8:19, 21, 22 ERV).

God has made the earth for the children of men, who were to be reflections of Himself and were to have dominion over the earth and all in it. Because of Adam's fall, the earth is now subject to decay, deterioration, corruption, and ruin. While under the dominion of the evil one, it groans in agony, awaiting a showing forth of the children of God for the presentation of the blessed redeemed of the Lord. God's eternal plan for restoration of born-again sons and daughters, for a family with whom he could have a loving, intimate relationship, is being fulfilled. His plan will be fulfilled for the redemption of the physical bodies by resurrection as His children put on immortality to live in joyous fellowship forever with Him in a restored and redeemed heaven and on earth.

All that Jesus, the first fruit of many brethren, paid for by His death, burial, and resurrection will be fully realized by those who are His own when your earthly body is gloriously brought to life again in resurrection. "But everyone will be raised to life in the right order. Christ was first to be raised. Then, when Christ comes again, those who belong to him will be raised to life" (1 Corinthians 15:23 ERV).

Travail and Birth Pains for a New Age of Peace

"God saw all that he had made, and it was very good. . ." (Genesis 1:31 NIV). But human rebellion and disobedience by the first man Adam has made creation subject to frustration. All of creation is now in continuous decline, deteriorating and decaying from the perfection of the Genesis 1:31 account. Ecological ruin, upheavals, climate change, natural disasters such as floods, earthquakes, volcano eruptions, tsunamis, hurricanes, storms, wildfires, mudslides, plagues, famines, droughts, and pestilence are becoming more prevalent throughout the earth. Plant and animal species both on land and in the sea have been altered, destroyed, endangered, or even become extinct. Specific plant food necessary for the survival of certain species of insects has almost disappeared.

The natural habitat of many animals has been deforested or razed as humans encroach into their territory. Concerns about air quality develop as pollution increases. Pesticides have caused death to unhatched bird populations and are also dangerous to the well-being of others among the earth's inhabitants. The earth's human population is threatened by blood-borne diseases and deadly viruses such as Ebola, HIV AIDS, Coronavirus and the disfiguring Zika Virus. Dread and naturally incurable diseases affect the quality of life of many families. Mental and emotional disturbances are increasingly prevalent as the cares and stresses of everyday living become unbearable.

The Travail of Creation

"For (even the whole) creation (all nature) waits expectantly and longs earnestly for God's sons to be made known (waits for the revealing, the disclosing of their sonship)" (Romans 8:19 AMPC). The whole created world of God travails in agony while eagerly expecting and looking forward to the delivery, freedom, and liberation from its bondage of corruption. "Because the creature itself also shall be delivered from the bondage of corruption into the glorious liberty of the children of God" (Romans 8:21 KJV).

"We know that the whole creation has been groaning as in the pains of childbirth right up to the present time" (Romans 8:22 NIV). Creation longs to be set free from decay and destruction with the birth of a new heaven and earth as God will bring forth a new habitat for His family. "But God made a promise to us. And we are waiting for what he promised—a new sky and a new earth. That will be the place where goodness dwells" (2 Peter 3:13 ERV).

Social Disorder—Human Depravity and Decadence

Jesus said, "Be careful! Don't let anyone fool you. Many people will come and use my name. They will say, 'I am the Messiah,' and they will fool many people. You will hear about wars that are being fought . . . [and] other wars beginning . . . Nations will fight against other nations. Kingdoms will fight against other kingdoms. There will be times when there is no food for people to eat . . . These things are only the beginning of troubles, like the first pains of a woman giving birth" (Mark 13:5-8 ERV).

". . . There are some terrible times coming in the last days. People will love only themselves and money. They will be proud and boast about themselves. They will abuse others with insults. They will not obey their parents. They will have no love for others and will refuse to forgive anyone. They will talk about others to hurt them and will have no self-control. They will be cruel and hate what is good. People will turn against their friends. They will do foolish things without thinking and will be so proud of themselves. Instead of loving God, they will love pleasure. They will go on pretending to be devoted to God, but they will refuse to let that 'devotion' change the way they live . . ." (2 Timothy 3:1-5 ERV).

Blood, Necessary for Physical Life—Shedding of Blood, Necessary for Spiritual New Life

Without the shedding of blood, there can be no natural physical birth. It begins with the bleeding of the mother as a result of the opening of her cervix in preparation and during the labor process. This first bloodshed is called "the bloody show." Additionally, some bloodshed occurs during delivery.

- CHAPTER 8 -

WHEN I SEE THE BLOOD

". . . The life of the body is in the blood" (Leviticus 17:11 ERV). Medically, there is a close, vital relationship and connection between human blood and a person's well-being or life itself. Physicians routinely order various types of blood tests as diagnostic tools to determine and treat health issues in patients. It is the life fluid flowing in the physical body. It is necessary for your continued existence while you are in this mortal body. The blood of Jesus, poured out and shed for you, was necessary for your new birth, life, and eternal existence as a child of God.

While the child is developing in the womb, the mother's blood never mixes with or enters the child's bloodstream. It does, however, receive warmth and nourishment as the blood of its mother encompasses and surrounds the placenta contained in the uterus. Restoration to divine favor, spiritual rebirth, is only by the shed blood of Jesus, God the Son, who came from the Father. Born-again believers are spiritually fathered from above through the shed blood of Jesus Christ.

In the physical birth process, some bloodshed occurs after delivery as a result of the process. At the very moment of spiritual rebirth, the born-again believer is protected and covered by the precious blood of Jesus from the divine judgment of God for sin and unrighteousness. You are forgiven from all your sins by the precious blood of Jesus. You are justified, just as if you'd never sinned, by the wonder-working blood of Jesus. You are sanctified, made holy, set apart, dedicated to God by the powerful blood of Jesus.

You are made righteous, in right standing with your heavenly Father by the outpoured blood of Jesus. You have complete access at any time to the very presence of God in heaven because the precious blood of Jesus has been shed for you. Now, you have been accepted by faith into the Father's loving family as a born-again child of God.

"But now in Christ Jesus, you who once were (so) far away, through (by, in) the blood of Christ have been brought near" (Ephesians 2:13 AMPC). You are brought back, reconciled into a harmonious, right relationship with a loving God who, in spite of everything, continually reaches out to you to draw you back to Himself. "In Him we have redemption (deliverance and salvation) through His blood, the remission (forgiveness) of our offenses (shortcomings and trespasses), in accordance with the riches and the generosity of His gracious favor" (Ephesians 1:7 AMPC).

Blood of Jesus the Son

Jesus shed His own life blood and gave up His sinless life as a sacrificial substitute for your sin: His life, the innocent, in exchange for your life, the guilty. Without the shed blood of Jesus, there is no spiritual re-birth and forgiveness of sin. ". . . Without the shedding of blood there is neither release from sin and its guilt nor remission of the due and merited punishment for sins" (Hebrews 9:22 AMPC).

"You must know (recognize) that you were redeemed (ransomed) . . . not with corruptible things (such as) silver and gold, but (you were purchased) with the precious blood of Christ (the Messiah), like that of a (sacrificial) lamb without blemish or spot" (1 Peter 1:18-19 AMPC).

Jesus, the perfect man, shed His life's blood from his back, head, face, hands, feet, and side. Also, prior to His arrest, trial, conviction, and death sentence, He shed blood as He prayed fervently to His Father. He travailed as He determined to complete His mission on earth.

"And being in an agony (of mind), He prayed (all the) more earnestly and intently, and His sweat became like great clots of blood dropping down on the ground" (Luke 22:44 AMPC). This experience could indicate what is called the "bloody sweat," an actual combination or mingling of the blood and sweat that may occur during times of extreme mental stress and conflict. After His arrest, He continued to shed His blood on many different occasions as he was beaten, abused, flogged, and pierced. "So then Pilate took Jesus and scourged (flogged, whipped) Him. And the soldiers, having twisted together a crown of thorns, put it on His head . . ." (John 19:1-2 AMPC).

"And they crucified him . . ." (Matthew 27:35 KJV). Jesus was nailed to a cross with hands and arms outstretched, with His feet nailed together so that His entire body weight was supported by those nails piercing His hands and feet. After His death, while yet suspended on the cross, He shed more blood. ". . . One of the soldiers pierced His side with a spear, and immediately blood and water came (flowed) out" (John 19:34 AMPC).

Just before their deliverance from captivity and slavery in Egypt, the families of the children of Israel were instructed by God to place the blood of a sacrificial lamb on three sides of the doorway, specifically on top and on both sides of the door posts. "But the blood on your houses will be a special sign. When I see the blood, I will pass over your house . . ." (Exodus 12:13 ERV).

Obedience to God's word would assure protection and security for them when the judgment of God came upon their captors.

It would pass over the houses with the blood, and all inhabitants within would survive. The blood was a sign and pledge of God's care and concern for His people. His goodness and merciful loving-kindness bring deliverance.

You also can be secure in your belief and faith in the work of Christ and His sacrificial blood shed for you. Repent, change your mind and ways; turn to Him and away from your disobedience and bondage to sin and unbelief. Your deliverance is assured.

Breaking the Water

Physical birth involves the water or fluid contained in the amniotic sac. During pregnancy, the unborn child is protected and cushioned in fluid as it is completely enclosed in a thin membrane, the amniotic sac. It breaks or bursts under pressure, usually at the onset of labor. When the fluid is released, it is called "breaking the bag of water." The expectant mother might say, "My water just broke." The rupture may result in a small trickle or a much greater gush of fluid escaping, signaling an expected and impending delivery. The breaking of the water is a definite sign that the baby is coming and physical birth will result.

"Jesus answered, 'Believe me when I say that everyone must be born of water and the Spirit. Anyone who is not born from water and the Spirit cannot enter God's kingdom. The only life people get from their human parents is physical. But the new life that the Spirit gives a person is spiritual'" (John 3:5-6 ERV).

". . . Christ loved the church and gave Himself for her, so that He might sanctify her, having cleansed her by the washing of water with the Word" (Ephesians 5:25-26 AMPC). Christ Jesus, motivated by His love for you, wholly and completely gave up His own life so that you might be born again. Here, water symbolizes the Word of God as the cleansing agent. The reborn child of God is set apart, dedicated for a special purpose and for service.

"He saved us because of his mercy, not because of any good things we did. He saved us through the washing that made us new people. He saved us by making us new through the Holy Spirit. God poured out to us that Holy Spirit fully through Jesus Christ our Savior. We were made right with God by his grace. God saved us so that we could be his children and look forward to receiving life that never ends" (Titus 3:5-7 ERV).

To be born of the Spirit, or the new birth, is an act of the Spirit of God. It is the Holy Spirit's convicting work to convince you of the sin of unbelief in the finished work of Jesus on the cross. It is the water, symbolic of the Word bringing salvation. It is the Word of God, the good news of the gospel, that you must believe in and trust for eternal life.

> "... You don't know what God can give you. And you don't know who I am, the one who asked you for a drink. If you knew, you would have asked me, and I would have given you living water ... Everyone who drinks this water will be thirsty again. But anyone who drinks the water I give will never be thirsty again. The water I give people will be like a spring flowing inside them. It will bring them eternal life" (John 4:10, 13-14 ERV).

This is the response of Jesus after He requested a drink of water from a natural well. He contrasts stored, non-moving cistern or well water with running water in a moving, refreshing stream or spring. The living water represents salvation and spiritual life in Christ Jesus. This living spring of water is poured out freely on the inside for personal salvation. As it gushes up, it overflows for the good of others.

"But when the soldiers came close to Jesus, they saw that he was already dead . . . But one of the soldiers stuck his spear into Jesus' side. Immediately blood and water came out" (John 19:33-34 ERV). The blood and water are the medical signs of death due to massive heart failure. In His humanity, Jesus was tormented and endured great physical suffering before and during His crucifixion. His natural heart may have also been ruptured as a result of the sorrow, grief, and mental agony when He took on in His own body the sin, sickness, and diseases of all mankind. When His side was pierced, blood flowed out from His broken heart. It mingled with the water or fluid from the membrane or sac enclosing His heart.

Through the Narrow Place

The baby travels through a narrow passageway, the birth canal, in order to be born and enter into a new physical life outside its mother's body. In physical birth, there is a miraculous breaking through from obscurity in a narrow, dark, constricted space into a bright, unrestricted new existence. In the new birth, there is also a miraculous breakthrough: from a life of bondage to sin in the kingdom of darkness and into a new life of light, love, and freedom in Christ Jesus.

Jesus Himself said: ". . . I am the Way and the Truth and the Life; no one comes to the Father except by (through) Me" (John 14:6 AMPC). There is only one way to make atonement (to be at one) with God Himself. That is through Jesus, and through Him alone are we restored to favor and reconciled back to God. The "way" is a means to get to a desired destination. That destination is a relationship with God the Father, a Person. Therefore, the "Way" is also a Person. Jesus is describing Himself when He states: "I am the Way." He does not say "I am one of many other possible ways or alternative ways," but "I am THE Way." He is the only way to the one true Father God. "And there is salvation in and through no one else, for there is no other name under heaven given among men by and in which we must be saved" (Acts 4:12 AMPC).

Every way or route has a specific point of entry. This way to the Father is only through a specific place, the entrance, the narrow gate. The Way is the Person of Jesus Christ, and the gate is belief or trust in His finished work on the cross. "Enter through the narrow gate. For wide is the gate and broad is the road that leads to destruction, and many enter through it. But small is the gate and narrow the road that leads to life . . ." (Matthew 7:13-14 NIV).

The way to destruction leads to eternal separation from a loving Father. Many people choose alternate unsuccessful attempts to reach God through various gates of unbelief. The narrow gate and the narrow way open up to eternal life, knowing God and Jesus Christ, the one He sent to pay the ultimate price on your behalf. From the moment of your new birth, now and forevermore throughout eternity, you can have a life of close personal relationship with God, your Father, and with Jesus Christ, God's firstborn Son. The way is clearly marked out in the Scriptures. There are no detours or alternate routes; He is the direct route to Life.

> *"If you openly say, 'Jesus is Lord' and believe in your heart that God raised him from death, you will be saved. Yes, we believe in Jesus deep in our hearts, and so we are made right with God. And we openly say that we believe in him, and so we are saved" (Romans 10:9-10 ERV).*

Salvation or the "born again" experience is through a narrow entrance. The way is the person of Jesus Christ. So, by faith, you can experience an instant, a single time of entry into God's family and kingdom. But then afterwards, the Christian walk—the walk of faith—is a process, a journey, a manner of living and conduct pleasing to your Father. While new birth is immediate, the new walk of life in the family of God is progressive. In fact, in Acts 9:2, early Christian believers were designated as "belonging to the Way (of life as determined by faith in Jesus Christ" (Acts 9:2 AMPC).

You don't need to map out or chart your own path or way. There is no other private or personal true revelation from any source other than the Scriptures. God will not reveal to anyone in a dream or vision a different way to Himself contrary to His own Word.

He does not say, "I am a portion of the way, so you must also perform certain rituals or complete additional religious ceremonies or rites to earn your own way." Salvation is available by what Jesus achieved for you through His death. It is not a result of your own achievement or self-effort.

The way is an open road to any and all who choose that path. No one is excluded or will be denied access or refused entry. Everyone has equal entrance and passage to the Father through faith in Jesus. "For there (is only) one God, and (only) one Mediator between God and men, the Man Christ Jesus, who gave Himself as a ransom for all (people) . . ." (1 Timothy 2:5-6 AMPC).

"Yes, God loved the world so much that he gave his only Son, so that everyone who believes in him would not be lost but have eternal life" (John 3:16 ERV). Right now, at this present time, the gate is ajar and the way is open to all who desire to come to the Father, the only true God. Enter in, choose life and that more abundant life. This is not achieved by natural birth or lineage but by the miraculous spiritual birth from above.

Through the straight gate is the place where we must enter, a single event when we become born again or saved. After the born-again experience, we enter into a new kind of life, which is a process that involves continuous growth and development in your Christian walk.

Now that you are born again, a child of God, your life is no longer your own to do with it as you will or as you please. You have been bought with a price. "... You are not your own, you were bought with a price ..." (1 Corinthians 6:19-20 AMPC).

The shed blood of Christ was the great price paid for your salvation. Since you are God's own treasured possession, all three members of the Godhead, God the Father, God the Son Jesus Christ, and God the Holy Spirit, continue to minister to and for you as you walk in the new way of life. You will not walk alone or be left to your own devices. God, your Father, promises His dear children, "Don't worry—I am with you. Don't be afraid—I am your God. I will make you strong and help you. I will support you with my right hand that brings victory" (Isaiah 41:10 ERV).

God the Son prays to God His Father, and yours, for His followers. "Now I am coming to you. I will not stay in the world, but these followers of mine are still in the world. Holy Father, keep them safe by the power of your name—the name you gave me. Then they will be one, just as you and I are one ... I pray not only for these followers but also for those who will believe in me because of their teaching" (John 17:11, 20 ERV).

He prays also for those who receive Christ throughout the world and through all the ages because of the Word, the Scriptures written by early followers of Christ as inspired by the Holy Spirit. "I leave you peace. It is my own peace I give you. I give you peace in a different way than the world does. So don't be troubled. Don't be afraid" (John 14:27 ERV). As believers walk the narrow way, you can be assured that you have the continued prayer of Jesus Christ as He intercedes for you. You have His legacy of peace to assist you in your walk.

Jesus also promised that believers would not be left alone as orphans, but that He would ask the Father to give them another Helper: "I will ask the Father, and he will give you another Helper to be with you forever. The Helper is the Spirit of truth . . . You know him. He lives with you, and he will be in you" (John 14:16-17 ERV).

The Helper is the Holy Spirit who indwells every child of God. He knows all about you, even better than you could possibly know yourself, because He dwells or lives in your innermost being. He will take you by the hand, walk alongside you, lead you, and guide you into all truth. He will teach you, comfort you, and counsel you. He will be just as real to you as Jesus was when He was physically here on Earth. He will be your tender, ever-present loving friend, helping you to live a life pleasing to God.

Jesus said also that He was Truth and the Life. He is the Truth of God to set you free, the way out of a life of sin and unbelief, and He is the way out of your season of fear, frustration, and failure. He said that He was the Life, the only source of an abundant life with God as your Father. He is the Way into an overcoming life of freedom and victory as a child of God.

Crowning

As an expectant mother enters into the second of the three stages of labor, the first visible appearance of the child's body is the crown of his head. This event is known as "crowning," and it signals that the birthing process is nearly complete. After the crowning, the child's entire head emerges. Next, the rest of the body follows and slips out without difficulty. The baby's head and its body are not separate but one in unity. Both as a living unit descend from identical, physical stock, with the same natural parentage and the same DNA. Both are part of the same physical body.

In physical birth, when the bottom, hinder part, or buttocks appears to emerge first instead of the crown of the head, this birthing situation establishes an unnatural order of things. Attempts are made to adjust and to restore the child's body back to the proper position before delivery. In the same way, any assembly, body of believers, church, or individual believer not acknowledging the spiritual headship of Jesus requires serious adjustment and restoration by the Holy Spirit back to God's divine arrangement.

> *"For the body does not consist of one limb or organ but of many . . . But as it is, God has placed and arranged the limbs and organs in the body, each (particular one) of them, just as He wished and saw fit and with the best adaptation. But if (the whole) were all a single organ, where would the body be? And now there are (certainly) many limbs and organs, but a single body"* (1 Corinthians 12:14, 18-20 AMPC).

The physical body has many different members or parts, with separate functions. Each is dependent upon the others, and each is necessary for fullness of life. The church, likewise, is a collection, a living organism of born-again believers, functioning separately but mutually dependent on each other. By following the lead of its head, Jesus Christ, the church, as the body of Christ, can complete the charge given to it by God to bless and minister to those in the world around it, as well as to each other. The head, Jesus Christ, has the God-given authority to lead and give direction. Because He is most prominent, the head rules or makes decisions and the body follows obediently.

Serious medical problems result whenever physical body parts or members are not controlled by the head or brain. Likewise, in the spiritual realm, God's perfect plan for mankind is not achieved when the church, the body of Jesus Christ, is not yielded to following the head. There can be no separation or division in the body. Members of the church must be united in harmony and cooperation, working together for the good of the body as well as for all others yet outside the body. "For as in one physical body we have many parts (organs, members) and all of these parts do not have the same function or use, so we, numerous as we are, are one body in Christ (the Messiah), and individually we are parts one of another (mutually dependent on one another)" (Romans 12:4-5 AMPC).

As with the physical body, God has placed and arranged the members of the church, the body of Christ, individually for His own use and to fulfill His purposes: ". . . God has so adjusted (mingled, harmonized, and subtly proportioned) the parts of the whole body . . . so that there should be no division or discord or lack of adaptation (of the parts of the body to each other), but the members all alike should have a mutual interest in and care for one another . . . Now you (collectively) are Christ's body and (individually) you are members of it, each part severally and distinct (each with his own place and function)" (1 Corinthians 12:24-25, 27 AMPC).

The head of the church and the church itself (His body) are one. Both have the same identity and are not separate, one from the other. Both share identical spiritual DNA and lineage; they are descended from the same line, either born or begotten as Jesus, or adopted as children, as you are, into the same spiritual family. All born-again believers are in Christ Jesus and make up the church, which is the body of Christ. The new creation body is the church, made up of those who are new creations. Each believer is a part of that body.

". . . Christ is head of the church; and He is the Savior of the body . . . The church is subject to Christ . . ." (Ephesians 5:23-24 NKJV). God appointed Jesus to be ". . . the universal and supreme Head of the church (a headship exercised throughout the church" (Ephesians 1:22 AMPC). Spiritually, Christ now operates in this present, natural world through the church, His body. Similarly, each distinctive characteristic of our human personalities functions through our physical bodies. The church serves under Christ. As He leads, we follow.

"He also is the Head of (His) body, the church; seeing He is the Beginning, the Firstborn from among the dead, so that He alone in everything and in every respect might occupy the chief place (stand first and be preeminent)" (Colossians 1:18 AMPC). Jesus is of primary importance in all things, since He is the center and source of life for the individual. Also, He is the head over all things for that which is beneficial and profitable for the church, His body, as a whole, and for each member in particular, including everything that touches or pertains to your individual life.

His headship extends to the time when all things will come together under one head, Jesus Christ. ". . . And He is the Head of all rule and authority (of every angelic principality and power)" (Colossians 2:10 AMPC).

> ". . . Our goal is to become like a full-grown man – to look just like Christ and have all His perfection. Then we will no longer be like babies...they will grow to be like Christ in every way. He is the head, and the whole body depends on him. All parts of the body are joined and held together, with each part doing its own work. This causes the whole body to grow and to be stronger in life" (Ephesians 4:13-15 ERV).

"And it is in union with him that you have been made full—he is the head of every rule and authority" (Colossians 2:10 Jewish New Testament). Jesus will be crowned Lord of all! Because when you belong to Christ, you are complete, having everything you need for life and godliness. Access this truth by remembering that the authority belonging to Christ, the head, also belongs to every individual member of the body. A song of David for praise to God: "Who redeems your life from destruction, who crowns you with lovingkindness and tender mercies" (Psalm 103:4 NKJV). Jesus Christ paid the price to bring you back to God, who encircles those who are His with all blessing available due His children and family. He shuts you up in His protective care. He surrounds and encloses you to shield and cover you with compassion, gentleness, and forgiveness. He watches over you as a patient mother diligently attends to the needs of her child, or as a mother hen protects and cares for her young brood of chicks. His all-encompassing love protects you in every situation or need in your new life when you are born again from above.

"Then Jesus said to his followers, 'If any of you want to be my follower, you must stop thinking about yourself and what you want. You must be willing to carry the cross that is given to you for following me" (Matthew 16:24 ERV). Since Jesus is the head of the spiritual body, the church, then as the body, His people, we carry out the will of the head. We allow Him to rule over our lives as followers of Christ. God will ultimately bring all things under one head, Christ Jesus.

> *"He put Christ over all rulers, authorities, powers, and kings. He gave him authority over everything that has power in this world or in the next world. God put everything under Christ's power and made him head over everything for the church. The church is Christ's body. It is filled with him. He makes everything complete in every way"* (Ephesians 1:21-23 ERV).

> *". . . God has highly exalted Him and has freely bestowed on Him the name that is above every name, that in (at) the name of Jesus every knee should (must) bow, in heaven and on earth and under the earth, and every tongue (frankly and openly) confess and acknowledge that Jesus Christ is Lord, to the glory of God the Father"* (Philippians 2:9-11 AMPC).

> *"And there was given Him (the Messiah) dominion and glory and kingdom, that all peoples, nations, and languages should serve Him. His dominion is an everlasting dominion which shall not pass away, and His kingdom is one which shall not be destroyed" (Daniel 7:14 AMPC).*

Jesus Christ will be crowned King of Kings and Lord of Lords as God's divine will is accomplished and brought forth, as He rules and reigns over all forever and ever. Eventually, according to God's divine plan, there will be a time when every principality, every ruler, and every authority will be subject and placed under the headship of Jesus. All will confess and acknowledge and declare Him to be the Son of God.

Revealed Through the Natural Delivery Process

"Upon You have I leaned and relied from birth. You are He Who took me from my mother's womb and You have been my benefactor from that day . . ." (Psalm 71:6 AMPC). God personally superintended and had oversight over your physical birth and delivery. He was intimately acquainted with you even before your conception. He knows and cares about every aspect, even the merest detail of your life and existence.

Natural delivery liberates a child from the confines of the old life before birth. It is a once-in-a-lifetime experience as the newborn is catapulted immediately into a new life in a brand-new world. Struggle and great physical effort are necessary during the natural birth process. During active childbirth, the baby is pushed down by contractions during the three stages of labor and finally to ultimate delivery. The mother assists in the strenuous process as she pushes to complete the delivery and birth. After birth, the newborn may need assistance to begin breathing. A smack on the baby's bottom helps, as the child fights and gasps with its very first breath outside the womb. All wait expectantly to hear that first cry indicating life.

However, there is no striving, effort, or struggle involved on your part in the new birth. Salvation is freely given and must be freely received by faith as a gift from God because of His great grace.

> *"For it is by free grace (God's unmerited favor) that you are saved (delivered from judgment and made partakers of Christ's salvation) through (your) faith. And this (salvation) is not of yourselves (of your own doing, it came not through your own striving), but it is the gift of God; not because of works . . . lest any man should boast. (It is not the result of what anyone could possibly do, so no one can pride himself in it or take glory to himself)" (Ephesians 2:8-9 AMPC).*

The child in the womb itself sets in motion or triggers the labor and delivery process. It had a previous life in the womb before its birth into a new, different life outside the womb of its mother.

"But when the fulness of the time was come, God sent forth His Son, made of a woman . . . to redeem . . . that we might receive the adoption of sons" (Galatians 4:4-5 KJV). Just at the right and proper time, God sent His beloved Son to earth to be born as a Deliverer and Savior and fulfill God's divine plan for the ages. Jesus, who always existed in the beginning with God and in the form of God, willingly left His heavenly home to be born on earth and take on a new life in human form. An unbeliever lives a life of sin and judgment, separated from a loving God. After you make a conscious choice to believe, confess, and receive a new life of faith in Christ Jesus, you are delivered from the family of Satan and gain entrance into the family of God.

- CHAPTER 9 -

SUPERNATURAL DELIVERANCE

Initial Deliverance

> *"When anyone is in Christ, it is a whole new world. The old things are gone; suddenly, everything is new!" (2 Corinthians 5:17 ERV).*

Spiritual rebirth is a one-time supernatural experience. You are translated immediately from the kingdom of darkness into God's kingdom of light, love, and life. You are set free from the family of Satan, who is the current prince of this world system, and delivered instantly into the family of the eternal, only true living God. When you are born again, you are instantly released and liberated from your dark past. You supernaturally become a brand-new creation, never in existence before, and fathered from above by the power of the Holy Spirit.

"(The Father) has delivered and drawn us to Himself out of the control and the dominion of darkness and has transferred us into the kingdom of the Son of His love" (Colossians 1:13 AMPC). You are freed from the restrictions of a sinful life without God that bound you and prevented you from enjoying the blessings of life in a loving family. God the Father has not only drawn you out of your past condition, but also has drawn you into a right relationship with Him. He brought you out to bring you in.

Ongoing Deliverance

> *"The righteous cry out, and the Lord hears them; he delivers them from all their troubles. The Lord is close to the brokenhearted and saves those who are crushed in spirit"* (Psalm 34:17-18 NIV).

He is faithful and true, and you can depend on His lovingkindness to keep you when you are sad and depressed. Those who are in right standing with God, His children, can be assured of His desire to deliver them now and in the future. He is always near to those who call out to Him in times of distress. Your heavenly Father God desires to make you content as He meets your needs and fulfills your desires, not only physically, but also emotionally and relationally.

Final Deliverance

Do not rely on yourselves, but depend upon the God "... who raises the dead. He has delivered us from such a deadly peril, and he will deliver us. On him we have set our hope that he will continue to deliver us" (2 Corinthians 1:9-10 NIV). All will eventually be resurrected, but only those who are His own will spend eternity with Him instead of experiencing the judgment and punishment of eternal separation from a loving God and Father.

Ultimate Deliverance of the Physical Human Body from Corruption, Decay, and Death

> *"... We have the Spirit as the first part of God's promise. So we are waiting for God to finish making us his own children. I mean we are waiting for our bodies to be made free"* (Romans 8:23 ERV).

The final stage in your adoption as God's children will be the resurrection of your bodies. Your mortal human bodies will be redeemed and delivered from death and decay. At that time, you will be just like His Son, Jesus Christ, who was the first raised from the dead.

Deliverance of All Creation from Decay—Restored Heaven and Earth

> *"Because the creation itself also will be delivered from the bondage of corruption into the glorious liberty of the children of God" (Romans 8:21 NKJV).*

All of creation shall be liberated and set free from the curse and bondage of decay and corruption, and shall again be made new. Its eternal state will then be suitable for a perfect habitation for Father God when He comes down to dwell on earth with His beloved family, those who have received their full inheritance.

> *"But in keeping with his promise we are looking forward to a new heaven and a new earth, the home of righteousness" (2 Peter 3:13 NIV).*

Breakthrough from Darkness to Light

The newborn infant progresses suddenly from the darkness and obscurity of its former life in the womb and is immediately birthed into a new life of light. It is propelled with great effort, labor pains and travail by the mother into a new world. The old restrictive environment allowed no possibility for continued growth and development. The familiar comfort of the mother's womb became increasingly uncomfortable and constricted. If the baby continued its life in that confining situation, the consequences for both child and mother would be certain death. At the moment of natural birth, the child usually emerges capable of functioning outside of the womb. Each new day presents opportunities for physical, mental, and emotional growth and maturation.

Just as a new child is plunged immediately from the darkness of its comfortable life sustained in the womb, in spiritual birth, the new believer is translated instantly from overwhelming darkness, without God, into a life of God's love and light. This new birth, however, involves no striving, self-effort, labor, struggle, or stress. It is not dependent on your own action, work, or performance. It comes only by faith and trusting in the completed work by Jesus Christ on your behalf.

In Genesis 1:3, God spoke and called forth light into a lifeless, chaotic, hopeless, unproductive earth, a place without form and void of His divine presence and purpose. At the time that God's creative spoken word went forth, the birth of the newly restored earth occurred. Darkness fled at the presence of light—it was dispelled, cleared away, and scattered. And light broke through and was separated from darkness.

It was God the Son's accomplished and completed work on the cross that made it possible for you to be redeemed back to Father God. He paid the price, the penalty required by a holy God. "When Jesus spoke again to the people, he said, 'I am the light of the world. Whoever follows me will never walk in darkness, but will have the light of life'" (John 8:12 NIV).

"For God, who said, 'Let light shine out of darkness,' made his light shine in our hearts to give us the light of the knowledge of the glory of God in the face of Christ" (2 Corinthians 4:6 NIV). Jesus came to earth from His Father's heavenly presence, the exact image and likeness of Him. He is the manifestation or representation of the radiance of God's divine glory. He is the light that came to earth to reveal to mankind the knowledge of God as Father, and to bring sinful men back to a right relationship with Him. "For God did not send the Son into the world in order to judge (to reject, to condemn, to pass sentence on) the world, but that the world might find salvation and be made safe and sound through Him" (John 3:17 AMPC).

"As people understand your word, it brings light to their lives. Your word makes even simple people wise" (Psalm 119:130 ERV). God leaves nothing to chance about His family's well-being. He left the Bible, His love letter to you, so you don't have to feel your way, searching or groping in the darkness and learning by trial and error. His Word clearly explains His plan for your life, the rewards for obedience, and the consequences and effects of willful disobedience.

> *"In the past you were full of darkness, but now you are full of light in the Lord. So live like children who belong to the light. This light produces every kind of goodness, right living, and truth. Try to learn what pleases the Lord. Have no part in the things that people in darkness do, which produce nothing good. . ." (Ephesians 5:8-11 ERV).*

Let your conduct and lifestyle draw others into the family of God. Let them see Christ in all that you do, as you are a living witness to unbelievers. Allow the Holy Spirit to assist you to be an obedient child who is well-pleasing to your heavenly Father, bringing glory and honor to God, and receive the blessing and promises of God in your life.

Jesus said that those who accompany Him as disciples or learners on the same path of life will have the light of life to flood and illuminate the way. "Your Word is a lamp to my feet and a light to my path" (Psalm 119:105 NIV).

Spiritual darkness represents evil, falsehood, disorder, destruction, chaos, and death. There is hopeless desperation, with no possible expectation of divine benefit or blessing in the present, the future, or for all eternity. "For every wrongdoer hates (loathes, detests) the Light, and will not come out into the Light but shrinks from it, lest his works (his deeds, his activities, his conduct) be exposed and reproved" (John 3:20 AMPC).

When anyone, as an unbeliever, receives with faith the revelation of God's Word and allows it to enter into his heart, light shines into that formerly dark place of sin and disbelief. Because people are living or walking in darkness, they cannot see or even know where they are or where they are heading. They are, therefore, unsure of the hopelessness of their current situation. As a result, without a light to guide them, they are lost and incapable of finding a way out of despairing circumstances.

It is the Word that makes clear the way to eternal life in Christ. It is the light of the glorious gospel that leads to salvation.

Jesus Spoke to Those with Blinded Minds

". . . Your father, the devil . . . when he speaks a falsehood, he speaks what is natural to him, for he is a liar (himself) and the father of lies and of all that is false" (John 8:44 AMPC). Because it is Satan's nature to lie and deceive, there can be no truth in him. He is utterly untrustworthy and unreliable, since his ultimate evil aim is to trick you and destroy your life and well-being now and forever.

"For the god of this world [Satan] has blinded the unbelievers' minds (that they should not discern the truth), preventing them from seeing the illuminating light of the Gospel. . ." (2 Corinthians 4:4 AMPC). They are spiritually blind, lack understanding, and choose to remain in darkness because of ignorance of Satan's devices and schemes.

"But you are . . . (God's) own purchased, special people . . . of Him Who called you out of darkness into His marvelous light" (1 Peter 2:9 AMPC). At the moment of spiritual rebirth, a totally new creation comes into existence as a miraculous transformation from within. You become a brand-new spiritual being indwelling a physical body. In your old life without God, spiritual growth is impossible, but in your new relationship as a child of God, your newly created spirit connects directly with God who is Spirit. It is in this atmosphere and in the light of His presence that you can flourish and thrive.

". . . If we walk in the light, as he is in the light, we have fellowship one with another, and the blood of Jesus Christ his Son cleanseth us from all sin. If we say that we have no sin, we deceive ourselves, and the truth is not in us. If we confess our sins, he is faithful and just to forgive us our sins, and to cleanse us from all unrighteousness" (1 John 1:7-9 KJV). A holy God is Light, absolutely pure, morally perfect, and there is no darkness in Him. You are His children who walk continually in the light of His Truth and Word and do not practice sin, but when you do sin, you have this hope.

"You are the light of the world . . . Let your light shine before men, that they may see your good deeds and praise your Father in heaven" (Matthew 5:14, 16 NIV). You are to reflect the light that comes from Jesus as you carry out His work on earth. People will be drawn to you as you share the good news of the gospel of Jesus Christ and depend on the Holy Spirit to convict them of unbelief. You will increase in reproductiveness as other children born from above are brought into God's family. Since you have been translated instantly from one life to another—from the family of the evil one, a family of death and destruction, and into God's marvelous family—you will not desire to continue to live in the old way.

To his firstborn nation Israel, God says, "And now, says the Lord . . . 'I will also give you for a light to the nations, that My salvation may extend to the end of the earth'" (Isaiah 49:5-6 AMPC). Almighty God foretells and reveals His promised redemptive plan for all nations. It is His grace, His loving-kindness and unmerited favor, and His great mercy and forgiveness that made provision for His light to shine throughout the earth.

Breath and Life

> *"By the word of the Lord the heavens were made, and by the breath of His mouth all their host . . . For He spoke, and it was done; He commanded, and it stood fast" (Psalm 33:6, 9 NASB).*

His breath, plus His Word of power, keeps all the universe, His creation, functioning together in their assigned places and orbits. The breath of God, the Holy Spirit, and the Word of power are creative forces. God the Father plans it, God the Son—the Word made flesh—speaks it, and God the Holy Spirit manifests and brings it into being. "The Lord, the true God . . . He created the sky and spread it out over the earth. He formed the earth and everything it produced. He breathes life into all the people on earth. He gives a spirit to everyone who walks on the earth" (Isaiah 42:5 ERV).

God is the source of all life. All life originates from Him; for He has life in Himself and all life belongs to Him. God himself breathed into lifeless man's nostrils the breath of life, "and man became a living soul" (Genesis 2:7 KJV). Man, made in the image of God, his body formed from the ground, lay lifeless. So God, from Himself, breathed into Adam the breath of life, and he became a living soul. Man became a breathing creation with a physical body, an intellectual soul, and an eternal spirit functioning and operating together for a new life on earth that God had lovingly prepared for him.

The Loving Heart of Father God

The Apostle Paul tells the people of Athens about the only eternal true and living God. "He is the God who made the whole world and everything in it . . . He is the one who gives people life, breath, and everything else they need . . . God began by making one man, and from him he made all the different people who live everywhere in the world. He decided exactly when and where they would live. God wanted people to look for him, and perhaps in searching all around for him, they would find him. But he is not far from any of us. It is through him that we are able to live, to do what we do, and to be who we are . . . We all come from him" (Acts 17:24-28 ERV).

All humans are God's offspring because all are descendants of the first man Adam. He was created by God to reproduce children like Himself to fill the earth. God, who is Creator, gives life and all things needed for existence. He rules all the nations of the world, as well as historical events. He determines where people and nations will settle and make their habitations.

Because He is a personal God who is love, He in turn seeks love from you as you seek Him. You are naturally His special offspring or child, but He deserves a closer, eternal, spiritual family relationship. He has more planned for you than your human existence on this earth—God has a divine plan for you to have a life fully in right relationship and fellowship with Him.

Jesus Christ, the Son of God, has been given the same kind of life the Father possesses. So, Jesus said, ". . . I came that they may have and enjoy life, and have it in abundance (to the full, till it overflows)" (John 10:10 AMPC).

"Life comes from the Father himself. So the Father has also allowed the Son to give life" (John 5:26 ERV). By the new birth, being born of God through faith in Jesus Christ His Son, your inner man or human spirit is newly created. The God-kind of life, His unchanging eternal nature and characteristics, are imparted into your spirit being.

"And this is eternal life: (it means) to know (to perceive, recognize, become acquainted with, and understand) You, the only true and real God, and (likewise) to know Him, Jesus (as the) Christ (the Anointed One, the Messiah) Whom You have sent" (John 17:3 AMPC). To know God and His Son Jesus is to live in loving fellowship and close communion together, now and forevermore. A personal God created a man Adam for personal fellowship. When Adam rebelled, God sent His only Son Jesus to reconcile man back to a right relationship with Him. God was in Christ Jesus, personally present, once again bringing peace between sinful man and Himself.

Eternal Life

All will continue to exist forever after physical death, either separated for eternity from a loving God or in union and harmony with the Father. This union is an intimate, personal knowledge of the Father God and the Son Jesus Christ who was sent by Him. It is enjoying close relationship and agreement together from the new birth, now in this life and forevermore as you live eternally with your Father. God desired a family. You can become part of that family and have a life abundant with all that your Father promises to those who are His own.

The angelic host looked on in great expectation and responded joyfully at the first sign of life on earth as a result of God's spoken Word. All heaven also awaits with eager anticipation as the Holy Spirit hovers and broods over unbelievers, awaiting the penetration of repentant hearts by the good news of the gospel, God's divine Word. The out-breathed spoken confession of faith, first believed in the heart, results in the new life in Christ Jesus.

> *"Because if you acknowledge and confess with your lips that Jesus is Lord and in your heart believe (adhere to, trust in, and rely on the truth) that God raised Him from the dead, you will be saved. For with the heart a person believes (adheres to, trusts in, and relies on Christ) and so is justified (declared righteous, acceptable to God), and with the mouth he confesses (declares openly and speaks out freely his faith) and confirms (his) salvation"* (Romans 10:9-10 AMPC).

Faith is the confident reliance on who God is and what He does, believing His promises, and depending solely on Him to live a new life pleasing to Him. Faith takes hold with assurance and conviction of the reality of those things not yet perceived or manifested to the senses.

Confess or agree with God's Word of Truth about the finished work of Jesus to bring you back into right relationship with the Father. Agree that you have need of a Savior because you cannot rely on your own efforts, deeds, works, or strength of character to attain salvation. Now, make Him Lord of your life, the One in complete control of your future and destiny. Recognize His authority and submit to Him in unreserved obedience.

After His resurrection, Jesus appeared to His disciples to give them authority to continue His work after He returned to His Father. "Jesus therefore said to them again, 'Peace be with you; as the Father has sent Me, I also send you.' And when He had said this, He breathed on them, and said to them, 'Receive the Holy Spirit'" (John 20:21-22 NASB).

A caring Father leaves nothing to chance to ensure the ultimate success of His children. He prepares and enables them to fulfill the God-given purpose destined for them. The heavenly

Father prepared a human body for His Son Jesus to come and live on earth. He was empowered and filled with the Holy Spirit to complete the work planned for Him. So, too, is it for those who are adopted into God's family. As the Father did, so did the Son when He sent His followers, His disciples, into the world. He gave them the same power and fullness of the Holy Spirit to do the work of the ministry.

> *"If then you have been raised with Christ (to a new life, thus sharing His resurrection from the dead), aim at and seek the (rich, eternal treasures) that are above, where Christ is, seated at the right hand of God. And set your minds and keep them set on what is above (the higher things), not on the things that are on the earth. For (as far as this world is concerned) you have died, and your (new, real) life is hidden with Christ in God. When Christ, Who is our life, appears, then you also will appear with Him in (the splendor of His) glory"* (Colossians 3:1-4 AMPC).

You are God's treasured one at the new birth, when your old self or nature is dead and you receive a new life or hidden man of the heart that is concealed, shielded, protected, and kept with Christ in God. Christ is your life because eternal life is in faith in Jesus Christ and Him alone. He will return for His brothers, those yet on the earth or in the earth who will meet Him in the air to return to His Father and yours. At that time, by resurrection, those who are believers will receive new life in their mortal bodies and be as He is for eternity. Then, the Father and His family, with Jesus your elder brother, will live together in peace and security forever and ever.

Agony, Then Joy

"Whenever a woman is in travail she has sorrow, because her hour has come; but when she gives birth to the child, she remembers the anguish no more, for joy that a child has been born into the world" (John 16:21 NASB). A mother submits to the pain and suffering of childbirth, enduring the agony and sorrow because the ultimate birth of her child is one of the most rewarding and joyous events she will experience. Family and friends join with her in celebrating the delightful occasion.

In the Scriptures, God again uses the familiar picture of the natural processes of physical labor endured by a woman during childbirth. Her travail, agony, and pain, followed by the glorious delight experienced by the mother afterward, represent the various aspects in the fulfillment of His divine, eternal purposes. You can envision God's perfect plan for the entire created world, for mankind, and also for you individually and personally.

"Jesus, Who . . . for the joy (of obtaining the prize) that was set before Him, endured the cross, despising and ignoring the shame, and is now seated at the right hand of the throne of God" (Hebrews 12:2 AMPC). Crucifixion was the most extreme, excruciating method of execution. The agonizing pain was prolonged, as Jesus—stripped of His clothing, beaten unmercifully, weary, hungry, thirsty, His hands and feet pierced by iron spikes to support His body weight—hung suspended in a very public place. He heard the ridicule and scorn of the unruly onlookers as He struggled to take each tortured breath before He ultimately gave up His own life for you.

The prize He obtained was that He redeemed you back to a holy God, paying the price of death so that you might have an eternal life of intimacy with a loving God, enjoying His presence for eternity. He obediently and willingly offered up Himself for your sins once and for all, completely and perfectly.

". . . He has no form or comeliness (royal, kingly pomp), that we should look at Him, and no beauty that we should desire Him. He was despised and rejected and forsaken by men, a Man of sorrows and pains, and acquainted with grief and sickness; and like One from Whom men hide their faces He was despised, and we did not appreciate His worth or have any esteem for Him. Surely He has borne our griefs (sicknesses, weaknesses, and distresses) and carried our sorrows and pains (of punishment), yet we (ignorantly) considered Him stricken, smitten, and afflicted by God (as if by leprosy). But He was wounded for our transgressions, He was bruised for our guilt and iniquities; the chastisement (needful to obtain) peace and well-being for us was upon Him, and with the stripes (that wounded) Him we are healed and made whole. All we like sheep have gone astray, we have turned every one to his own way; and the Lord has made to light upon Him the guilt and iniquity of us all . . .

Yet it was the will of the Lord to bruise Him; He has put Him to grief and made Him sick. When You and He make His life an offering for sin (and He has risen from the dead . . .) He shall see His (spiritual) offspring . . . and the will and pleasure of the Lord shall prosper in His hand. He shall see (the fruit) of the travail of His soul and be satisfied . . . [and] justify many and make many righteous (upright and in right standing with God), for He shall bear their iniquities and their guilt (with the consequences, says the Lord)" (Isaiah 53:2-6, 10-11 AMPC).

". . . Our great God and Savior, Jesus Christ, who gave himself for us to redeem us from all wickedness and to purify for himself a people that are his very own . . ." (Titus 2:13-14 NIV). The sacrificial death of Jesus, a sinless man, on the cross and His resurrection defeated and judged Satan, the prince of this world system. As a result of His finished work He, Jesus, sat down in triumph at the right hand of God; the right hand is symbolic of a place of power, strength, and honor. The fact that He sat down indicates that His redemptive work for God's creation and His created beings was completed. His work is complete; therefore, no self-effort or work is necessary for you to accomplish in order for you to be in right standing with a holy God. This is the good news of the gospel of Jesus Christ: believe, trust in, and rely on what Jesus accomplished on the cross.

"Looking away (from all that will distract) to Jesus, Who is the Leader and the Source of our faith (giving the first incentive for our behalf) and is also its Finisher (bringing it to maturity and perfection). He, for the joy (of obtaining the prize) that was set before Him, endured the cross, despising and ignoring the shame, and is now seated at the right hand of the throne of God" (Hebrews 12:2 AMPC). Focus and concentrate on Jesus, who is the beginner who pioneers your faith, and also the one who perfects it and makes it complete. Focus your thoughts on His once-and-for-all sacrifice.

". . . There is joy in the presence of the angels of God over one sinner who repents" (Luke 15:10 NKJV). A joyous celebration erupts in heaven whenever just one person believes in the truth of God's word and repents, changes his mind and ways, and accepts Jesus as his Savior and Lord. God counts as most precious even one soul brought into His family and household of faith. The transition from unbelief and slavery to sin to true Sonship is a time for exhibitions of delight and rejoicing.

> *"The Spirit Himself (thus) testifies together with our own spirit, (assuring us) that we are children of God. And if we are (His) children, then we are (His) heirs also: heirs of God and fellow heirs with Christ (sharing His inheritance with Him); only we must share His suffering if we are to share His glory." (Romans 8:16-17 AMPC).*

The indwelling Spirit of God confirms and seals your personal relationship and restoration back into fellowship and favor with Father God. As His beloved child, you are assured of your full legal rights of inheritance. In the future, you will receive your promised resurrection body. It will be the same as the one your joint heir, Jesus Christ, possesses. At that time, your adoption process will be complete. There is nothing, no trial, tribulation, or suffering now endured in your current situation that can compare to the joy of your glorious eternal destiny.

"For our light and momentary troubles are achieving for us an eternal glory that far outweighs them all. So we fix our eyes not on what is seen, but on what is unseen. For what is seen is temporary, but what is unseen is eternal" (2 Corinthians 4:17-18 NIV). Your temporary physical body is in a state of continuous decay, but the eternal inner man, the real YOU, your spirit person, is continually being renewed daily.

Focusing on what is seen or experienced during this short period of your natural lifetime can easily cause desperation or fear. The more important pursuit should be on the unseen, the eternal and unfailing promises of God which are real, more real than the things that are visible or tangible to the senses. Your troubles and trials in this world are insignificant in comparison to the glory of the future planned for you by your Father. These afflictions are accomplishing that glorious purpose and plan conceived by your heavenly Father before time began.

> *"Now to Him Who is able to keep you without stumbling or slipping or falling, and to present (you) unblemished (blameless and faultless) before the presence of His glory in triumphant joy and exultation (with unspeakable, ecstatic delight)—To the one only God, our Savior through Jesus Christ our Lord, be glory (splendor), majesty, might and dominion, and power and authority, before all time and now and forever (unto all the ages of eternity). Amen (so be it)"* (Jude 24-25 AMPC).

God is capable of protecting, guarding, and keeping you, His beloved child, from falling. When you put your trust completely in Him, you will be secure until the return of Jesus Christ. You will be presented without blame or fault before God's presence and glory. This will be a time of exceeding great joy and unspeakable delight.

> *"Now we know that if the earthly tent we live in is destroyed, we have a building from God, an eternal house in heaven, not built by human hands. Meanwhile we groan, longing to be clothed with our heavenly dwelling . . . Now it is God who has made us for this very purpose and has given us the Spirit as a deposit, guaranteeing what is to come"* (2 Corinthians 5:1-2, 5 NIV).

Your frail human body, your earthly house inherited from your natural parents, is temporary and weak. Although your inner spirit man is being renewed with each passing day, your natural forces are slowly degrading and wasting away with time and age. But God the Father has prepared a permanent resurrected body, a glorious heavenly dwelling for you to inhabit eternally.

"When Christ, Who is our life, appears, then you also will appear with Him in (the splendor of His) glory" (Colossians 3:4 AMPC). When Christ Jesus returns to the earth with believers whose old selves have been crucified and whose new lives now are in Christ, when He comes again to establish His kingdom, you children of God, will joyously share in His marvelous glory.

Jesus encourages His followers before His death and resurrection: ". . . In the world you have tribulation and trials and distress and frustration; but be of good cheer (take courage; be confident, certain, undaunted)! For I have overcome the world. (I have deprived it of power to harm you and have conquered it for you)" (John 16:33 AMPC).

After the first man Adam turned over to Satan the title deed to the earth because of his disobedience and rebellion, Jesus came as a man to redeem mankind back to God. When He defeated Satan at the cross, he gave power and authority in heaven and on earth to those who believe. But this current world system continues to remain under the control of the "prince" of the power of the air or the "god" of this world. Although he is a defeated foe, he is constantly on the attack against the true and living God and His eternal purpose. "And indeed, all who desire to live godly in Christ Jesus will be persecuted" (2 Timothy 3:12 NASB).

> *"For I consider that the sufferings of this present time (this present life) are not worth being compared with the glory that is about to be revealed to us and in us and for us and conferred on us!" (Romans 8:18 AMPC).*

Jesus said, "I have told you these things so that you can have peace in me. In this world you will have troubles. But be brave! I have defeated the world!" (John 16:33 ERV). "After Jesus said these things, he looked toward heaven and prayed,

'Father, the time has come. Give glory to your Son so that the Son can give glory to you. You gave the Son power over all people so that he could give eternal life to all those you have given to him. And this is eternal life: that people can know you, the only true God, and that they can know Jesus Christ, the one you sent. I finished the work you gave me to do. I brought you glory on earth. And now, Father, give me glory with you. Give me the glory I had with you before the world was made" (John 17:1-5 ERV). His work as a man on earth, to bring "many sons to glory," was completely completed, perfectly perfected.

> *"Let us fix our eyes on Jesus, the author and perfecter of our faith, who for the joy set before him endured the cross, scorning its shame, and sat down at the right hand of the throne of God" (Hebrews 12:2 NIV).*

All during your Christian walk of faith there will be struggles as you obediently trust in God. He will carry you through to the end of the course He has prepared for you. Keep your eyes focused on Jesus, who led the way to go before you. Follow the example of His patient endurance while despising the disgrace of a public execution on the cross. He completed the journey on earth as a man and achieved the prize, and He is now seated with His Father in the heavenly place of honor and power. Therefore, whatever your present trials suffered today for the gospel's sake, they cannot be compared to the joy of the glory of the future when you receive your eternal rewards.

> *"Assured that He Who raised up the Lord Jesus will raise us up also with Jesus and bring us (along) with you into His presence . . . Therefore we do not become discouraged (utterly spiritless, exhausted, and wearied out through fear). Though our outer man is (progressively) decaying and wasting away, yet our inner self is being*

(progressively) renewed day after day. For our light, momentary affliction (this slight distress of the passing hour) is ever more and more abundantly preparing and producing and achieving for us an everlasting weight of glory (beyond all measure, excessively surpassing all comparisons and all calculations, a vast and transcendent glory and blessedness never to cease!)" (2 Corinthians 4:14, 16-17 AMPC).

In Genesis 3, after the first man Adam's rebellion, Satan gained dominion and is now in control over this ungodly world system. The man Christ Jesus came down to earth and at the cross defeated, judged, and sentenced Satan and all his demonic forces. As he awaits his eventual eternal punishment, he continually attempts to frustrate a loving God's desire to bring you into His family. Satan will lose control when Christ Jesus returns triumphantly to the earth as conquering King and Lord of all.

In the Genesis 1 account, after God looked at everything He had made, He saw that it was good. By divine design, the earth was prepared as a perfect habitation for mankind who, made like God Himself, was created to have intimacy and fellowship with God. As a result of Adam's sin and disobedience, the whole creation has now become frustrated in its ineffectiveness to operate according to God's original plan and purpose. As it increasingly deteriorates by pollution, contamination, and decay, creation anticipates and looks forward to its promised restoration. Then, all God's creation will be able to participate in the same freedom and enjoy together God's glory with His crowning achievement, mankind—His precious possessions, His own children.

"But in keeping with his promise we are looking forward to a new heaven and a new earth, the home of righteousness" (2 Peter 3:13 NIV). ". . . The creation itself will be liberated from its bondage to decay and brought into the glorious freedom of the children of God" (Romans 8:21 NIV).

"I am creating a new heaven and a new earth. The troubles of the past will be forgotten. No one will remember them. My people will be happy and rejoice forever and ever because of what I will make . . ." (Isaiah 65:17-18 ERV). The new heaven and earth will be so awesome and wonderful that people will not regret or long for the old order of things. They will not think about or meditate on past situations but will focus on the wonderful, eternal changes made by God.

Umbilical Cord Cut

The umbilical cord connects the unborn child with the placenta, which supplies all of the nourishments and sustenance necessary for life in the uterus. When the umbilical cord is cut immediately after delivery, it is a one-time act to sever the dependent connection of the child to its mother. The baby is instantly free and able to sustain life on its own. The newborn passes instantly from the old environment inside the womb to a new one outside the mother's body. There is a direct transfer from the old life support and supply system, from one way of living, to another completely different way of life. Ties are cut from the former existence of isolation and darkness to a new existence in the light of life.

"When anyone is in Christ, it is a whole new world. The old things are gone; suddenly, everything is new!" (2 Corinthians 5:17 ERV). A new believer passes immediately from the bondage of the old order into a new life in Jesus Christ. Ties are cut, severing the relationship with the prince of this current evil world. Connections are suddenly removed from membership in the family of the father of lies and his realm of darkness, destruction, and death.

At the moment of rebirth, a one-time event, the born-again believer is translated into the family of God. At the new birth, there is a separation from a former self-sufficient and independent lifestyle without God, and the believer moves into a new life of freedom from past history. Jesus now becomes Lord and Master of all that concerns you. He is now the one to be in control of your life, so there is no need for an existence solely dependent on your own individual efforts and ability.

Separation: New Lifestyle, New Environment, New Source of Nourishment and Life

"We sinned against him, but he didn't give us the punishment we deserved. His love for his followers is as high above us as heaven is above the Earth. And he has taken our sins as far away from us as the east is from the west" (Psalm 103:10-12 ERV). For those who put their trust in Jesus, God promises not only to forgive their sins and the resulting punishment, but to forget their sins and never see or remember them anymore.

> "... Through Christ, God made peace between himself and us ... God was in Christ, making peace between the world and himself. In Christ, God did not hold people guilty for their sins ... Christ had no sin, but God made him become sin so that in Christ we could be right with God" (2 Corinthians 5:18-19, 21 ERV).

"I, even I, am He Who blots out and cancels your transgressions, for My own sake, and I will not remember your sins" (Isaiah 43:25 AMPC). At the time of the prophet Isaiah's writing, when a debt was fully paid, all charges against that person were canceled, blotted out, or erased completely. At the moment of the new birth, God separates and disconnects you from your past sin with its consequences of guilt, shame, and condemnation.

> *"Blessed (happy, fortunate, prosperous, and enviable) is the man who walks and lives not in the counsel of the ungodly (following their advice, their plans and purposes), nor stands (submissive and inactive) in the path where sinners walk, nor sits down (to relax and rest) where the scornful (and the mockers) gather. But his delight and desire are in the law of the Lord, and on His law (the precepts, the instructions, the teachings of God) he habitually meditates (ponders and studies) by day and night" (Psalm 1:1-2 AMPC).*

Be Separated Unto God Your Father

"You must not ever become unequally yoked with unbelievers; for would some mix righteousness and iniquity, or some the fellowship of light with darkness? . . . or what has a believer in common with an unbeliever? . . . For we are a sanctuary of the Living God. Just as God said that 'I will dwell and I will walk among them, and I will be their God and they will be my people' and 'I will be a Father to you, and you will be sons and daughters to me,' says the Lord of Hosts" (2 Corinthians 6:14-16, 18 PNT).

Be separated unto God as a new creation, never in existence before. So, completely give your entire self and life to God, and you will not desire to "hang out" or join in activities with those who are unbelievers. You will no longer be enticed by their ungodly lifestyles. They will no longer be your "bosom buddies" or very close friends and confidants. Although you are in the world system, you are not of it.

> *". . . Nothing can separate us from God's love—not death, life, angels, or ruling spirits. I am sure that nothing now, nothing in the future, no powers, nothing above us or nothing below us—*

> *nothing in the whole created world—will ever be able to separate us from the love God has shown us in Christ Jesus our Lord"* (Romans 8:38 ERV).

At one time, before your rebirth from above, you were separated from God the Father. Now you can be assured with absolute certainty that no one, nothing in the seen or unseen world, can ever at any time separate you from your Father's love which is in Christ Jesus. His love is everlasting, limitless, and unconditional, even when you had separated yourself from His loving-kindness. It is that love and goodness that causes unbelievers to change their minds and ways and turn toward God in faith.

While in the womb, the pre-born child is nourished by the physical structure, the placenta. After delivery or natural birth, a new source of life-sustaining supply is necessary. Therefore, at that time, the placenta is expelled from the mother's body as the afterbirth. After the spiritual new birth, the old spirit man, the old nature, and the power of sin expire and are supernaturally displaced. Those things you formerly depended on and trusted in are replaced by a new life support source: your newly created hidden man of the heart. That old nature, supported and satisfied by those desires, appetites, and habits, has passed away, and all things have become new.

A New Source of Supply: The All-Sufficient One

An unborn child eventually outgrows its enclosed living space. In addition, the God-given physical and chemical resources of the life-sustaining support system during those stages are discontinued and depleted. As a result, the next phase of the development process begins as the baby moves into the birth canal in preparation for delivery.

There also must be a time or season in your own life when you decide that "there must be something more." The first step is dissatisfaction in your current life situation and condition. The next phase is the realization that you have exhausted the inadequate human resources of your own self-efforts and self-sufficiency. There is Someone who is more than enough—another source of supply who is accessible and available at all times to meet every need necessary for your total well-being: spirit, soul, and body. Spiritual rebirth by faith assures you of the unlimited resources and provision of the All-Sufficient One, your heavenly Father.

Revealed Through Adoption into the Family—Physical and Spiritual

An adopted child is specially sought out beforehand, selected and chosen by parents because of their great desire for a family. The son or daughter is welcomed, readily accepted, and receives all rights, privileges, love, and support given any child born of natural descent. In the same way, you are legally entitled to all of the promises of God if you are in union with Jesus Christ. Jesus, the Son of God, the firstborn, is the elder brother of all those adopted as God's sons. Therefore, all His children are joint heirs with equal rights and privileges, as well as the responsibilities of sonship.

". . . But ye have received the Spirit of adoption . . ." (Romans 8:15 KJV). ". . . The Spirit that we have makes us God's chosen children. And with that Spirit we cry out, '*Abba*, Father.' And the Spirit himself speaks to our spirits and makes us sure that we are God's children" (Romans 8:15-16 ERV).

As with your original ancestor, Adam, you are fathered in God's image and likeness. Just as you inherit the traits and characteristics of your natural parents, as God's spiritual children, you have received the Spirit and nature of God because you are fathered from above. As His beloved child, you have the privilege of calling your heavenly Father by a very personal, intimate name. "Abba" (that is, "Dear Father") (Romans 8:15 Jewish New Testament).

Divine Conception

> ". . . God loved the world so much that he gave his only Son, so everyone who believes in him would not be lost but have eternal life. God sent his Son into the world. He did not send him to judge the world guilty, but to save the world through him. People who believe in God's Son are not judged guilty. But people who do not believe are already judged, because they have not believed in God's only Son" (John 3:16-18 ERV).

The Word was God, and therefore had no beginning, but in His humanity, He was physically born in a particular place at a certain time to a human mother. The Word became flesh, born of flesh in a human body, and came as a temporary resident of this earthly realm. He was the exact image, the total representation, identical in character and essence to God the Father. Because He is the Word, and the Word is God, He understands and experiences God in His fullness, all that He is and does.

Before Jesus was betrayed and crucified, He encouraged His followers, and He prayed for them as well as for those of us who would come into the family later. When Jesus talked to His followers about death, burial, and resurrection, He comforted them, saying, "After I go and prepare a place for you, I will come back. Then I will take you with me, so that you can be where I am. You know the way to the place where I am going . . . I am the way, the truth, and the life. The only way to the Father is through me. If you really knew me, you would know my Father too. But now you know the Father. You have seen him" (John 14:3-7 ERV).

Jesus came to earth as a human to reveal and to demonstrate the Father's heart of love and compassion for you. "This is how God showed his love to us: He sent his only Son into the world to give us life through him" (1 John 4:9 ERV).

"Love is expressed by this, not because we loved God, but because He loved us and sent His Son to be an atonement for our sins" (John 4:10 PNT). Jesus loved us and became the atoning sacrifice for our sins. His death on the cross canceled man's hostility and ill will toward God and reconciled mankind back to goodwill and friendship with a loving and forgiving God.

"In the beginning (before all time) was the Word (Christ), and the Word was with God, and the Word was God Himself. He was present originally with God" (John 1:1-2 AMPC). "And the Word (Christ) became flesh (human, incarnate) and tabernacled (fixed His tent of flesh, lived awhile) among us . . ." (John 1:14 AMPC).

> "... The angel Gabriel was sent from God to a town in Galilee named Nazareth, to a girl ... and a virgin engaged to be married to a man whose name was Joseph, a descendant of the house of David; and the virgin's name was Mary ... And the angel said to her, 'Do not be afraid, Mary, for you have found grace (free spontaneous, absolute favor and loving-kindness) with God. And listen! You will become pregnant and give birth to a Son, and you shall call His name Jesus. He will be great (eminent) and will be called the Son of the Most High ...'" (Luke 1:26-27, 30-32 AMPC).
>
> "And Mary said to the angel, 'How can this be,

> *since I have no (intimacy with any man as a) husband?' Then the angel said to her, 'The Holy Spirit will come upon you, and the power of the Most High will overshadow you (like a shining cloud); and so the holy (pure, sinless) Thing (Offspring) which shall be born of you will be called the Son of God' . . . Then Mary said . . . 'Let it be done to me according to what you have said.' and the angel left her"* (Luke 1:34-35, 38 AMPC).

Mary believed the message from God given to her by the angel Gabriel. In her spoken reply, her words confirmed and gave birth and life to God's plan and purpose for her. Christ, the Eternal Word, supernaturally became a seed in the womb of Mary his mother by the power of the Most High God the Holy Spirit.

But before that, Mary had been promised to Joseph, a good and upright man. ". . . An angel of the Lord appeared to him in a dream, saying, 'Joseph, descendant of David, do not be afraid to take Mary (as) your wife, for that which is in her is of (from out of) the Holy Spirit. She will bear a Son, and you shall call His name Jesus (. . . which means Savior), for He will save His people from their sins (that is, prevent them from failing and missing the true end and scope of life, which is God) . . . Behold, the virgin shall become pregnant and give birth to a Son, and they shall call His name Emmanuel—which, when translated, means, "God with us"'" (Matthew 1:20-21, 23 AMPC).

The Word became flesh and became the divine expression to mankind of who God is, a revelation of His essential character, nature, ways, and works. Throughout His life on earth, Jesus modeled for all to see God's ways of expressing Himself, His decrees and declarations, His creative ability, and His dominion over all creation. The humanity of Jesus is confirmed when He speaks lovingly of His relationship with His Father God before and after His natural birth as the Son of man.

> *"God, the truth is, you are the one who brought me into this world. You made me feel safe while I was still at my mother's breasts. You have been my God since the day I was born. I was thrown into your arms as I came from my mother's womb" (Psalm 22:9-10 ERV).*

> *"Jesus, the one who makes people holy, and those who are made holy are from the same family. So he is not ashamed to call them his brothers and sisters . . . These children are people with physical bodies. So Jesus himself became like them and had the same experiences they have . . . Jesus became like these people and died so that he could free them . . . Then he could bring forgiveness for the people's sins" (Hebrews 2:11, 14-15, 17 ERV).*

Paul's letter to the Philippians says regarding Messiah Jesus: "Who was in the form of God, yet didn't think that this equality with God was to be eagerly clung to or retained, but emptied Himself of His Own equality, taking the form of a servant, when He came in a likeness of men. And when He was found in a manner of life as a man, He humbled Himself, becoming obedient unto death, even of a death on the cross" (Philippians 2:6-8 PNT).

Adoption Physical and Spiritual

A family welcomes and accepts an adopted child into the family. It receives all of the same rights, inheritance, privileges, and responsibilities as one born into the family. In the natural realm, a decision to adopt may be made if conception is not physically possible and if other medical options and interventions are not acceptable or successful. This process most often involves long waiting periods and consultations with adoption and other social agencies. Legal issues can also complicate matters before that special, chosen child is received and accepted into a loving family. Many people desperately desire a biological child when infertility problems or issues prevent conception. Other options are explored, including expensive medical procedures and interventions that are not available to most because of the cost involved.

However, the born-again experience and resulting adoption into God's family is freely given and must be freely received. "For it is by grace you have been saved, through faith—and this not from yourselves, it is the gift of God—not by works, so that no one can boast" (Ephesians 2:8-9 NIV). Grace is God's forgiving love, His unearned and unmerited favor, His loving-kindness to and for you. It is a gift. ". . . Do not think of yourself more highly than you ought, but rather think of yourself with sober judgment, in accordance with the measure of faith God has given you" (Romans 12:3 NIV).

That saving faith is a gift from God. It is the power of God to trust, believe, and totally rely on the finished work on your behalf of Jesus on the cross. "Yes, God loved the world so much that he gave his only Son, so that everyone who believes in him would not be lost but have eternal life" (John 3:16 ERV).

Jesus, your Savior, is the most priceless gift from God: He gave His only Son. Jesus, in turn, willingly shed His precious blood and gave His life willingly to redeem you back to God. It cost all He had to pay the debt you owed but that He did not owe. You can't do it your way, by your own efforts, works, or performance. If you could, then you would have something to brag about.

> *"Even as (in His love) He chose us (actually picked us out for Himself as His own) in Christ before the foundation of the world . . . For He foreordained us (destined us, planned in love for us) to be adopted (revealed) as His own children through Jesus Christ, in accordance with the purpose of His will (because it pleased Him and was His kind intent"* (Ephesians 1:4-5 AMPC).

It was God Himself who personally and intentionally picked you out especially to be adopted into His own family. His thoughts were always about you and for your good. So, even before He laid the foundation of the world, He chose you and invited you to be a member of His family. He joyfully and carefully designed a plan to accomplish His purposes. However, it is your own personal choice to accept and receive His gracious offer. "And it was of His own (free) will that He gave us birth (as sons) by (His) Word of truth . . ." (James 1:18 AMPC).

"Before the world began, the Word was there. The Word was with God, and the Word was God. He was there with God in the beginning. Everything was made through him, and nothing was made without him" (John 1:1-3 ERV). The Word, the eternal Christ, is the second member of the Godhead, God's spokesperson, God's Word in action, Christ Jesus who does the work and who is God, the Father's expression of Himself. The Word that was made flesh became a man and was born of a woman. He, Jesus, had an earthly mother and an earthly family. It is through Him and by the Holy Spirit that adoption into God's family is possible for you.

"For (the Spirit which) you have now received (is) not a spirit of slavery to put you once more in bondage to fear, but you have received the Spirit of adoption (the Spirit producing sonship) . . ." (Romans 8:15 AMPC). You are no longer bound by fear of separation and alienation from God.

God's Desire for a Family: Spiritual Descendants

> *"God—the one who made all things and for whose glory all things exist—wanted many people to be his children and share his glory. So he did what he needed to do. He made perfect the one who leads those people to salvation. He made Jesus a perfect Savior through his suffering. Jesus, the one who makes people holy, and those who are made holy are from the same family. So he is not ashamed to call them his brothers and sisters"* (Hebrews 2:10-11 ERV).

Jesus, when He walked on Earth as a man, suffered as all other men, yet without sin. Additionally, He endured for all men the ultimate suffering of death on a cross. He became the perfect sacrifice to restore to fellowship with God what Adam lost. Jesus, the only begotten Son of God, is the firstborn of all who by faith receive Him as Savior and Lord. All, then, belong to God's family. He is pleased to acknowledge you as His beloved brothers and sisters.

"The Son of Man came to find lost people and save them" (Luke 19:10 ERV). He came to earth to lift fallen mankind out of sin and disobedient rebellion and to restore you back to life and hope. Jesus, the Son of man, therefore emphasized His humanity and His feelings of compassion for lost man separated from the Father by experiencing in every way the same tests and trials as other humans.

> *"He was like God in every way, but he did not think that his being equal with God was something to use for his own benefit. Instead, he gave up everything, even his place with God. He accepted the role of a servant, appearing in human form. During his life as a man, he humbled himself by being fully obedient to God,*

even when that caused his death—death on a cross" (Philippians 2:6-8 ERV).

Because Jesus was fully God as well as fully man, He could bridge the gap between God and man to bring you together into one family. God, who is rich in mercy and loving-kindness, is willing to restore those who put their trust in Him. The Christian faith is not an organizational system of religion with different denominational beliefs and practices. Rather, it is a relationship with a loving God, a Father with a maternal heart who desires to adopt you into His family. He desires for you to enjoy all the benefits as joint heirs with Jesus. He yearns for a family of His image bearers, Christ-like followers, saved by His grace through faith.

> *"We know that in everything God works for the good of those who love him. These are the people God chose, because that was his plan. God knew them before he made the world. And he decided that they would be like his Son. Then Jesus would be the firstborn of many brothers and sisters. God planned for them to be like his Son. He chose them and made them right with him. And after he made them right, he gave them his glory" (Romans 8:28-30 ERV).*

God knew and determined in advance His perfect plan for a spiritual family. He established His purposes in ages past. They are presently made known, manifested, and expressed in your life when by faith you receive Him as your Savior. You can have confident expectation that His will for you will be completely fulfilled in the future. But in the present, Jesus came that you might live this life to the fullest measure, enjoying all the promises and blessings possible as a child of the heavenly Father.

- CHAPTER 10 -

CRY OF THE NEWBORN

The newborn child is utterly dependent on the mother. It cries out for help at any time, day or night, whenever or whatever the need, physical or emotional. Whenever it needs nourishment, is distressed or uncomfortable, or simply needs the consoling tenderness of its mother's presence, it expects and requires immediate attention and care.

". . . The Lord, the Maker of heaven and earth . . . he who watches you . . . will neither slumber nor sleep" (Psalm 121:2-4 NIV). Your heavenly Father never needs to be awakened, for He is constantly watchful every moment of your life. He is always there. He hears you when you call out to Him. With His maternal heart of compassion and comfort, He is the only being in the universe who is completely trustworthy and entirely dependable. Know that you are helpless and hopeless without Him.

> *"How blessed is he whose help is the God of Jacob, whose hope is in the Lord his God; who made heaven and earth, the sea and all that is in them; who keeps faith forever; who executes justice for the oppressed; who gives food to the hungry. The Lord sets the prisoners free. The Lord opens the eyes of the blind; the Lord raises up those who are bowed down; the Lord loves the righteous; the Lord protects the strangers; He*

supports the fatherless and the widow; but He thwarts the way of the wicked. The Lord will reign forever . . ." (Psalm 146:5-10 NASB).

The Lord is our help, our strength, our deliverer, the protector of the defenseless and hopeless. He is faithful, just, good, and full of mercy and loving-kindness. He is whatever you need Him to be in every aspect of your life.

A child confidently expects to receive from natural parents. A child of God can confidently and eagerly expect to receive abundantly all of the promises and blessings of Father God through Christ Jesus. He will not withhold or keep any good thing from you.

> *"Let us then fearlessly and confidently and boldly draw near to the throne of grace (the throne of God's unmerited favor . . .) that we may receive mercy (for our failures) and find grace to help in good time for every need (appropriate help and well-timed help, coming just when we need it)" (Hebrews 4:16 AMPC).*

As God's beloved child, you can come to His heavenly throne into His presence at any time, for any need. You can come without fear of rejection, guilt, shame, or condemnation. When you pray in the name of Jesus, who paid the ultimate price for your right standing with God, you need have no feelings of unworthiness or self-consciousness as you draw near to cry out for help like a child when it needs or wants its mother.

". . . From whence shall my help come? My help comes from the Lord, Who made heaven and earth. He will not allow your foot to slip or to be moved; He Who keeps you will not slumber" (Psalm 121:1-4 AMPC). He is always readily available right here and right now, at this very moment, ever listening, aware, in tune, and abundantly capable.

"God is our refuge and strength, a very present help in trouble . . . Therefore we will not fear. . ." (Psalm 46:1-2 NASB). He is more than able to protect and keep you secure at all times. You need not be afraid that He will leave you forsaken and alone. In your greatest hour of need, know that He is there to strengthen and uphold you.

"How kind the Lord is! How good he is! So merciful, this God of ours! The Lord protects those of childlike faith . . ." (Psalm 116:5-6 NLT). Those who are helpless and utterly dependent on God the Father's nurturing care and protection can run into His arms of love. He will continually care for you at all times and in every situation.

Childlike Faith

When people brought their little children to Jesus so that He could bless them, His followers discouraged them. But Jesus said, "'Let the little children come to me. Don't stop them, because God's kingdom belongs to people who are like these little children. The truth is, you must accept God's kingdom like a little child accepts things, or you will never enter it.' Then Jesus held the children in his arms. He laid his hands on them and blessed them" (Mark 10:14-16 ERV).

As small child is entirely dependent and unable to provide adequately for any of its own needs. It has a genuinely trusting nature; it holds no preconceived ideas and notions that might limit all that is freely offered for its nurture and care. It will receive expectantly without question everything that is offered or provided. It confidently relies on its mother and father to provide for its welfare. Its wants and needs are either anticipated by others or it makes known, in no uncertain terms, its discomfort in any area. A child will accept or take hold of any gift or good thing graciously offered. It does so without thought of the need to earn it by work or self-effort. An innocent child also runs eagerly with outstretched arms to the one who offers nurturing comfort and security. It joyously reacts with delight as it is received and lifted up to be enfolded in the embrace of a loving father or mother.

You must accept by faith the good news of the gospel of God's Word of truth to a lost world. You must be as a child who accepts God's free gift of salvation. Believe and receive Jesus Christ as Savior and Lord of your life. Accept confidently all the gifts and blessings you are promised as a child of God.

"I mean that you have been saved by grace because you believed. You did not save yourselves; it was a gift from God. You are not saved by the things you have done, so there is nothing to boast about" (Ephesians 2:8-9 ERV). It is by God's grace, His divine loving-kindness and favor. You did not—and could not—earn by doing.

A child must totally depend on others because it has no power or strength to sustain, support, or protect itself. God is gracious, righteous, and merciful. He will come to the aid of those who realize their own inability and lack of strength, and who trust in and rely solely on His ability and power.

> *"The teaching about the cross seems foolish to those who are lost. But to us who are being saved it is the power of God. As the Scriptures say, 'I will destroy the wisdom of the wise. I will confuse the understanding of the intelligent.' So what does this say about the philosopher, the law expert, or anyone in the world who is skilled in making clever arguments? God has made the wisdom of the world look foolish. This is what God in his wisdom decided: Since the world did not find him through its own wisdom, he used the message that sounds foolish to save those*

> *who believe it . . . Even the foolishness of God is wiser than human wisdom. Even the weakness of God is stronger than human strength"* (1 Corinthians 1:18-21, 25 ERV).

Salvation is not about clever debate or philosophical argument but about simple truth in God's Word. There is absolutely no foolishness in God's character or in His thoughts and actions. But even if that possibility existed, man's wisdom could never compare favorably. There is no weakness in any aspect of God's nature. If, however, that were possible, it would still be stronger than human strength.

> *"But this is what the Scriptures say about being made right through faith . . . 'God's teaching is near you; it is in your mouth and in your heart.' It is the teaching of faith that we tell people. If you openly say, 'Jesus is Lord' and believe in your heart that God raised him from death, you will be saved. Yes, we believe in Jesus deep in our hearts, and so we are made right with God. And we openly say that we believe in him, and so we are saved"* (Romans 10:6, 8-10 ERV).

"Therefore humble yourselves (demote, lower yourselves in your own estimation) under the mighty hand of God, that in due time He may exalt you" (1 Peter 5:6-7 AMPC). Stop depending on your own self-effort and self-sufficiency. Submit to God and His eternal plan for you, and realize that a right relationship with God is not by your human works and achievement, but by what Jesus Christ achieved by His sacrificial death on the cross on your behalf. ". . . Christ Jesus died for us, but that is not all. He was also raised from death. And now he is at God's right side, speaking to him for us" (Romans 8:34 ERV).

Now that Jesus has completed His work on earth, He continues working for you while He is in heaven with His Father. Before He ascended into heaven, He asked Father God to send the Holy Spirit to be a helper, companion, and friend to those who trusted Christ as Savior and Lord. Believers are not left as orphans without comfort and assistance, because there is another One like Himself indwelling them. Now, He is in heaven until the appointed time of His return for His church to forever be with Him where He is. He suffered agonies on earth, and He continues to suffer with His brethren on earth as you struggle to overcome temptations and conform to the will of God.

> *"For because He Himself (in His humanity) has suffered in being tempted (tested and tried), He is able (immediately) to run to the cry of (assist, relieve) those who are being tempted and tested and tried (and who therefore are being exposed to suffering)" (Hebrews 2:18 AMPC).*

> *"For we do not have a High Priest Who is unable to understand and sympathize and have a shared feeling with our weaknesses and infirmities and liability to the assaults of temptation, but One Who has been tempted in every respect as we are, yet without sinning. Let us then fearlessly and confidently and boldly draw near to the throne of grace (the throne of God's unmerited favor to us sinners), that we may receive mercy (for our failures) and find grace to help in good time for every need (appropriate help and well-timed help, coming just when we need it)" (Hebrews 4:15-16 AMPC).*

You have a representative in heaven, a go-between for you when you sin. You have Jesus Christ, who defends you before God the Father. And now, after His resurrection and ascension back to heaven, He can help those now on earth who are tempted. He is able to help you because He suffered the same tests and trials and was tempted Himself. Jesus showed you the example of an obedient Son doing the will of His Father and pleasing Him in all aspects of His life. As your elder brother who has experienced all the tests, the firstborn endured the trials and temptations of human life. You can look to Him as a model of what your heavenly Father has planned for your life.

> *"So Christ can save those who come to God through him. Christ can do this forever, because he always lives and is ready to help people when they come before God"* (Hebrews 7:25 ERV).

Revealed through Times of Rest and Refreshing After Labor, Work, and Self-Effort

A new mother, weary and weakened physically, mentally, and emotionally, has ceased from her agonizing travail and labor during the birth process and delivery of the child. With a sense of accomplishment and satisfaction, she quietly and tranquilly rests for renewal, recovery of spirit, soul, and body. She has ceased the exertion of bringing to birth the child of her womb, and she now rests quietly, knowing that she can focus totally on her newborn. She enjoys peace of mind, quiet, and tranquility as her strength is renewed and restored. She is revived and satisfied that her task has been completed.

The newborn child has also been through an intense struggle through the narrow birth canal into the immediate shock of plunging into a new environment. It gasps for the breath necessary for survival. Then it is placed in the loving arms of its mother and is nestled against the warmth and security of her breast. It rests undisturbed in the bosom of the one who gave it birth, a time of refreshing and recovery.

"For he who has once entered (God's) rest also has ceased from (the weariness and pain) of human labors, just as God rested from the labors peculiarly His own" (Hebrews 4:10 AMPC). His work was completed after He restored the earth out of darkness and its chaotic state. Your work to achieve self-righteousness ends when you trust and rely on him for your salvation.

Jesus offers these promising words in the Gospel of Matthew: "Come to me all of you who are tired from the heavy burden you have been forced to carry. I will give you rest. Accept my teaching. Learn from me. I am gentle and humble in spirit. And you will be able to get some rest. Yes, the teaching that I ask you to accept is easy. The load I give you to carry is light" (Matthew 11:28-30 ERV).

A born-again believer has ceased from depending upon self and trying to make it without God and His eternal plan for your salvation. No more laboring to achieve your own self-righteousness, struggling and striving in your own strength and exhaustive effort to obtain what God through Jesus and the power of the Holy Spirit have already accomplished for you.

". . . You will find rest (relief and ease and refreshment and recreation and blessed quiet) . . ." (Matthew 11:29 AMPC). You can rest assured and undisturbed in His Word of truth. His loving message and teaching will comfort you as He draws you closely to His breast, to a safe place, undisturbed security, and accepting approval.

"The eternal God is your refuge and dwelling place, and underneath are the everlasting arms . . ." (Deuteronomy 33:27 AMPC). You have been immediately transferred from an often chaotic, restless, empty, disorderly, and sometimes destructive existence into the rest and intimacy of the reality of God's presence. You will find rest from the pain, frustration, and discouragement of human labor and self-effort to achieve peace and good will with God. God gives you a place of security and safety. He will guard you and keep you safe and secure in His arms of love.

There is a rest when you come to Jesus by faith and cease from the exertion of your own ineffective self-effort. God comforts and encourages those who are His own chosen ones. He joyfully makes known to you His great pleasure in your close relationship. "The Lord your God is with you . . . He will take great delight in you, he will quiet you with his love, he will rejoice over you with singing" (Zephaniah 3:17 NIV). You can sincerely know that, as you are His child, He is not counting or holding your sins against you. His love is lavished on you as He reacts joyously in high-spirited response to the triumphant victory over all those who are against God and His chosen ones.

In Christ Jesus, you are free from your past life. He paid the price to redeem you back to right relationship with God. So rest in the knowledge of His forgiving grace and mercy. You need no longer attempt to achieve right standing with God by your own labor and self-effort.

As a child is a source of joy to its mother, you as a born-again child of God are a source of exceeding great expressive joy to Father God. There is mutual pleasure and satisfaction when a loving God communicates with His beloved. They, in return, express heartfelt love and sincere adoration and gratitude for His tender care. "In peace I will both lie down and sleep, for You, Lord, alone make me dwell in safety and confident trust" (Psalm 4:8 AMPC).

At all times, you can utterly depend on His care and concern for your welfare. He is faithful and true to His promises. You can rest securely and sleep, knowing that He "shall neither slumber nor sleep" (Psalm 121:4 KJV). Therefore, you don't have to lie awake at night fretting, tossing and turning, worrying about situations and things you cannot control. Your heavenly Father is watching protectively over you. He has you covered; rest in his watchful attention. He will never leave you alone, unguarded, or defenseless in your most vulnerable moments.

"Your Protector will not fall asleep . . . does not get tired. He never sleeps. The Lord is your Protector . . ." (Psalm 121:3-5 ERV). As a contented child rests comfortably in its mother's arms, you can be confidently satisfied when you are most susceptible to be affected by fear about anything or anyone in opposition to Father God's purposes for your life.

"Repent therefore and return, that your sins may be wiped away, in order that times of refreshing may come from the presence of the Lord" (Acts 3:19 NASB). Change your mind and your way of doing things, and turn to God in total submission and dependence on the finished work of Jesus. When you come into right relationship with God, you will enjoy peace and tranquility and revival of body, mind, and soul because of your union with Him.

"The Lord your God . . . He will rest (in silent satisfaction) and in His love He will be silent and make no mention (of past sins, or even recall them) . . ." (Zephaniah 3:17 AMPC). When you accept God's plan and His will for your life, He is faithful to keep His promises. You, by faith, became His beloved child. It was accomplished because God's just demands have been met and accomplished by the blood of Jesus. He is content that you are in right standing with Him and have all the privileges of membership in His family.

"Surely I have calmed and quieted my soul; like a weaned child with his mother, like a weaned child is my soul within me (ceased from fretting)" (Psalm 131:2 AMPC). Desire to be satisfied and content in the intimacy of your personal relationship with God, your Father. Rest and be refreshed in His presence. Bask secure in the tender warmth of His maternal love and return that love as it is awakened within you during those precious quality moments.

"(Resting) in the hope of eternal life, (life) which the ever truthful God Who cannot deceive promised before the world or the ages of time began" (Titus 1:2 AMPC). God's eternal plan was to restore man back to fellowship with Himself. You become a family member, His beloved child, from the moment of your miraculous rebirth and continuing throughout all eternity.

". . . Just being with you will bring complete happiness . . ." (Psalm 16:11 ERV). A mother's regular, rhythmic physical heartbeat is first sensed by the unborn child while in the womb. Immediately after birth, the baby is placed in its mother's welcoming arms. That same familiar rhythm of life is a comforting sound when the baby is cradled at her breast. It recognizes and responds to her assuring heartbeat as it rests in its new environment of life on the outside of her body.

Revealed Through Discipline and Child Training

In any earthly family, in order for children to grow, develop, thrive, and mature, they must do so in a loving and caring atmosphere. Rights, privileges, duties, responsibilities, and expectations must be specific and age-appropriate, with consequences for negative behavior and positive rewards for all clearly stated and understood.

Father God has provided in His Word full instructions for child training and discipline. Also included in the Scriptures is the perfect example of Jesus Christ, who personally modeled acceptable behavior in every life situation He experienced while here on earth.

A good parent sets boundaries and limits in the child's life for their protection and welfare. Father God would certainly be actively involved in the training and teaching of His own family, the household of faith. Look to the Bible, His Word, as the final authority expressing the absolute truth of God's will for your life and for all those who are under His care and leadership.

The writers of Scripture were men who were especially selected by God to speak for Him. They were inspired and directed by the Holy Spirit when they recorded God's Word as He spoke through them. The Bible is an owner's manual for the discipline and training of His children.

We purify ourselves outwardly as we are pure inwardly. We aim toward holiness as He is holy. We walk in the truth of God's revealed word as followers of Christ Jesus. We do not practice sin willingly and without restraint, because of our new life in Christ. True Biblical repentance is to change your mind and receive the power to change your actions. But if you slip, fall, or stumble in your Christian walk, you have a Helper, the One who speaks on your behalf and pleads your case before your Father. The most familiar example in the natural realm is that of an attorney addressing the judge in a courtroom in defense of his client. Only Jesus, sinlessly perfect, the only begotten Son of God can petition your Father for you. Only He understands our weakness and temptations. Only as a perfect sinless human can Jesus be a substitute to pay the penalty of death to reconcile a sinful you back to restoration to a holy God.

Your loving Father desires that you fulfill the destiny planned for you. He gives you everything you need for that purpose. He makes provision for the instruction and training for those in His care. He works out all things for your good.

At the moment of your new birth into His family, He sends someone special to dwell inside of you. He gifts you with His Spirit, the Holy Spirit, to comfort, assist, encourage, and empower you in your new life. He will lead and guide and show you how to live a life pleasing to your Father. He will teach you and help you remember and understand the truth of the Word of God.

"Loving God means obeying his commands. And God's commands are not too hard for us, because everyone who is a child of God has the power to win against the world. It is our faith that has won the victory against the world. So who wins against the world? Only those who believe that Jesus is the Son of God" (1 John 5:3-5 ERV). The Father's commands are His teachings and His Word. His Word instructs you so that His will and purpose for your life are clearly known.

> "... The most important command is this ... 'Love the Lord with all your heart, all your soul, all your mind, and all your strength.' The second most important command is this: 'Love your neighbor the same as you love yourself.' These two commands are the most important" (Mark 12:28-31 ERV).

There is no other commandment greater than these two. If you are God-centered, if your life is influenced, first of all, by the Word of God and His unconditional love for you, that love will be returned to Him when you give to Him your all, your total being.

"We love him, because he first loved us" (1 John 4:19 KJV). He loved you while you were estranged from Him, when your thoughts were far from Him. He drew you to Him by His unconditional love.

The Love of God Motivates

When you are God's enemy, it is His love and goodness that leads you to turn away from unbelief and toward Him. That unconditional love of God is then outpoured into the hearts of believers by the Holy Spirit, and in response, that love is to be returned back to Him. He is love, yet as a Person, He desires to be loved. Then, that God-kind of love overflows abundantly to others through the discipline and training of His children in order to reflect the Father's character. ". . . God has poured out his love into our hearts by the Holy Spirit, whom he has given us" (Romans 5:5 NIV).

He makes all things possible; therefore, God doesn't ask you to do anything that He doesn't enable you to do. In obedience, you work out that love from the inside so that it is evident and available to Him, your Father, and to others. Discipline and training are necessary to activate and accomplish that outworking of God's divine love.

God loved the world system so much that He gave His very best, His most precious Son, for the good of all mankind. Jesus Christ gave His all, His life, to pay a debt He did not owe. He sacrificed Himself because of His love for sinful man and His desire to please His Father.

The first commandment of Jesus in Mark 12 requires that you love and serve God with your entire being: your heart, soul, mind, and strength. This includes your innermost being, your heart, your mind, the intellect, will, and your conscience. The soul is the area involving feeling, passions, and emotions. Display your love for God as you obey His instructions regarding your physical body as it is bombarded continually through the senses.

Love and care for others as much as you are interested and concerned for your own personal well-being and welfare. Love yourself as you realize how amazingly special you are to your heavenly Father. While you were forming in your mother's womb, He was carefully designing and crafting you to be the wonderful person you are.

To enable you to achieve His divine purpose, He has given you special abilities and talents to make you uniquely different. No other individual in this world is exactly like you.

Just as in the natural created realm, each snowflake pattern is unlike any other, to you, His crowning achievement, He has given distinctive, identifiable fingerprints differing from all other humans. These prints were formed in the earliest months after conception and change only in size.

Your worth or value certainly is not based on your own efforts, achievements, or accomplishments. Your personal physical appearance or mental ability and intellectual knowledge is not the foundation of your extraordinary value. God proved your worth to Him when He gave His own beloved Son as a sacrifice to bring you into His maternal care. Jesus Christ willingly paid with His own life the ultimate price for you.

God's Grace Teaches and Trains

> *"For the grace of God that brings salvation has appeared to all men. It teaches us to say 'No' to ungodliness and worldly passions, and to live self-controlled, upright and godly lives in this present age, while we wait for the blessed hope—the glorious appearing of our great God and Savior, Jesus Christ, who gave himself for us to redeem us from all wickedness and to purify for himself a people that are his very own, eager to do what is good" (Titus 2:11-14 NIV).*

God's grace, His unmerited, unearned and undeserved favor and blessing trains us, just as we are saved by grace through faith. It's the complete package. God leaves nothing to chance when it pertains to His family.

Grow Up

Luke writes about Jesus: "And He went down with them"—Mary, His mother and Joseph her husband—"and came to Nazareth and was (habitually) obedient to them . . . And Jesus increased in wisdom (in broad and full understanding) and in stature and years, and in favor with God and man" (Luke 2:51-52 AMPC). Jesus was born on earth, and as He lived, He grew physically and matured spiritually to be a sinless example to mankind.

"God is Spirit" (John 4:24 NKJV). He is a Spirit Being, and you are spirit. Your spirit man is ensheathed in your physical body, which is a perfect image of your spirit body. God formed your physical body to connect with the natural physical world through your five senses.

"The only life people get from their human parents is physical. But the new life that the Spirit gives a person is spiritual" (John 3:6 ERV). "We get our new life from the Spirit, so we should follow the Spirit" (Galatians 5:25 ERV). You are born again in your spirit-man, created to connect with the eternal spiritual realm.

"You should know that your body is the temple for the Holy Spirit that you received from God and that lives in you. You don't own yourselves. God paid a very high price to make you his. So honor God with your body" (1 Corinthians 6:19-20 ERV). Your temporary body is God's spiritual house, His temple where He dwells. The Spirit of the Living God, the Spirit of Jesus Christ, lives in you if you are a born-again child of God. He speaks, Spirit to spirit, to guide and teach and assist you in your Christian walk. You have become children of God by faith in the finished work of Christ, but to become a mature son or daughter, you must be led by the Spirit of God.

Your physical body wants its sensual, fleshly desires to be indulged and gratified. Additionally, the soul—your mind, will, and emotions—constantly reminds you of its wants and needs. ". . . Because of the great mercy God has shown us, offer your lives as a living sacrifice to him—an offering that is only for God and pleasing to him. Considering what he has done, it is only right that you should worship him in that way . . . Let God change you inside with a new way of thinking. Then you will be able to understand and accept what God wants for you. You will be able to know what is good and pleasing to him and what is perfect" (Romans 12:1-2 ERV).

Put God first in your life by completely giving yourself, spirit, soul, and body over to Him. Allow His Spirit to lead you as He quietly speaks from His heart to yours, gives you direction, and leads you in the way you should go.

". . . He sent his own Son to earth with the same human life that everyone else uses for sin. God sent him to be an offering to pay for sin. So God used a human life to destroy sin . . . People who live following their sinful selves think only about what they want. But those who live following the Spirit are thinking about what the Spirit wants them to do. If your thinking is controlled by the Spirit, there is life and peace . . . The true children of God are those who let God's Spirit lead them" (Romans 8:3, 5-6, 14 ERV). When Jesus returned to the Father, He said He would ask Him to send another helper, the Holy Spirit, to be your constant companion to live with and to be in you. He will help you grow and mature.

> ". . . *Our goal is to become like a full-grown man—to look just like Christ and have all his*

perfection. Then we will no longer be like babies . . . We will grow to be like Christ in every way. He is the head, and the whole body depends on him. All the parts of the body are joined and held together, with each part doing its own work. This causes the whole body to grow and be stronger in love . . ." (Ephesians 4:13-16 ERV).

"Rather, let our lives lovingly express truth (in all things, speaking truly, dealing truly, living truly). Enfolded in love, let us grow up in every way and in all things unto Him Who is the Head, (even) Christ (the Messiah, the Anointed One)" (Ephesians 4:15 AMPC).

The Pattern of God the Father's Discipline and Instruction

"Those whom I (dearly and tenderly) love, I tell their faults and convict and convince and reprove and chasten (I discipline and instruct them). So be enthusiastic and in earnest and burning with zeal and repent (changing your mind and attitude)" (Revelation 3:19 AMPC).

"For whom the Lord loves He corrects, even as a father corrects the son in whom he delights" (Proverbs 3:12 AMPC).

". . . My son, you must not make, not ever, make lightly of the discipline of the Lord and you must not ever lose courage by His reproving: for whom the Lord loves, He disciplines, and punishes every son whom He accepts. Endure discipline. God deals with you as sons. For what son is there whom a father does not discipline . . . And indeed, no discipline at the time seems to be joy

> *but grief, and later it would yield the peaceful fruit of righteousness to those who are trained by it" (Hebrews 12:5-7, 11 PNT).*

Discipline and child training are necessary to help you fulfill God's purpose and divine plan for your own life. It is ultimately for His glory, but it is also for your own personal good so that you can be all that He has called you to be and fulfill your unique destiny. God gets the glory when His purposes are fulfilled.

> *"Now if you are exempt from correction and left without discipline in which all (of God's children) share, then you are illegitimate offspring and not true sons (at all)" (Hebrews 12:8 AMPC).*

All God's children are equally loved and accepted in His sight. All are legally heirs of the Father, joint heirs with Jesus Christ. All are loved as He loves Jesus, His only begotten Son. Therefore, His plans for you, individually, are for your welfare and are designed to make you more than overcomers, to give you a future and a hope.

> *"Fathers, do not provoke or irritate or fret your children (do not be hard on them or harass them), lest they become discouraged and sullen and morose and feel inferior and frustrated. (Do not break their spirit)" (Colossians 3:21 AMPC).*

God's discipline and training plan includes encouragement and instruction, inspiring you to correct mistaken and wrong thinking patterns and behavior. God is not an oppressive tyrant afar off, or someone who must be appeased to be pacified. His training is not intended to oppress or to cause undue pain or suffering. His teaching is designed to correct, strengthen, aid, and mold you as you develop to maturity.

His limits are an expression of His unlimited love. Enclosed in His boundaries are His bountiful blessings. Within His set parameters is the perfect peace of God not understood by those outside His family. His guidelines represent His great grace toward you, His favor, unearned and undeserved.

"Fathers, do not irritate and provoke your children to anger (do not exasperate them to resentment), but rear them (tenderly) in the training and discipline and the counsel and admonition of the Lord" (Ephesians 6:4 AMPC). As you learn from the Scriptures and experience God's way of training His born-again children to follow His example. God is "slow to anger" and therefore does not act unreasonably when correcting, disciplining, or training His family. God corrects His children in love and not in anger. He is long-suffering and patient, merciful, and kind to all who put their trust in Him.

His loving discipline proves to His children that they are true sons with every legal right and privilege due legal heirs. Included in child training is the accepting of responsibility for conduct, as well as the consequences resulting from any behavior.

"Train up a child in the way he should go (and in keeping with his individual gift or bent), and when he is old he will not depart from it" (Proverbs 22:6 AMPC). God has already blessed each of us with individual gifts, talents, aptitudes, and abilities. Therefore, each child is already inclined to develop in a particular direction according to its natural tendencies and the specific way its character and abilities are already focused. A loving parent initiates, arranges, and surrounds each child with responsibilities, activities, and opportunities to encourage advancement in that God-given bent or leaning. When the child is older, he will not depart from the right way of wisdom. When he is responding to chaos, by his own will, he selects the right path for himself.

In writing a pastoral letter to Timothy—whose mother and grandmother were also Christians, and who had been taught the Scriptures by them from his childhood—the Apostle Paul encourages and strengthens him: "But as for you, continue to hold to the things that you have learned and of which you are convinced, knowing from whom you learned (them). And how from your childhood you have had a knowledge of and been acquainted with the sacred Writings, which are able to instruct you and give you the understanding for salvation which comes through faith in Christ Jesus (through the leaning of the entire human personality on God in Christ Jesus in absolute trust and confidence in His power, wisdom, and goodness)" (2 Timothy 3:14-15 AMPC).

> "... Train yourself toward godliness... (keeping yourself spiritually fit). For physical training is of some value (useful for a little), but godliness (spiritual training) is useful and of value in everything and in every way, for it holds promise for the present life and also for the life which is to come" (1 Timothy 4:7-8 AMPC).

An unborn child begins its physical exercise program while yet in the womb. Frenzied arm and leg movements are often felt by the expectant mother. The child also makes complete changes in bodily position at times. During infancy, rapid arm and leg movements in joyful response to recognition of loved ones develop strength in those limbs. Play and sport activities during childhood years also promote growth in strength and stamina.

All adults are encouraged to discipline themselves to have regular exercise and physical fitness programs. The new birth is an instant event that requires no work or effort, but in the process of the Christian walk to spiritually mature, you must consciously and actively put forth effort to live a life pleasing to God, your Father.

Be intentional in your desire to spend quality time in fellowship with Him. Practice the ways and actions of Jesus as He walked on the earth, faithful and obedient to His Father's word. Exercise or use the God-given gifts of service for the good of others. The results of these spiritual activities are not of brief value, only for a season or a short duration, but have eternal results. In this day where man's wisdom and knowledge are increasing rapidly, the reliable and unchanging truth of God's word is eternal. Feed on that word and allow your mind and your thinking to be renewed.

Various physical fitness and exercise programs for self-discipline are readily available. They are necessary to develop bodily strength and endurance for this temporary life on earth. The natural body, the temple of the indwelling Holy Spirit, is to be cared for and available for the Father's use while we serve as His agent on this earth.

Spiritual self-discipline is developed by training through the practice of obedience to the true word of God. This training and instruction has eternal consequences and rewards. "But the fruit that the Spirit produces in a person's life is love, joy, peace, patience, kindness, goodness, faithfulness, gentleness, and self-control . . ." (Galatians 5:22-23 ERV). These character traits are those that are seen in Jesus Christ, the one who came to earth to reveal the Father and His true nature. Spiritual fruit, as with natural fruit, matures progressively and develops as it is nurtured and cared for.

"For once you were darkness, but now you are light in the Lord; walk as children of Light (lead the lives of those native-born to the Light). For the fruit (the effect, the product) of the Light or the Spirit (consists) in every form of kindly goodness, uprightness of heart, and trueness of life" (Ephesians 5:8-9 AMPC). Let your conduct and lifestyle draw others to Christ, as you are a living witness to unbelievers. Allow the Holy Spirit to help you to be an obedient child who is well pleasing to your Father God, as Jesus was to His Father and yours.

In Paul's letter to the Romans, he writes: "The true children of God are those who let God's Spirit lead them. The Spirit that we received is not a spirit that makes us slaves again and causes us to fear. The Spirit that we have makes us God's chosen children . . ." (Romans 8:14-15 ERV). And as you are God's chosen child, it pleases Him when you are obedient to His Word.

God expressed His approval about the man Christ Jesus during His earthly walk after his baptism by John the Baptist: "And lo a voice from heaven, saying, 'This is my beloved Son, in whom I am well pleased" (Matthew 3:17 KJV).

After Jesus completed His work on earth to receive the punishment you deserved, the just for the unjust, He was raised again from the dead by the power of God the Holy Spirit and was received to His heavenly home.

Now, "Jesus . . . is able to understand our weaknesses. When Jesus lived on earth, he was tempted in every way. He was tempted in the same ways we are tempted, but he never sinned" (Hebrews 4:15 ERV). Because Jesus, God the Son, was born to an earthly mother and walked on this earth in bodily human form, Jesus Son of man, He is able to be in touch with and share in your feelings as you walk daily in the new life of intimacy and fellowship with God. You, therefore, have a mediator, a go-between, with the Father in the heavenlies, the man Christ Jesus who can sympathize with and understand all of our weaknesses. John the Apostle writes, "My little children, these things write I unto you, that ye sin not. And if any man sin, we have an advocate with the Father, Jesus Christ the righteous" (1 John 2:1 KJ21).

You were created to be a reflection of God, and to accomplish that purpose, you must know who He is and what He is like.

The Scriptures reveal His holiness, the moral perfection of every aspect of His being. As His child, your inward condition, your newly created spirit man is holy and set apart for His purposes. Therefore, your behavior illustrates holy living, reflecting your Father's nature and character.

God speaks to Job: "Can you bring out the other constellations at the right times? . . . Do you know the laws that control the sky? Can you put each star in its place above the earth" (Job 38:32-33 ERV). Since God keeps the heavenly bodies in their predictable courses as they rotate and revolve in constant motion in their established orbits, surely He can fix, direct, and order your life.

A good mother does not criticize her child's first attempts to walk, but applauds and encourages so that it will be secure and confident. As it grows and matures, the mother holds its hand as the child walks confidently at her side. Later, it independently lets go and walks alone, comfortably assured that her assistance is readily available. She carefully watches over her cherished offspring.

The Lord, ever present and unchanging, says, "Fear not, for I am with you; be not dismayed, for I am your God. I will strengthen you, yes, I will help you, I will uphold you with My righteous right hand" (Isaiah 41:10 NKJV). You need not be afraid or lose hope when you despair or are discouraged, for God is your strength in the time of weakness. He will come to your aid and lift you up when you falter or stumble.

"For I am the Lord, your God, who takes hold of your right hand and says to you, 'Do not fear; I will help you'" (Isaiah 41:13 NIV). As a loving father or mother cares for a child, God also lovingly takes your hand to guide and encourage you as you try out new behaviors during your Christian walk. He is always there to keep you from falling as He protects you from any hurt, danger, harm, or a sudden false step.

"Establish my steps and direct them by (means of) Your word; let not any iniquity have dominion over me" (Psalm 119:133 AMPC). Allow God, your Father, to guide and lead you in the way He has prepared for you. He will make your steps fixed, steady, and constant when you are obedient to His Word of truth. You will not stray off the course and the way set before you. Follow His direction so that those tests and trials necessary for your progress will not cause you to be distracted and wander off aimlessly from that path.

"The steps of a (good) man are directed and established by the Lord when He delights in his way (and He busies Himself with his every step). Though he falls; he shall not be utterly cast down, for the Lord grasps his hand in support and upholds him" (Psalm 37:23-24 AMPC). Before your birth, God had already charted His plan for your life. He points out the right path for you to follow to fulfill your destiny. He is constantly at work to keep you on course, steadfast and without wavering as you trust that He will uphold you in every situation. He will lead and guide you as He directs your every step.

> *". . . Your hand will guide me, your right hand will hold me fast" (Psalm 139:10 NIV).*

No matter where you are in your walk of faith, no matter your current situation, God thoughtfully and protectively watches over you with loving care and concern.

After the initial born-again experience by saving faith, continue to walk in faith as you are led by the Holy Spirit. Be assured that your faithful heavenly Father will always be present to hold you up with His powerful, steady hand.

Cleansing

The newborn infant is thoroughly cleaned outwardly by others after birth. The baby cannot and does not clean itself, either externally or internally, in order to get ready for natural birth. It is absolutely impossible to do so by its own efforts. At birth, it completely leaves behind its past. The former life experiences in the womb are history. The child is born into a brand-new life situation, one never experienced before.

> *"But when the goodness and loving-kindness of God our Savior to man (as man) appeared, He saved us, not because of any works of righteousness that we had done, but because of His own pity and mercy, by (the) cleansing (bath) of the new birth (regeneration) and renewing of the Holy Spirit, which He poured out (so) richly upon us through Jesus Christ our Savior. (And He did it in order) that we might by justified by His grace (by His favor, wholly undeserved), (that we might be acknowledged and counted as conformed to the divine will in purpose, thought, and action), and that we might become heirs of eternal life according to (our) hope"* (Titus 3:4-7 AMPC)

God speaks of His loving care for the people of His chosen capital city Jerusalem in terms of the responsible attention given by the care givers to a newborn child. "Then I washed you with water; yes, I thoroughly washed away your (clinging) blood from you and I anointed you with oil" (Ezekiel 16:9 AMPC). He uses familiar terms of physical birth in the visible temporary world to describe the reality of His eternal care in the spiritual realm.

After the birth of a baby in the natural world, those responsible for delivery and aftercare remove from its physical body any residue remaining after it is delivered from the old life. ". . . But you were washed clean, you were made holy, and you were made right with God in the name of the Lord Jesus Christ and by the Spirit of our God" (1 Corinthians 6:11 ERV). A spiritually reborn child of God has no past history and comes with nothing remaining of the old inner life or nature. The hidden man of the heart, the spirit man, is a brand new creation of God. It is impossible for you to clean yourself by your own efforts before coming to the Father at rebirth. You can't change yourself for the better or "get straight" or "get right." You are incapable of getting yourself or your act together. God the Father accepts and receives you exactly as you are with all your past and present weaknesses, faults, and failures. When you accept and receive Jesus as Savior and Lord of your life, God makes you acceptable in His sight. You are justified by faith, just as if you had never sinned. You are made righteous, in right standing with God as you are pronounced to be clean through the shed blood of Jesus Christ.

> *"Christ died for us when we were unable to help ourselves. We were living against God, but at just the right time Christ died for us. Very few people will die to save the life of someone else, even if it is for a good person . . . But Christ died for us while we were still sinners, and by this God showed how much he loves us. We have been made right with God by the blood sacrifice of Christ . . ." (Romans 5:6-9 ERV).*

"Sprinkled with the blood of Christ, our hearts have been made free from a guilty conscience, and our bodies have been washed with pure water" (Hebrews 10:22 ERV). Water, here, refers to cleaning by the pure and unadulterated Word of God. ". . . Christ loved the church and gave himself up for her to make her holy, cleansing her by the washing with water through the word, and to present her to himself as a radiant church, without stain or wrinkle or any other blemish, but holy and blameless" (Ephesians 5:25-27 NIV).

". . . Ye are clean through the word . . ." (John 15:3 KJV). Immediately at the new birth, you are a new creation, never existing before; old things are passed away. All things in the old nature, the spirit and power of sin, are passed away replaced by purity of heart and a new life within. Only Jesus Christ through His blood and the word of faith can wash you personally free from sin and purify your heart through belief in His work on the cross. The new birth is a divine act of God's Spirit; it is an act of being made new, not by religious traditions, ceremony, and rites, nor by human works or self-effort, but by faith and faith alone in the Word of God.

The church, the called-out ones, are those set apart to be His very own. After the spiritual new birth, the Scriptures or Word of God corrects and cleanses your life as it is read, studied, absorbed, and obeyed, and as you allow the Holy Spirit within to guide, teach, and lead you in your Christian walk.

". . . God is light . . . But if we walk in the light, as he is in the light, we have fellowship with one another, and the blood of Jesus, his Son, purifies us from all sin" (1 John 1:5-7 NIV). When your daily life continually and faithfully conforms to God's standard of holiness and truth, the blood of Jesus continually cleanses you from sin.

The body of believers is spiritually cleansed inwardly by the means of the washing of the Word, as they are physically cleansed outwardly by pure water. As with outward cleansing of the physical body, so must a believer be regularly cleansed by the Word.

Cleanse Yourself

> ". . . We should make ourselves pure—free from anything that makes our body or soul unclean. Our respect for God should make us try to be completely holy in the way we live" (2 Corinthians 7:1 ERV).

Since you receive a new nature, a brand new spirit, and the power over sin at the birth from above, your responsibility is to adjust and submit your physical body and its conduct and desires to obedience to the Word of God. Your natural mind, will, and emotions will continue to think, reason, choose, and react in ways not pleasing to your Father.

"If we claim to be without sin, we deceive ourselves and the truth is not in us. If we confess our sins, he is faithful and just and will forgive us our sins and purify us from all unrighteousness" (1 John 1:8-9 NIV). Only Jesus lived a perfect sinless life as He walked on earth. A true believer does not deliberately and continually practice sin, but when you miss the mark and ask forgiveness, God will do so. Not only are your sins forgiven by Him, but He will remember them no more. Additionally, the stain of sin and guilt is removed.

"Beloved, we are (even here and) now God's children; it is not yet disclosed (made clear) what we shall be (hereafter), but we know that when He comes and is manifested, we shall (as God's children) resemble and be like Him, for we shall see Him just as He really is. And everyone who has this hope (resting) on Him cleanses (purifies) himself just as He is pure (chaste, undefiled, guiltless)" (1 John 3:2-3 AMPC).

The purifying process begins with God; your response is to purify yourself so that your body, mind, and will are in line with the leading of your re-created spirit. "So whoever cleanses himself (from what is ignoble and unclean, who separates himself from contact with contaminating and corrupting influences) will (then himself) be a vessel set apart and useful for honorable and noble purposes, consecrated and profitable to the Master, fit and ready for any good work" (2 Timothy 2:21 AMPC).

You Are Clean Through the Blood of Jesus

> "... God is light, and in him, there is no darkness. So if we say that we share in life with God, but we continue living in darkness, we are liars, who don't follow the truth. We should live in the light, where God is. If we live in the light, we have fellowship with each other, and the blood sacrifice of Jesus, God's Son, washes away every sin and makes us clean. If we say that we have no sin, we are fooling ourselves, and the truth is not in us. But if we confess our sins, God will forgive us. We can trust God to do this. He always does what is right. He will make us clean from all the wrong things we have done" (1 John 1:5-9 ERV).

When you walk continually in the light of the truth of God's Word, then you can have the assurance that the blood of Jesus continually cleanses you when you confess your sins. The light of God's Word that reveals sin is that same light that reveals the way out of the continued practice of disobedience to the Father's plan and purpose for you, His child. To walk in the light is to make a deliberate and continuous effort to live a life in conformity to God's Word. Additionally, Jesus Christ, His Son, came to reveal the Father. He is an exact reflection of God, who is light.

Examined for Imperfection

To determine if any prevention or corrective measures are necessary, the physically newborn child is carefully examined for imperfections. Are all organs and systems fully developed and functioning properly? The new mother's first question is usually, "How many fingers and toes?" Any evident outward imperfections at birth or any genetic abnormalities are duly noted and treatment prescribed.

The spiritually born-again believer is a new creation, completely guilt-free, blameless, with all sins forgiven, past, present, and future. You have no imperfections in your newly created inner man, the hidden man of the heart.

". . . Being made righteous freely by His grace through the redemption that is by means of Messiah Jesus" (Romans 3:24 PNT). You have been justified, "just as if" you had never sinned. You have been declared righteous, by faith in Christ Jesus.

At your born-from-above rebirth, you bring with you no past to condemn you. You have become a brand-new creation, never in existence before. You become God's supernatural masterpiece, His marvelous created work of art.

> *"When anyone is in Christ, it is a whole new world. The old things are gone; suddenly, everything is new! . . . I mean that God was in Christ, making peace between the world and himself. In Christ, God did not hold people guilty for their sins . . . Christ had no sin, but God made him become sin so that in Christ we could be right with God"* (2 Corinthians 5:17, 19, 21 ERV).

Your born-again spirit, newly created spirit man, has no flaws, faults, or deficiencies. It is by the grace of God, His unearned, unmerited favor that you are considered righteous with the righteousness of Jesus Christ. Your right standing with God is a gift because all your sins were placed on Jesus, who was sinless. He was punished in your place with the ultimate death penalty. In exchange, you were made His righteousness: the righteousness of Jesus was placed on sinful you.

This was made possible because Jesus Christ lived the perfect, sinless life. Jesus lived the life we could not live and died the death we should have died. The innocent was punished for the guilty. He did no sin, but God made Him to be so, and to be an offering for sin. In exchange, we who deserve punishment for our sin, God has made us righteous in Christ Jesus. "For God did not send the Son into the world in order to judge (to reject, to condemn, to pass sentence on) the world, but that the world might find salvation and be made safe and sound through Him" (John 3:17 AMPC).

Salvation and eternal life in intimacy and fellowship with your Father includes peace, favor, deliverance, safety, victory, provision, wholeness, soundness, and preservation. Sin causes separation from God, who is holy, but His greatest desire is to reconcile you back to Himself. Therefore, He sent His Son into a sinful world to save us, not to condemn us and judge us guilty. He does not record our faults, sins, and transgressions because we are reconciled to God by faith. Our sins were placed on Jesus and His righteousness placed on us. He was made sin, and we are made righteous; this is how our Father sees us.

> *"As far as the east is from the west, so far has He removed our transgressions from us. As a father loves and pities his children, so the Lord loves and pities those who fear Him (with reverence, worship, and awe)" (Psalm 103:12-13 AMPC).*

"Who is a God like You, Who forgives iniquity . . . because He delights in mercy and loving-kindness. He will again have compassion on us; He will subdue and tread underfoot our iniquities. You will cast all our sins into the depths of the sea" (Micah 7:18-19 AMPC). God is not the one who continually brings up your past to cause you to have feelings of guilt, shame, condemnation, and rejection. He has cast them into the sea of forgetfulness. You are no longer required to carry the burden of sin or pay its penalty.

- Chapter 11 -

Examine Your Heart

"You must test yourselves to see if you are in the faith. You must continually examine yourselves . . ." (2 Corinthians 13:5 PNT). Look into the mirror of God's Word. Check out your life in all its areas to see if they line up with the truth found in the Scriptures. Does your image reflect Jesus Christ, the Word made flesh, who lived among us? Although the born-again experience is an instantaneous event, an immediate translation from darkness to light, the next steps are the walk of faith.

The Holy Spirit had already begun His satisfying work from the inside, setting you apart for God. By His convicting and convincing work on your behalf, He brings you to belief in Jesus Christ as your Savior and Lord.

Jesus explains the functions of the Holy Spirit as He works in union with Him and God to convict the world of sin, righteousness, and judgment: "When the Helper comes, he will show the people of the world how wrong they are about sin, about being right with God, and about judgment . . . He will show them how wrong they are about how to be right with God . . . And he will show them how wrong their judgment is, because their leader has already been condemned" (John 16:8, 10-11 ERV).

The evil leader of this current world system is Satan. When you choose Jesus, you join the family of God. If you continue with Satan and remain in his family as his child, you are destined for eternal separation from God. Jesus speaks about Satan's fatherhood: "You are of your father, the devil, and it is your will to practice the lusts and gratify the desires (which are characteristics) of your father . . ." (John 8:44 AMPC).

At the very moment of rebirth and salvation, your Helper the Holy Spirit comes to dwell inside you in order to continue His sanctifying work. He will teach you, lead you, and guide you into all truth of God's word. He has done and will continually do His part, and you as a born-again believer have a responsibility to live a life in conformance to that word. Examine yourself as you willingly give your physical body over to God, your Father, in complete submission and obedience.

". . . Offer your lives as a living sacrifice to him—an offering that is only for God and pleasing to him . . ." (Romans 12:1 ERV). But first, before you can present your body and your life to God, there must first be a continual process of renewing of the mind and its thoughts and attitudes. Choose not to come into agreement with current worldly standards but to allow God the Holy Spirit to teach, lead, and guide you.

> "Do not change yourselves to be like the people of this world, but let God change you inside with a new way of thinking. Then you will be able to understand and accept what God wants for you. You will be able to know what is good and pleasing to him and what is perfect" (Romans 12:2 ERV).

New ways of thinking will eventually reflect a new way of life, conduct, and actions. Listen attentively to the Holy Spirit, the voice of God, who will not speak on His own authority, but will only speak what He hears from God your Father. He will not seek to bring glory to Himself, but will reveal and glorify the Son. By this, you become more and more like Jesus. He is your perfect example of leading an overcoming life as He experienced the same tests, temptations, and trials you undergo now.

"Looking away (from all that will distract) to Jesus, Who is the Leader and the Source of our faith (giving the first incentive for our belief) and is also its Finisher (bringing it to maturity and perfection) . . ." (Hebrews 12:2 AMPC). Submit yourself to God, your heavenly Father, who is always approachable, available for and accepting of His beloved children. So He gladly welcomes you as you draw near to Him freely and confidently, without fear of disapproval, whenever or however help is needed.

"Let us then fearlessly and confidently and boldly draw near to the throne of grace (the throne of God's unmerited favor) . . . that we may receive mercy (for our failures) and find grace to help in good time for every need (appropriate help and well-timed help, coming just when we need it)" (Hebrews 4:16 AMPC).

Did He not choose you before the foundation of the world, knowing beforehand how you would act in response to the good news of the gospel of Jesus Christ? Did He not have previous knowledge about your Christian walk and your responses to those experiences, both positive and negative?

Turn completely away from all diversions that hinder your faith walk. Focus and concentrate on Jesus Christ, who has experienced and endured all that you go through in this life and more. He knows and understands all your human weaknesses and daily struggles. The Bible, His story, details His thoughts, words, deeds, and responses to all people in every situation.

Footprinted

The image made by the footprint of the newborn positively identifies it as the child of its biological parents. It bears witness to and proves that this individual child will not be confused with any other child of any other biological parents.

> *"And you also were included in Christ when you heard the word of truth, the gospel of your salvation. Having believed, you were marked in him with a seal, the promised Holy Spirit, who is a deposit guaranteeing our inheritance . . ."* (Ephesians 1:13-14 NIV).

In Biblical times, a seal proved legal ownership and was used for security purposes to prove that a document was authentic and valid. It also authorizes the correctness of the document's contents. Each stamp or seal had a distinct private or personal mark or design that could not be broken or tampered with without discovery, thereby providing assurance of the completion of a promised obligation.

God has "set his seal of ownership on us, and put his Spirit in our hearts as a deposit, guaranteeing what is to come" (2 Corinthians 1:22 NIV). When God seals you as His own, no one else, no other thing, can break that bond of security. God, the Holy Spirit, indwells you, marks you out, puts His stamp of approval on you, and brands you as God's child. You are now assured that all of your inheritance and the promises of God in Christ Jesus are available to and for you. God appropriates and acknowledges you as His own when He confirms you into His family by sending you His indwelling Spirit. You know without a doubt who you are and whose you are. You also know that the Scriptures, the Renewed Testament, the will and testament of your inheritance cannot be contested. You will eventually receive all that is legally due you because you already have His Holy Spirit as down payment.

"But the firm foundation of (laid by) God stands, sure and unshaken, bearing this seal (inscription): The Lord knows those who are His . . ." (2 Timothy 2:19 AMPC). You can rest and be secure in God's unchanging Word of truth. The Holy Spirit has been given as a down payment confirming that the resurrected Jesus would return for you. Born-again believers will be raised up with Him in glorified bodies and will forever be with Him.

> ". . . You heard the true message, the Good News about the way God saves you. When you heard that Good News, you believed in Christ. And in Christ, God put his special mark on you by giving you the Holy Spirit that he promised. The Spirit is the first payment that guarantees we will get all that God has for us. Then we will enjoy complete freedom as people who belong to him . . ." (Ephesians 1:13-14 ERV).

Paul writes to the believers in Philippi: "And I am convinced and sure of this very thing, that He Who began a good work in you will continue until the day of Jesus Christ (right up to the time of His return), developing (that good work) and perfecting and bringing it to full completion in you" (Philippians 1:6 AMPC). The Holy Spirit's indwelling presence is the divine pledge insuring that His promised full payment will be satisfied.

In modern times, manufactured products often received a "seal of approval" for excellence. Those spiritually born again from above have received the seal of ownership and approval from their heavenly Father because of positional righteousness in Christ Jesus. This seal is a down payment, a deposit, a foretaste received beforehand, confident in your anticipation of greater things to come.

God has ". . . put his mark on us to show that we are his. Yes, he put his Spirit in our hearts as the first payment that guarantees all that he will give us" (1 Corinthians 1:22 ERV).

> ". . . We ourselves, who have the first fruits of the Spirit, groan inwardly as we wait eagerly for our adoption as sons, the redemption of our bodies" (Romans 8:23 NIV).

We have the first part of God's promise, and we have the assurance that He will be faithful to complete His promise that our physical mortal bodies will be redeemed and set free and suitable for inhabiting the new Heaven and Earth. "So it is with the resurrection of the dead. (The body) that is sown is perishable and decays, but (the body) that is resurrected is imperishable (immune to decay, immortal)" (1 Corinthians 15:42 AMPC).

After resurrection, those who are not in God's family will experience eternal separation from Him, but those of you who are His children will spend eternity with God after being raised to newness of life. "When the body is 'planted,' it is without honor. But when it is raised, it will be great and glorious. When the body is 'planted,' it is weak. But when it is raised, it will be full of power. The body that is 'planted' is a physical body. When it is raised, it will be a spiritual body . . ." (1 Corinthians 15:43-44 ERV).

> "As the Scriptures say, 'The first man, Adam, became a living person.' But the last Adam [Jesus] is a life-giving spirit. The spiritual man did not come first. It was the physical man that came first; then came the spiritual. The first man came from the dust of the earth. The second man [the last Adam] came from heaven. All people belong to the earth. They are like that first man of earth. But those who belong to heaven [born-again children of God] are like

> *that man of heaven. We were made like that man of earth, so we will also be made like that man of heaven'" (1 Corinthians 15:45-49 ERV).*

The glorious good news of the gospel of Jesus Christ, that sure Word of truth, is supported and upheld by the church of the Living God. Born-again believers from above are the called-out ones, the family and household of faith that make up the church.

God's seal confirms and guarantees His ownership. You belong to Him, so you are not your own. You have been purchased by the precious blood of Jesus, God's own Son. Therefore, you can be secure in the knowledge that you belong to God as His dearly beloved child. God chose and called you; He is for you, so who can triumph over or prevail against you (Romans 8:31)? Your Father God cares for those who are His, so He is with you and will never, ever leave or forsake you. He also came to live inside you, to make His home in you at the very moment of your new birth. God the Holy Spirit dwells in you to teach, guide, counsel, and comfort you.

Weighed

When a child is born, it is weighed on accurate scales or balances to determine if the birth weight of the infant compares favorably to the established standard of the average birth weight of other newborns. Weight gain or loss is carefully monitored after delivery.

All mankind is weighed by God's absolute standard of perfection according to the accurate, unchanging instrument, the truth of God's word and by Jesus Christ, the Living Word, who is the ultimate example of unfailing sacrificial love. "... For the Lord sees not as man sees; for man looks on the outward appearance, but the Lord looks on the heart" (1 Samuel 16:7 AMPC).

In the Bible, the book of Daniel tells the story of how Belshazzar, King of Babylon, failed to honor the only true God, who had decisive power over his life and all that he had. Instead, he proudly and defiantly turned against Him to honor the false idols of the land. As a result, God sent him a message: ". . . The Most High God rules in the kingdom of men and . . . He appoints and sets over it whomever He will. And you ... O Belshazzar, have not humbled your heart and mind . . . And you have lifted yourself up against the Lord of heaven . . . God has numbered the days of your kingship and brought them to an end" (Daniel 5:21-23, 26 AMPC). Ultimately, King Belshazzar suffered the consequences of his lack of faith and trust in the Most High God.

God's warning to him had been, "You have been weighed on the balances and have not measured up." (Daniel 5:27 NLT)

"All the ways of a man are pure in his own eyes, but the Lord weighs the spirits (the thoughts and intents of the heart)" (Proverbs 16:2 AMPC). You have been weighed on the scales, the standard of God's perfection, and are found wanting or not good enough in your own vain efforts of self-righteousness. Only Jesus Christ, as He walked in human flesh on this earth, lived up to God's sinless standard that you could not attain or earn. He died the death you deserved through His sacrificial death on your behalf. He Himself, who knew no sin, died so that in exchange, you in your unrighteousness became His righteousness. You can stand faultless before God when you believe and trust in the finished work of Christ on the cross. ". . . Those who receive (God's) overflowing grace (unmerited favor) and the free gift of righteousness (putting them into right standing with Himself) . . ." (Romans 5:17 AMPC).

"Men of low degree (in the social scale) are emptiness (futility, a breath) and men of high degree (in the same scale) are a lie and a delusion. In the balances they go up; they are together lighter than a breath" (Psalm 62:9 AMPC). It does not matter your current state or condition in life or what you do or fail to do. It does not matter how great your accomplishments or your lack of achievement or progress in this world system. On the scales of God's standard, all of your combined weight is lighter than a breath or a gentle puff of air. All of your self-confident, self-centered self-righteousness equals nothing, avails nothing, and carries no weight in God's estimation. Only Jesus, the living Word, and the Bible, God's written Word, are perfectly balanced.

". . . To those who put their trust in his person and power, he gave the right to become children of God, not because of bloodline, physical impulse or human intention, but because of God" (John 1:12-13 Jewish New Testament). You have been born into your earthly family not by your own choice but by the decisions of your natural parents. You are born again into your heavenly family by your decision, your faith in Christ Jesus, and by God's eternal law of spiritual reproduction. Your faith makes you a son and an heir of Father God with all rights, benefits, and privileges as all other children, no matter the color, culture, ethnic group, sex, position, class, status, or situation in life. All are one in unity and one in Christ Jesus.

Measured

Newborns are measured to compare them to a reliable standard for the average length of full-term babies. Measurements are recorded periodically to determine growth and progression.

You alone cannot measure up to God's glorious ideal and absolute standard of righteousness as revealed in the Scriptures, "for all have sinned and fall short of the glory of God" (Romans 3:23 NIV). But a loving, compassionate God had a plan even before your conception to reconcile you back to Himself without self-effort.

> "... *The righteousness of God which comes by believing with personal trust and confident reliance on Jesus Christ . . . All who believe . . . are justified and made upright and in right standing with God, freely and gratuitously by His grace (His unmerited favor and mercy), through the redemption which is (provided) in Christ Jesus . . . Then what becomes of (our) pride and (our) boasting?" (Romans 3:22, 24, 27 AMPC).*

Because of the original sin of Adam, the first man, all mankind is guilty. We all have inherited our common ancestor Adam's sin nature; therefore, all mankind is under the sentence of death, condemnation, and separation from God. All fall short or miss the mark of His honor and approval. Each one of us fails to attain the image of the majesty, greatness, and goodness of His glory.

But whosoever believes and trusts in the sacrificial atoning death of Jesus and His resurrection from the dead will be regarded in God's sight as forgiven and righteous. Christ died for the sins of mankind, so the penalty has already been paid. Man's sin would now be unbelief and the refusal to accept this free gift of restoration back to a loving God.

God's perfect standard of measurement for all things and in every aspect of life is clearly stated in the Bible, His communication with mankind. There is no doubt of His will in any situation we encounter.

"When they measure themselves by themselves and compare themselves with themselves they are not wise" (2 Corinthians 10:12 NIV). When people measure themselves to others by deceptive human standards, which are ever changing, they often say things like "Everyone is doing it!" "I did it my way!" "If it feels good, do it!" "I'm not like those people!" But God is the same yesterday, today, and forever, and His truth never changes. It was, is, and will be; it will endure forever and all throughout eternity.

"Jesus Christ is the same yesterday, today, and forever" (Hebrews 13:8 NKJV). He never changes, and He is the only person who measures up to God's perfect established redemptive model. God's standard is sure, unchanging, and dependable. There is no possibility of variation in the truth of His Word.

". . . The Father who made all the lights in the sky. But God never changes like the shadows from those lights. He is always the same" (James 1:17 ERV). Our Father in heaven neither shifts nor moves from His sure position in order to suit the individual occasion or for your special convenience.

Swaddled, Wrapped, Enclosed to Comfort

> *"And she gave birth to her firstborn, a son. She wrapped him in cloths and placed him in a manger . . ." (Luke 2:7 NIV)*

When the newborn leaves its familiar life in the womb, it is plunged immediately into a completely different environment. It goes suddenly from the comfortable former life into a brand-new physical lifestyle. Afterwards, it is quickly wrapped and enclosed securely within a blanket or cloth. This process imitates the warmth and the protective, enclosed, totally contained safety of the womb. The baby is quieted and comforted as it rests contentedly and serenely on the mother's breast as they bond in loving intimacy.

The tightly wrapped cloth also serves to help strengthen the child's back and bones in order to assure proper physical growth and development. Therefore, swaddling has benefits for the natural body as well as for emotional welfare.

At the new birth, you are immediately welcomed within the security of God's family circle. There, you will be entirely encased in His everlasting love. He tenderly and totally surrounds you in the warmth of His unfailing love.

When the physical newborn leaves a secure and familiar place, the womb, it needs to be placed in another similar place of comfort and security. The new believer leaves the old, comfortable, self-centered life of sin and unbelief and is instantly indwelt by the Comforter, God the Holy Spirit, the third Person of the Godhead.

Another Comforter: The Promise of the Holy Spirit

"And I will ask the Father, and He will give you another Comforter (Counselor, Helper, Intercessor, Advocate, Strengthener, and Standby), that He may remain with you forever" (John 14:16 AMPC). ". . . I will send Him to you (to be in close fellowship with you)" (John 16:7 AMPC).

Jesus told His followers and believers that He was returning to His Father after His resurrection. He would ask God the Father to send the Holy Spirit to be another Comforter and Counselor to dwell on this Earth, another Person like Himself to be with them and in them in His absence.

The Holy Spirit is called alongside you to help you, to live in you, to gently lead, guide, teach, empower, and comfort you, and to be your loving, constant companion. He will always be present with you, an ever-loving friend, tenderly holding your hand as you mature and develop toward the character of Jesus, evidenced by the fruit of the Spirit in your life. "For all who are led by the Spirit of God are sons of God" (Romans 8:14 AMPC). Sons of God have grown and matured from the newborn and childish stages.

> *"But the fruit of the (Holy) Spirit (the work which His presence within accomplishes) is love, joy (gladness), peace, patience (an even temper, forbearance), kindness, goodness (benevolence), faithfulness, gentleness (meekness, humility), self-control (self-restraint, continence) . . . If we live by the (Holy) Spirit, let us also walk by the Spirit. (If by the Holy Spirit we have our life in God, let us go forward walking in line, our conduct controlled by the Spirit" (Galatians 5:22-23, 25 AMPC).*

Jesus, knowing that the time had come for His crucifixion, death, burial, and resurrection, assured those who were His own of His utmost love for them. Comforting His followers, He promised to send another one like Himself: "And I will ask the Father, and He will give you another Comforter (Counselor, Helper, Intercessor, Advocate, Strengthener, and Standby) that He may remain with you forever—the Spirit of Truth . . . You know and recognize Him, for He lives with you (constantly) and will be in you. I will not leave you as orphans (comfortless, desolate, bereaved, forlorn, helpless); I will come (back) to you" (John 14:16-18 AMPC).

He had completed His temporary residence and assignment on Earth and was physically returning to His loving Father in Heaven. But, He first wanted them to know that they would not be utterly forsaken. When he gave them the promise of the Holy Spirit, God the Holy Spirit was called alongside them to walk with and encourage them. ". . . I am telling you nothing but the truth when I say it is profitable (good, expedient, advantageous) for you that I go away. Because if I do not go away, the Comforter (Counselor, Helper, Advocate, Intercessor, Strengthener, Standby) will not come to you (into close fellowship with you) . . ." (John 16:7 AMPC).

"... You know and recognize Him, for He lives with you (constantly) and will be in you" (John 14:17 AMPC). He will look after you and care for you. He will act as your Helper, Teacher, Counselor, and Guide to assist you in every area of need. He will also support, strengthen, and sustain you spiritually as you grow, develop, and mature in your Christian walk. The Holy Spirit was given to dwell inside you and to be your constant companion, your divine friend called to walk alongside you, to talk with you, and to help you live your new life in Christ.

You need never feel lonely or solitary, bereaved or deprived, abandoned, or unloved, for you are a child of the loving God. Jesus is your brother who gave up His life on your behalf to reconcile you back to God.

The Spirit of Truth, God's Spirit, guides you into all truth and teaches you when you listen attentively to His still, small voice. He will gently speak only what He hears and not speak His own message or glorify Himself. He will not bring honor to His own Person, but will reveal Jesus. "But when the Spirit of truth comes, he will lead you into all truth. He will not speak his own words. He will speak only what he hears and will tell you what will happen in the future. The Spirit of truth will bring glory to me by telling you what he receives from me. All that the Father has is mine. That is why I said that the Spirit will tell you what he receives from me" (John 16:13-15 ERV).

Jesus explained the work of the Holy Spirit before His departure from the earth: "But the Comforter . . . The Holy Spirit, Whom the Father will send in My name (in My place, to represent Me and act on My behalf), He will teach you all things. And He will cause you to recall (will remind you of, bring to your remembrance) everything I have told you" (John 14:26 AMPC). ". . . He (Himself) will testify regarding Me" (John 15:26 AMPC).

God the Holy Spirit is the representative of the Godhead now on earth. He is the Comforter who indwells believers to assist God's children in the direction of life's journey, empowering you to do the work God has prepared for you and to understand God's truth. He is the One who is sent and called alongside to help you with encouragement, consolation, exhortation, and support. The believers, those who put their trust in Jesus Christ, were walking ". . . in the comfort of the Holy Spirit . . ." (Acts 9:31 NASB).

"For in Christ Jesus you are all sons of God through faith" (Galatians 3:26 AMPC). "And the Spirit himself speaks to our spirits and makes us sure that we are God's children" (Romans 8:16 ERV). How comforting it is to have the indwelling Holy Spirit of God reminding and assuring you that you are the beloved child of God.

> ". . . Walk and live (habitually) in the (Holy) Spirit (responsive to and controlled and guided by the Spirit); then you will certainly not gratify the cravings and desires of the flesh (of human nature without God). For the desires of the flesh are opposed to the (Holy) Spirit, and the (desire of the) Spirit are opposed to the flesh (godless human nature); for these are antagonistic to each other (continually withstanding and in conflict with each other) . . ." (Galatians 5:16-17 AMPC).

A new believer is surrounded and enclosed completely by the comforting loving-kindness, compassion, and consolation of the Godhead. You can be confident of the encouragement and support of God the Father and God the Holy Spirit. In your times of distress, testing, and temptation, you are wrapped safely in their tender, protective care. The Apostle Paul speaks to the church at Corinth: "The grace of the Lord Jesus Christ, and the love of God, and the fellowship of the Holy Spirit, be with you all" (2 Corinthians 13:14 NIV).

The closest of spiritual intimacy with the children of God is possible because of the communion, sharing together, participation and friendship with God the Father, God the firstborn Son Jesus, and God the Holy Spirit.

The Garments of Salvation, the Robe of Righteousness

An Old Testament prophet, Isaiah, speaks of things that would be fulfilled in the life and ministry of Jesus Christ, the good news of salvation. "I will greatly rejoice in the Lord, my soul shall be joyful in my God; for He has clothed me with the garments of salvation, He has covered me with the robe of righteousness . . ." (Isaiah 61:10 NKJV).

For the born-again believer, immediately at spiritual rebirth or salvation, you become the righteousness of God in Christ Jesus through faith. You have right standing with God. Jesus, who knew no sin, was made to be sin for your sinfulness. As a result, you, who know no righteousness, became the righteousness of God.

Through Him, you are spiritually clothed with the garment of salvation as you are completely covered with God's total provision, spirit, soul, and body. All this is made possible through the sacrificial work of Jesus on the cross. You will also be wrapped all around with a robe of righteousness, enclosed securely in the assurance of your acceptance by a holy God.

Clothing, Garments, Coverings for the Physical Body

In the natural, physical realm, a person can often be identified by specific, distinctive clothing or apparel. What someone wears is usually appropriate and suitable for the individual's age, rank, locality, calling, occupation, role or position, life situation, period, or special occasion. Notable examples include judicial robes, protective clothing, prison garb, sportswear, business attire, service uniforms, baby clothes, riding habits, religious robes, and nun's habits. A newborn is immediately wrapped tightly and comfortably in a blanket or swaddling clothes, as was the custom at the birth of Jesus: Mary ". . . brought forth her firstborn son, and wrapped him in swaddling clothes . . ." (Luke 2:7 KJV).

The child leaves the old familiar darkness and constriction of the security of the womb, entering into a new life of light and openness outside its mother's body. It is immediately wrapped, and covered tightly, where it experiences a new peaceful, protected, warm and secure environment necessary for its well-being. It is the appropriate clothing for a newborn infant.

Spiritual Covering

The first man Adam's own efforts to partially cover and clothe himself and his wife Eve were not suitable or adequate. Only God Himself could provide the proper blood sacrificial covering. "Unto Adam also and to his wife did the Lord God make coats of skins, and clothed them." (Genesis 3:21 KJV).

They had covered themselves with fig leaves. But only the shedding of blood of the innocent animal for the guilty provided an acceptable sacrifice to God. "This is because the life of the body is in the blood . . . It is the blood that makes a person pure" (Leviticus 17:11 ERV).

Christ Clothed Himself In Humanity

Christ was there in the beginning before the world began. He was with God, and He was God. Everything was made through Him, and without Him nothing was made. Yet He humbled Himself and laid aside His glory, and He gave up everything to clothe Himself in frail humanity, appearing on earth, born in human form and likeness.

Jesus clothed Himself and humbled Himself as a servant. By clothing Himself in human flesh, He took on Himself the outward form and characteristics of sinful man. "Who, being in very nature God, did not consider equality with God something to be grasped, but made himself nothing, taking the very nature of a servant, being made in human likeness. And being found in appearance as a man, he humbled himself and became obedient to death—even death on a cross!" (Philippians 2:6-8 NIV).

Jesus laid aside His divine privileges in heaven and, in a sense, removed His godly garment to exchange it for the lowly attire of a servant. In those days, the Romans made slaves of many people from many lands. One special garment worn to set them apart as servants was an apron depicting their lowly status. Jesus, as a man, changes His clothing to wash His disciples' feet: "He . . . knew that he had come from God. And he knew that he was going back to God. So while they were eating, Jesus stood up and took off his robe. He got a towel and wrapped it around his waist. Then he poured water into a bowl and began to wash the followers' feet. He dried their feet with the towel that was wrapped around his waist" (John 13:3-5 ERV).

In those days, people wore sandals as they walked for long distances on dirty roads. Washing the feet of people was a social custom, and this task was usually done by the lowest level of servant or slave.

Put On and Assume a New Lifestyle—Put Off the Old

In the spiritual realm, to "put on" means to assume the characteristics of Christ Jesus. To "put off" means to discard old habits as a garment: to put aside behaviors, thoughts, or words not pleasing and conforming to the Word of God. Old habits, customs, or practices acquired by use and repetition are unsuitable for the new life as a child in the family of God.

Those activities of the old way of living repeated continuously are called "habitual." Believers, born-again ones, are clothed in garments befitting their new spiritual positions in Christ Jesus.

In the new life of the Spirit, at spiritual rebirth, the newborn one is covered supernaturally by the precious blood of Jesus. You are surrounded by the peace of God, the contentment and satisfaction in life, the wholeness and completeness in Him. You are totally secure and wrapped up in the unconditional love of your Father God.

When you change your garments, it indicates a change from your current situation or conditions in life to another. Those old habits, enjoyable and pleasurable for a season, are not appropriate for your new lifestyle, one that instead brings eternal benefits and great joy for both you and your heavenly Father.

"For in Christ Jesus you are all sons of God through faith. For as many (of you) as were baptized into Christ (into a spiritual union and communion with Christ, the Anointed One, the Messiah) have put on (clothed yourselves with) Christ . . . For you are all one in Christ Jesus" (Galatians 3:26-28 AMPC). When you clothe yourself wholly and completely with Him, you will eventually take on the qualities of His person and character. You will continually be changed into His image so that when people see you, they see the qualities of Jesus. When others are around you, they will know that you are in a relationship with Him.

"I delight greatly in the Lord; my soul rejoices in my God. For he has clothed me with garments of salvation and arrayed me in a robe of righteousness . . ." (Isaiah 61:10 NIV). Salvation includes all the redemptive acts purchased by the finished work of Jesus on the cross. You are stripped immediately of the old nature of sin and unbelief, and in exchange, you are given a new nature of life in Christ. Victory, welfare, forgiveness, deliverance, safety, health, wholeness, and prosperity all comprise the believer's total outfit. At the instance of the new birth, your initial clothing and garments are supernaturally provided by God.

Once saved, the child of God is justified, just as if you had never sinned. You are made righteous at the same time Jesus was made sin on your behalf. But now, since you are made righteous in Christ Jesus, the Holy Spirit will assist you as you put on spiritual clothing, fitting your new life as God's chosen child. Put away, put off, and renounce your old way of life, and now live in accordance with your new position and status. "Strip yourselves of your former nature (put off and discard your old unrenewed self) which characterized your previous manner of life and becomes corrupt through lusts and desires that spring from delusion . . . And put on the new nature (the regenerate self) created in God's image, (Godlike) in true righteousness and holiness" (Ephesians 4:22, 24 AMPC).

"But now put these things out of your life: anger, losing your temper, doing or saying things to hurt others, and saying shameful things" (Colossians 3:8 ERV). Remove from your manner of life, by an act of your will, those tendencies that are harmful to both you and others. Uncontrolled, burning anger; a nature that viciously desires to hurt or harm others; and slanderous, abusive speech intended to downgrade or belittle others indicate how you used to live before your rebirth from above. These habits are to be cast off as unclean garments unsuitable for a child of the King.

> *". . . You have taken off those old clothes—the person you once were and the bad things you did then. Now you are wearing a new life, a life that is new every day. You are growing in your understanding of the one who made you. You are becoming more and more like him" (Colossians 3:9-10 ERV).*

You will grow because of your close, ongoing personal relationship with your heavenly Father. Your experiences with Him as you fellowship together will allow you to take on His character. You will put off old, ungodly habits, as you would an ill-fitting, unclean, or inappropriate garment, as you are led and guided by the indwelling Holy Spirit.

Freedom in Christ Jesus

> *"The Spirit of the Lord God is on me. The Lord has chosen me to tell good news to the poor and to comfort those who are sad . . . I will take away their sadness, and I will give them the oil of happiness. I will take away their sorrow, and I will give them celebration clothes . . ." (Isaiah 61:1, 3 ERV).*

For the faint, feeble, and weak, or for those burdened down with the cares of life, Jesus promises to give you a "garment of praise," suitable spiritual clothing for those who trust completely in Him. Instead of depression and despair, you can assume a life of joy, gratitude, and thanksgiving for all He has freely given you.

Isaiah writes about what Jesus would be empowered to do: "To comfort all who mourn . . . giving them . . . the mantle of praise instead of a spirit of fainting . . ." (Isaiah 61:2-3 NASB). A mantle is a garment designed for enveloping, enfolding, and covering the body. The finished work of Jesus is a cause for celebration, for expressive praise and magnifying God, replacing the despair, depression, heaviness, and weakness apparent in your old life outside of God's family.

Clothed with Power

". . . Clothed with power from on high" (Luke 24:49 AMPC). After Jesus' resurrection from the dead, immediately before He ascended into heaven, He instructed His followers about the ministry they were to continue to share, the good news of the gospel. Since He was leaving them, He reminded them of the Father's promise to send them the coming power-giver, the Holy Spirit. They had already received the indwelling Holy Spirit at the new birth. Now, they would be filled to overflowing to enable them to do the works that Jesus did, because they would be equipped with supernatural power from heaven.

> *"And [Jesus] said to them, Thus it is written that the Christ (the Messiah) should suffer and on the third day rise from (among) the dead. And that repentance (with a view to and as the condition of) forgiveness of sins should be preached in His name to all nations, beginning from Jerusalem. You are witnesses of these things. And behold, I will send forth upon you what My Father has promised . . . you are clothed with power from on high"* (Luke 24:46-49 AMPC).

God the Father sends the Holy Spirit to provide the power for born-again believers to do the work of the ministry. You are to be a witness not only by word and testimony, but also by your lifestyle as you are led by the Spirit, and as you do the mighty works of Jesus. When you are equipped with the power and presence of the Holy Spirit, you will be enabled with supernatural testimony, signs, wonders, and miracles to impact the lives of others.

> *". . . All of you, clothe yourselves with humility toward one another, because, 'God opposes the proud but gives grace to the humble.' Humble yourselves, therefore, under God's mighty hand, that he may lift you up in due time. Cast all your anxiety on him because he cares for you"* (1 Peter 5:5-7 NIV).

The acceptable attitude of your new life is self-humbling, as Jesus did by willingly trusting in His Father's purpose for good to all mankind. Develop and assume a friendly and helpful attitude toward others. Then your actions toward them will be performed with patient and hopeful expectation for good. You will be able to act with loving restraint in unpleasant or unproductive situations.

"Clothe yourselves therefore, as God's own chosen ones (His own picked representatives), (who are) purified and holy and well-beloved (by God Himself, by putting on behavior marked by) tenderhearted pity and mercy, kind feelings, a lowly opinion of yourselves, gentle ways, (and) patience (which is tireless and long-suffering, and has the power to endure whatever comes, with good temper) . . . And above all these (put on) love and enfold yourselves with the bond of perfectness (which binds everything together completely in ideal harmony)" (Colossians 3:12, 14 AMPC).

The most important part of your new life is that you make a decision to love one another, for out of love flows the motivation for the Christ-like lifestyle, and it is that which ties or holds all things in perfect unity.

"I tell you this, brothers and sisters; Our bodies of flesh and blood cannot have a part in God's kingdom. Something that will ruin cannot have a part in something that never ruins. But listen, I tell you this secret: We will not all die, but we will all be changed. It will only take the time of a second. We will be changed as quickly as an eye blinks. This will happen when the last trumpet blows. The trumpet will blow and those who have died will be raised to live forever. And we will all be changed. This body that ruins must clothe itself with something that will never die. So the body that ruins will clothe itself with that which never ruins. And this body that dies will clothe itself with that which never dies . . ." (1 Corinthians 15:50-54 ERV).

Believers will be raised to life, just as Jesus Christ was raised from the dead to newness of life. The resurrected body will be eternally clothed gloriously with honor and power. This is the final change.

- CHAPTER 12 -

WHO AND WHOSE ARE YOU?

Presentation

The newborn child, after a brief separation, is brought to and presented to its own mother by those who have assisted her in the labor and delivery process. Next, the new mother joyously presents her infant to the proud father, and later to adoring family and friends. She desires to "show off" her wonderful child for all to admire and celebrate the miracle of natural birth.

At His birth, Jesus was presented to the world by angelic host. "And the angel said to them, 'Do not be afraid; for behold, I bring you news of great joy which shall be for all the people; for today in the city of David there has been born for you a Savior, who is Christ the Lord' . . . And suddenly there appeared with the angel a multitude of the heavenly host praising God, and saying, 'Glory to God in the highest, and on earth peace among men with whom he is pleased'" (Luke 2:10-11, 13-14 NASB).

This birth was foretold by the prophet Isaiah: "For a child will be born to us, a son will be given to us . . ." (Isaiah 9:6 NASB). With the birth of Jesus, a new agreement between God and man would be established. The favor of God's presence was to be restored through "Immanuel" (God with us): ". . . A virgin will be with child and bear a son, and she will call His name

Immanuel" (Isaiah 7:14 NASB). His birth was to bring peace, harmony, contentment, satisfaction, and complete well-being in all areas of life to those who are in accord with the will of God.

God the Son, Jesus, born physically to a human mother, during His life on earth, experienced all the tests, trials, and temptations that all other humans endure. Although He came that you ". . . may have and enjoy life, and have it in abundance (to the full, till it overflows)" (John 10:10 AMPC), at His birth and all throughout His lifetime on earth, Jesus was unwelcome and unreceived and unaccepted by some. But to those who did welcome, receive, and accept Him, He gave them the right to become the children and heirs of God.

> *"He came into the world, and though the world was made through Him, the world did not recognize Him (did not know Him). He came to that which belonged to Him (to His own—His domain, creation, things, world), and they who were His own did not receive Him and did not welcome Him. But to as many as did receive and welcome Him, He gave the authority (power, privilege, right) to become the children of God, that is, to those who believe in (adhere to, trust in, and rely on) His name—who owe their birth neither to bloods nor to the will of the flesh (that of physical impulse) nor to the will of man (that of a natural father), but to God. (They are born of God!)" (John 1:10-13 AMPC).*

David said, "I will not offer . . . to the Lord my God of that which costs me nothing" (2 Samuel 24:24 AMPC), and likewise, God did not offer the world something that cost Him nothing. He so greatly loved and prized the world that He gave His most precious possession, His only Son, who left His presence to come earth and die a horrible, agonizing death.

Jesus Christ, God the Son, loved you so much that He gave His life to die on an instrument of torture. Before He gave up His life, He took all of your sins in His own body. He willingly gave up His divine form and humbled Himself to become a sacrificial lamb on your behalf.

"At one time you were separated from God. You were his enemies in your minds, because the evil you did was against him. But now he has made you his friends again. He did this by the death Christ suffered while he was in his body. He did it so that he could present you to himself as people who are holy, blameless, and without anything that would make you guilty before him" (Colossians 1:21-22 ERV).

Jesus, who is head of the church, will present His reborn ones to God, His Father and yours. He will joyfully and proudly exhibit those who are His body of believers, who are His brethren in the family for which the Father yearned.

"But God, who is rich in mercy, for his great love wherewith he loved us, even when we were dead in sins, hath quickened us together with Christ, (by grace ye are saved;) and hath raised us up together, and made us sit in heavenly places in Christ Jesus: that in the ages to come he might show the exceeding riches of his grace in his kindness toward us through Christ Jesus . . . For we are his workmanship, created in Christ Jesus" (Ephesians 2:4-7, 10 KJV).

You are God's newly created masterpiece. He wants to exhibit you, show you off to the rest of His creation because you are a tangible sign of His marvelous grace, kindness, and goodness of heart. You will be a demonstration piece to show your Father's great grace, love, mercy, and wisdom toward all who believe and trust in His word.

". . . Make a decisive dedication of your bodies (presenting all your members and faculties) as a living sacrifice, holy (devoted, consecrated) and well pleasing to God" (Romans 12:1 AMPC). "So I beg you, brothers and sisters, because of the great mercy God has shown us, offer your lives as a living sacrifice to him—an offering that is only for God and pleasing to him . . ." (Romans 12:1 ERV).

Because of His tender loving-kindness and compassion, He was moved by His distress at your separation from Him because of unbelief. In His desire to draw you close to Him, He sent His only begotten, unique Son Jesus to be a sacrificial offering for your sin and mine. Jesus Himself willingly left the glories of heaven to come down to earth in human flesh, and offered up His own body on the cross to pay the ultimate price.

You, in return, as a born-again believer, are to present yourself over to God. Offer to Him your own physical body with all its human needs, wants, and desires. Submit to God your total being, including mind, will, and emotions, all to be ruled and governed from within, by your newly created spiritual nature.

Now you are redeemed by the blood of Jesus and reconciled back to favor with God, ". . . by the death Christ suffered while he was in his body. He [God] did it so that he could present you to himself as people who are holy, blameless, and without anything that would make you guilty before him" (Colossians 1:22 ERV). As a born-again believer, return His love by completely giving yourself over to God: your body, mind, will, and emotions. In this way, you also present to this prevailing world system who you are in Christ Jesus by the new life you lead in this current age.

"Everything that God made is waiting with excitement for the time when he will show the world who his children are. The whole world wants very much for that to happen" (Romans 8:19 ERV). All creation has been negatively affected by man's rebellion and the resulting curse and corruption. Therefore, the whole creation will again be made new and perfect when the children and heirs of God are revealed in their glorious eternal state.

> *"Now to Him Who is able to keep you without stumbling or slipping or falling, and to present (you) unblemished (blameless and faultless) before the presence of His glory in triumphant joy and exaltation (with unspeakable, ecstatic delight). To the only God, our Savior through Jesus Christ our Lord, be glory (splendor), majesty, might and dominion, and power and authority, before all time and now and forever (unto all the ages of eternity). Amen (so be it)"* (Jude 24-25 AMPC).

Accepted in the Beloved Jesus Christ

The mother joyfully receives and accepts as her own the newborn infant as it is presented to her. She lovingly embraces that child for whom she has labored and travailed in birth. She experiences great pleasure and satisfaction as she holds her child close to her heart. They, at this moment, begin to bond and form a new and more familiar, intimate relationship.

". . . Having predestined us to adoption as sons by Jesus Christ to Himself, according to the good pleasure of His will, to the praise of the glory of His grace, by which He made us accepted in the Beloved" (Ephesians 1:5 NKJV). Our heavenly Father not only receives you into His family, but joyously welcomes you as His dear child. You experience much more than His receiving and welcoming: you are, by His grace, mercy, and goodness, also highly favored.

Before the world was made, God chose you, marked you out individually beforehand to make you His very own child. This is what pleased Him, and this is what He desired to make Him happy. So when you heard the good news of the gospel and believed in Christ Jesus, His Son, He embraces you as He does His only begotten Son. God has no unwanted, second-class, unplanned children; all are highly regarded and esteemed. No one is illegitimate in His sight. Whosoever comes to Him will be welcomed into His loving arms.

It was Jesus "Who took away our sins Himself by means of His body on the tree (cross), so that by dying to our sins, we can live in righteousness." (1 Peter 2:24 PNT). He gave up His own innocent life for your sinful life. Father God accepts this transfer done on your behalf. It is a loving God's good pleasure to accept a born-again believer into His own family, but also to receive you with favor, approval, and special honor. It is the finished work of Jesus Christ that makes this possible.

In Matthew 3, the Father validated His only begotten Son after Jesus was baptized by John the Baptist, thereby personally affirming His Sonship: "This is My Son, My Beloved, in Whom I delight!" (Matthew 3:17 AMPC). God the Father not only declared Jesus to be His Son at the sea, very early, but later also affirmed and gave His divine approval on the mountain, when Jesus went there with Peter, James, and John to pray: "Then there came a voice out of the cloud, saying, 'This is My Son, My Chosen One or My Beloved; listen to and yield to and obey Him!'" (Luke 9:35 AMPC).

God, who is a Person, has spirit, soul, and body. Since He possesses a soul, He therefore has and expresses emotions, feelings, desires, and passions. God loves His spiritual children with the same love He has for His only unique Son, Jesus, who is the first of many children now adopted by spiritual rebirth into the Father's family.

". . . Let the world know that you sent me and have loved them even as you have loved me" (John 17:23 NIV). Because you are God's child, you are beloved, affirmed, and accepted not according to your own performance or lack thereof, but because of your unfailing trust, belief in, and reliance on the finished work of Jesus.

God the Father calls Jesus Christ His Son, His Chosen, His Beloved, ". . . My Elect One in whom My soul delights . . ." (Isaiah 42:1 NKJV). As His child, you are His chosen one, His elect, selected and set apart to be with Him forever. You are dearly beloved and highly valued by Him and precious in His sight because you are His very own. You give Him great joy and satisfaction because of your relationship and fellowship together.

God planned before time, in the beginning, that His adopted children would ". . . be molded into the image of His Son (and share inwardly His likeness) . . ." (Romans 8:29 AMPC). All of those children will eventually be resurrected in glorious new bodies, like Jesus, the first raised from the dead.

". . . Now we are children of God. We have not yet been shown what we will be in the future. But we know that when Christ comes again, we will be like him. We will see him just as he is" (1 John 3:2 ERV). Jesus Christ, your elder brother, will return to those who have a family resemblance to Him. You will live in a spiritual resurrected body just as He does. All God's family members will live together in unity on the restored earth.

"Do your best to be the kind of person God will accept, and give yourself to him. Be a worker who has no reason to be ashamed of his work, one who applies the true teaching in the right way" (2 Timothy 2:15 ERV). After the new birth during your Christian walk and work, you will be tested and tried about your obedient faithfulness to God's word. Be able to present yourself to God, approved and unashamed.

Jesus Speaks to the People

"All whom My Father gives (entrusts) to Me will come to Me; and the one who comes to Me, I will most certainly not cast out (I will never, no never, reject one of them who comes to Me)" (John 6:37 AMPC).

So come to Jesus in faith, right now, at this very moment. Come without hesitation. Come exactly as you are, no matter your past or present condition, knowing that He will joyously receive you and will not send you away or refuse you. He will welcome you with total acceptance.

El Shaddai

"... I am God All-Powerful..." (Genesis 17:1 ERV). Almighty God is everything you need Him to be in every area of your life. One of His names is *El Shaddai*, from the Hebrew word *Shad*, meaning "female breast" (Strong's Concordance 7699). "El" means Strong One, God of Power and Might, and "Shaddai" signifies Breasted One, so this name reveals that He is All-Sufficient, Supplier of needs, Nourishing One, All Bountiful, Satisfier, Life Giver and Nurturer. El Shaddai is the One who pours out His unlimited blessings. He is more than enough, complete and perfect, having integrity.

In the book of Genesis, Jacob, a natural father, blesses his family of twelve sons and foretells their specific futures. "These are the twelve families of Israel. And this is what their father said to them. He gave each son a blessing that was right for them" (Genesis 49:28 ERV). To one of his sons, Joseph, Jacob said, "... The Almighty who blesses you with blessings of heaven above, blessings of the deep that lies beneath, blessings of the breasts and of the womb" (Genesis 49:25 NASB). To Joseph, Jacob promises prosperity from the earth's natural resources, watered by the rain from above and from water springing up from below the earth. His descendants would reproduce bountifully and would be blessed with numerous flocks and herds. All these provisions would be supplied by the Mighty God who is more than enough, who pours forth blessings, who promised to be the source of Joseph's strength and that of his descendants.

The Apostle Peter writes to born-again believers: "Like newborn babies, crave pure spiritual milk, so that by it you may grow up in your salvation, now that you have tasted that the Lord is good" (1 Peter 2:2-3 NIV). The unsuppressed need of a hungry baby is expressed loudly without restraint. So should new believers earnestly desire and diligently pursue the study of the unadulterated Word of God. Just as natural milk is necessary and appropriate for the physical nurture and nourishment of the body, so is pure spiritual milk, the Word of God, essential for spiritual growth and development in intimacy with your heavenly Father.

The warm emotional bonding resulting from the close personal contact between mother and child as it is nourished at the breast is unequaled in all other human relationships. Almighty God, with a maternal heart, nurtures His children, providing and caring for you as a devoted mother cares for her child nestled at her breast. He pours out His unlimited blessings, the strength, nourishment, and comfort that you need to be sustained and to flourish. He gives the very best from His magnificent, bountiful, abundant supply as you feed daily on His Word of truth.

The prophet Isaiah describes God's maternal care as He moves in historical events: "Rejoice with Jerusalem and be glad for her . . . that you may nurse and be satisfied from her consoling breasts, that you may drink deeply . . . Then you will be nursed, you will be carried on her hip and trotted (lovingly bounced up and down) on her (God's maternal) knees. As one whom his mother comforts, so will I comfort you . . ." (Isaiah

66:10-13 AMPC). God, through Isaiah, speaks of a new nation in terms of the pain before giving birth to a child. As a result, those who rejoice with her, Zion, will benefit and be satisfied, just as a child receives nourishment and is delighted by its mother's playful, nurturing care.

"Anyone who lives on milk is still a baby and is not able to understand much about living right. But solid food is for people who have grown up. From their experience they have learned to see the difference between good and evil" (Hebrews 5:13-14 ERV). Newly regenerated or born-again children need to learn the basic and fundamental principles of the faith, simple and easily understood. "Like newborn babies you should crave (thirst for, earnestly desire) the pure (unadulterated) spiritual milk, that by it you may be nurtured and grow into completed salvation, since you have (already) tasted the goodness and kindness of the Lord" (1 Peter 2:2-3 AMPC).

To grow physically, a human infant requires milk as the first food it is given. It is easily taken in, digested, and absorbed. It contains all of the nutrients needed by a child at that initial stage of life outside of the womb. As new born-again believers, you require the pure milk of the Word of God for your spiritual growth and maturation.

You have already experienced the goodness of Jesus, who paid the ultimate price for your salvation when you received knowledge of the truth of God's Word. So, when you become a member in the family of God, His Word will teach you how to live your new life in Christ Jesus in obedience to His will and purposes. Desire first to search and accept the basic principles, the foundational truths of the Christian walk of faith, so that you can grow and develop spiritually. After that, you will be capable of understanding other truths of God's Word that lead to maturity.

Satisfying Food and Water

God said to John, ". . . To the thirsty I (Myself) will give water without price from the fountain (springs) of the water of life. He who is victorious shall inherit all these things, and I will be God to him and he shall be My son" (Revelation 21:6-7 AMPC). Your spiritual need is pictured here as thirst. God your Father provides water from the fountain of life to satisfy that need.

"Wait and listen, everyone who is thirsty! Come to the waters; and he has no money, come, buy and eat! Yes, come, buy (priceless, spiritual) wine and milk without money and without price (simply for the self-surrender that accepts the blessing)" (Isaiah 55:1 AMPC). Salvation is free because the penalty has already been paid by Jesus, who died for your sins and for mine. God is reaching out to you with arms of love. Those who know they have need of a Savior will run to Him as a child runs to his father.

"The (Holy) Spirit and the bride (the church, the true Christians) say, 'Come!' . . . And let everyone come who is thirsty (who is painfully conscious of his need of those things by which the soul is refreshed, supported, and strengthened); and whoever (earnestly) desires to do it, let him come, take, appropriate, and drink the water of Life without cost" (Revelation 22:17 AMPC). This is an invitation addressed to all men to accept the free gift of salvation by drinking freely of the spiritual water of life. The Holy Spirit and believers are in agreement with Jesus the Son in this invitation to choose life.

As a believer grows and develops in his Christian walk, additional, more advanced teaching is needed for spiritual growth in order to be changed and conformed to the image of Jesus Christ. David, the Psalmist, writes, "Surely I have calmed and quieted my soul; like a weaned child with his mother, like a weaned child is my soul within me (ceased from fretting)"

(Psalm 131:2 AMPC). A child, as it matures, is content merely resting in its mother's arms. It snuggles securely in satisfaction, without a care or concern. It basks in the loving tenderness it receives without striving or frustration at futile attempts to meet its own needs. There is no crying, whimpering, or fuss to continue being nursed from the breast. The comforting presence of its mother is all that is necessary to nurture and sustain the child at this stage of growth and development.

"O taste and see that the Lord is good; How blessed is the man who takes refuge in Him!" (Psalm 34:8 NASB). Allow the Lord to show you how much He values you as His own child. He desires to bless you and prove to you how good He is to those who depend on His loving-kindness and tender mercy to sustain them.

As you mature spiritually and are able to progress from milk, the basic truths of the Word, to solid food, take time to savor, enjoy, and discern the living Word of God. Chew slowly and thoroughly in order to digest, absorb, and assimilate the full measure of God's eternal plan for your life, spirit, soul, and body. He wants you to experience His strength, which is perfect to meet your every need in the times of greatest weakness.

"How sweet are your words to my taste, sweeter than honey to my mouth!" (Psalm 119:103 NIV). Delight in His Word, for it is pleasant and agreeable.

"But God's strong foundation never moves, and these words are written on it: 'The Lord knows those who belong to him.' Also, these words are written there: 'Everyone who says they believe in the Lord must stop doing wrong'" (2 Timothy 2:19 ERV). The church has a double seal of ownership and has an inscription written on it stating that God knows and will acknowledge only those who belong to Christ, and God's children know they are His.

You know you are His because God the Holy Spirit within us confirms with our own newly created inner man, the hidden man of the heart, that we are His children.

A Mother Knows Her Own Child

Mother and child spend so much personal shared time together that she is aware of the child's emotional and physical needs. She is watchfully attentive to its facial expressions and the sound of its cries. She is aware of its physical, emotional, and relational needs. She knows and anticipates, sometimes instinctively, how to respond and to comfort or satisfy its various requirements and desires. She, in return, finds personal pleasure and gratification as a result of her maternal care.

A child knows its own mother. A baby coos, gurgles, moves its arms up and down vigorously whenever its mother comes close, or when it hears her voice or senses her presence. It responds with pleasure when it receives her attention and tender concern for its complete welfare.

Family Resemblance

Immediately after a child's birth, attention and discussion turns toward determining family resemblance. "He has his father's eyes, his mother's nose. He looks exactly like Uncle Bob when he was a baby! He's going to be a doctor like his father. She gets her good looks from her mother. She's high spirited like Grandma. He's got long legs and will be athletic like Uncle Joe."

"And God said, 'Let us make man in our image, after our likeness' . . . So God created man in his own image, in the image of God created he him; male and female created he them" (Genesis 1:26-27 KJV). God created man to be like Himself, to be His image bearers, to be singularly unique reflections of Himself. Man was created as a spirit being, but also able to exist in the natural, physical, and intellectual realm or world. He resembled God, His Creator in form and shape, and also in having a mind, a will to make choices, and emotions and feelings and passions. Man received God's ability, nature, and life. He was also created to have dominion and control over his environment, as well as over his physical and soulish nature and all that affects him in every aspect of his being.

> *"This is the book of the generations of Adam. In the day when God created man, He made him in the likeness of God. He created them male and female, and He blessed them and named them Man in the day when they were created. When Adam had lived one hundred and thirty years, he became the father of a son in his own likeness, according to his image, and named him Seth" (Genesis 5:1-3 NASB).*

The first man Adam was created in the perfect likeness of God and was placed in a perfect place of habitation. Adam's son Seth was born by natural reproduction in the imperfect likeness of his father and lived in a cursed place. All generations born after him are also subject to the curse, the evil consequences resulting from Adam's rebellion. All creation is affected by the choice Adam made to be in rebellion against God's original divine plan.

> *"We know that in everything God works for the good of those who love him. These are the people God chose, because that was his plan. God knew them before he made the world. And he decided they would be like his Son. Then Jesus would be the firstborn of many brothers and sisters. God planned for them to be like his Son . . ." (Romans 8:28-30 ERV).*

> "God—the one who made all things and for whose glory all things exist—wanted many people to be his children and share his glory. So he did what he needed to do. He made perfect the one who leads those people to salvation. He made Jesus a perfect Savior through his suffering . . . These children are people with physical bodies. So Jesus himself became like them and had the same experiences they have . . ." (Hebrews 2:10, 14 ERV).

Jesus the Son, Elder Brother

". . . He is the perfect imprint and very image of (God's) nature . . ." (Hebrews 1:3 AMPC). Jesus, because He is God, is not a mere reflection as man was to be, but a true representation of God's being. "(Now) He is the exact likeness of the unseen God (the visible representation of the invisible) . . ." (Colossians 1:15 AMPC).

"Jesus became like these people and died so that he could free them . . . For this reason, Jesus had to be made like us, his brothers and sisters, in every way . . ." (Hebrews 2:15, 17 ERV). Legally, in order to pay the ultimate price for man's disobedience, Jesus, the Lord, became flesh and identified with man. He was made in the likeness of man; He came down to earth to resemble man and to be an example or a pattern for His brothers and sisters. His ultimate aim is for them to be like Him as they are brought into harmony or changed and conformed into His image.

". . . As He is, so also are we in this world" (1 John 4:17 NASB). Jesus Christ, firstborn by the power of the Holy Spirit, became the only begotten Son of God. He is the first of many brothers who are now adopted by spiritual rebirth into God's own family. All of those children will eventually, in time, be resurrected after death or taken up in glorious new physical bodies as was Jesus, the Son, who was the first one raised from the dead and glorified.

"... The government that rules us is in heaven. We are waiting for our Savior, the Lord Jesus Christ, to come from there. He will change our humble bodies and make them like his own glorious body . . ." (Philippians 3:20-21 ERV). He will change our physical bodies—weak, mortal, subject to death—and make them like His flesh-and-bone spiritual body. It will be powerful, glorious, and eternal.

"The Father has loved us so much! This shows how much he loved us: We are called children of God. And we really are his children . . . Now we are children of God. We have not yet been shown what we will be in the future. But we know that when Christ comes again, we will be like him. We will see him just as he is" (1 John 3:1-2 ERV).

When Jesus comes back in the air to take His Father's children with Him to heaven, all resurrected believers or those raptured alive will have a great bodily change. Your new spiritual body will be comparable and similar in form to the glorious body of Jesus. This miraculous transformation will occur instantly.

Jesus explained to Philip, one of his followers: "'If you had known Me (had learned to recognize Me), you would also have known My Father. From now on, you know Him and have seen Him.' Philip said to Him, 'Lord, show us the Father (cause us to see the Father—that is all we ask); then we shall be satisfied.' Jesus replied, 'Have I been with all of you for so long a time, and do you not recognize and know Me yet, Philip? Anyone who has seen Me has seen the Father . . ." (John 14:7-9 AMPC)

Jesus came to earth to reveal the Father to man. All that His Father was lived fully in Jesus when He walked in human flesh on the earth. Therefore, He could disclose and open up to view for all to see, hear, and know what God was like. ". . . He

[Jesus] is able to do only what He sees the Father doing, for whatever the Father does is what the Son does in the same way (in His turn). The Father dearly loves the Son and discloses to (shows) Him everything that He Himself does . . ." (John 5:19-20 AMPC).

A child attempting to walk in the footsteps of his natural father will endeavor to take giant steps, to move, walk, and model his behavior after that of his ideal. "Therefore be imitators of God (copy Him and follow His example), as well-behaved children (imitate their father)" (Ephesians 5:1 AMPC).

Given a Name

Parents select a first name, "a given name," for the newborn child. The last name, "the family name," comes down the father's line. The heritage and history of the family is reflected in that last name. Each child born into a family has the legal right to be known by that name, and any child officially adopted into the family also has an equal right to that name.

All true children are entitled to be identified and called by the name of their father. They are authorized to use that name for any purpose and in all life situations. "See what (an incredible) quality of love the Father has given (shown, bestowed on) us, that we should (be permitted to) be named and called and counted the children of God! And so we are! . . ." (1 John 3:1 AMPC).

It is written in Ephesians 3:15 that every fatherhood—the state of being a father, the head of family—whether in heaven or on earth, gets its true name from God the Father, for it is He who generates, produces, and originates all life in the unseen spiritual realm and in the visible physical realm. The Lord of heaven and earth, God of power and might, a Father who rules in the affairs of men, of nations, and in the entire course of history, He also planned specific, particular events for your individual, personal life. He set that divine plan in motion in the following narrative:

God Gives His Son the Name Above Every Name

An angel came in a dream to Joseph, promised husband of Mary, a virgin who was discovered to be pregnant: "But as he was thinking this over, behold, an angel of the Lord appeared to him in a dream, saying, 'Joseph, descendant of David, do not be afraid to take Mary (as) your wife, for that which is conceived of her is of (from, out of) the Holy Spirit. She will bear a Son, and you shall call His name Jesus . . . (which means Savior), for He will save His people from their sins (that is, prevent them from failing and missing the true end and scope of life, which is God). All this took place that it might be fulfilled which the Lord had spoken through the prophet, 'Behold, the virgin shall become pregnant and give birth to a Son, and they shall call His name Emmanuel—which, when translated, means, God with Us' (Isaiah 7:14). Then Joseph, being aroused from his sleep, did as the angel of the Lord had commanded him: he took (her to his side as) his wife. But he had no union with her as her husband until she had borne her firstborn Son; and he called His name Jesus" (Matthew 1:20-25 AMPC).

Jesus is the name given to God's Son. It is His earthly name, referring to His humanity and His purpose on the earth. The name Jesus means "God is salvation." That name represents His role in this world, that is, to save the lost. "Emmanuel" means that God was personally present in Christ Jesus, "God with us." ". . . God was in Christ, making peace between the world and himself. In Christ, God did not hold people guilty of their sins . . ." (2 Corinthians 5:19 ERV).

". . . All of God lives in Christ fully, even in his life on earth" (Colossians 2:9 ERV). All that God is, His fullness, lives in Jesus Christ, the Son of God, as He walked on earth as a man.

He was completely God and completely man.

"And there is salvation in and through no one else, for there is no other name under heaven given among men by and in which we must be saved" (Acts 4:12 AMPC). There is no other way to salvation other than through Jesus and in the belief that He paid the penalty to reconcile you back to God. "And it shall be that whoever shall call upon the name of the Lord (invoking, adoring, and worshiping the Lord–Christ) shall be saved" (Acts 2:21 AMPC).

After His resurrection, God gave Jesus all power in heaven and earth. Jesus, then, gave believers, those who believe and call on His name, the same authority, the legal power and right to use that name to continue His work on the Earth, ". . . that repentance (with a view to and as the condition of) forgiveness of sins should be preached in His name to all nations . . ." (Luke 24:47 AMPC).

Jesus went back to the Father, His followers could not ask Him anything personally; but you have the right to ask your Father for what you need in the name of Jesus. "Ask in My Name (as presenting all that I AM)" (John 16:23 AMPC). Before the return of Jesus to His Father, He added, "Until now you have not asked for anything in my name. Ask and you will receive, and your joy will be complete" (John 16:24 NIV). So your prayer should end, "In the name of Jesus, Amen" ("So be it").

"These things have I written unto you that believe on the name of the Son of God; that ye may know that ye have eternal life, and that ye may believe on the name of the Son of God. And this is the confidence that we have in him, that, if we ask any thing according to his will, he heareth us. And if we know that he hear us, whatsoever we ask, we know that we have the petitions that we desired of him (1 John 5:13-15 KJV).

Authority of His Name

Jesus said before He ascended back to His Father in heaven: "All authority (all power of rule) in heaven and on earth has been given to Me" (Matthew 28:18 AMPC). He has given us of the family of God the authority and right to use His name and to share that God-given power and authority with Him. We step confidently into His authority when we speak or call upon the name of Jesus.

The ultimate origin or source of a believer's power is the name of Jesus, and you have the privilege and authority to use that name. You have been given the power of attorney, the legal authorization by the written word of truth, to conduct for another person, with all lawful and rightful power, the official family and kingdom business. This is as Jesus is doing the work Himself, as we continue His work done while He was on earth. His name, when used by believers, brings immense power into every life situation.

After His resurrection, Jesus said, ". . . If anyone steadfastly believes in Me, he will himself be able to do the things that I do; and he will do even greater things than these, because I go to the Father. And I will do (I Myself will grant) whatever you ask in My Name (as presenting all that I AM), so that the Father may be glorified and extolled in (through) the Son. (Yes) I will grant (I Myself will do for you) whatever you shall ask in My Name (as representing all that I AM)" (John 14:12-14 AMPC)

"And whatever you do (no matter what it is) in word or deed, do everything in the name of the Lord Jesus and in (dependence upon) His Person, giving praise to God the Father through Him (Colossians 3:17 AMPC). "At all times and for everything giving thanks in the name of our Lord Jesus Christ to God the Father" (Ephesians 5:20 AMPC).

> "... During his life as a man, he humbled himself by being fully obedient to God, even when that caused his death—death on a cross. So God raised him up to the most important place and gave him the name that is greater than any other name. God did this so that every person will bow down to honor the name of Jesus. Everyone in heaven, on earth, and under the earth will bow. They will all confess, 'Jesus Christ is Lord,' and this will bring glory to God the Father" (Philippians 2:7-11 ERV).

God gives His Son a name that explains His authority and character. After Jesus had humbled Himself to become a man born to die on a cross, after His resurrection from the dead, God rewarded Him for His obedience. He exalted Him highly, above all others, and set Him in a high position of glory, honor, and power. He gave Him a name above every other name. All will eventually recognize, acclaim, and submit to Him as Lord and Master of all.

Birth Certificate

A birth certificate is a legal document usually issued for every natural birth. It registers the name and gender of the newborn child and the order of birth. It records the name of the father and mother and includes the exact time and place of this important event. It also lists other details, such as ethnic origin, viewed as necessary information from a human perspective. It is the written testimony of the truth of the birth of a child. Official records are stamped or marked with a seal used to authenticate and guarantee that the contents of the document are correct.

The Bible is a legal document including two testaments, God's covenants or agreements with man. The Old Testament is the agreement God made with Israel and details His desire to bless that nation and to make it a blessing to the entire world. Specific detailed genealogies and lines of descent are recorded for His chosen people.

The New Testament is God's renewed agreement and plan to bless all people who are given an opportunity to respond to His loving-kindness as revealed through Jesus Christ. Those who accept will be born again from above to become by spiritual reproduction children of God and members of His own family. The New Testament includes some of the details of the spiritual birth certificate of all God's children. It is proof of who you are and whose you are in Christ Jesus.

"Who am I? Who were my people? What is my history?" These are questions people often ask when expressing interest in finding out about the ancestry and lineage of the family into which they were born. Family histories are also very important to God. Throughout Scripture, genealogies are prominently and faithfully recorded until they ultimately lead to the birth of Jesus Christ, the only begotten Son of God. The Scriptures all eventually point to His story.

The family history of Jesus, by direct descent through Joseph, Mary's husband, goes through David back to Abraham, as documented in Matthew 1:1. ". . . The generations of Jesus Christ the son of David, the son of Abraham" (Matthew 1:1 KJV). Luke 3:23-38 records the genealogy of Mary, His mother, and her natural descent back to Adam, the son of God by creation. ". . . Adam was the son of God" (Luke 3:38 ERV). In the beginning of humanity, it was only the first man, Adam, who was God's son by creation. After that, all of Adam's descendants were sons conceived and born by God's natural laws of reproduction. ". . . And Mary was the mother of Jesus, who is called the Messiah" (Matthew 1:16 ERV).

The Bible records the birth of Jesus, God's own Son, in the Gospel of Luke: "And the angel said unto them, 'Fear not; for, behold, I bring you good tidings of great joy, which shall be to all people. For unto you is born this day in the city of David a Savior, which is Christ the Lord'" (Luke 2:10-11 KJV).

This record certifies that the birth of Jesus occurred on a definite day, "this day," and in a definite place: Bethlehem, the city where His ancestor David was also born. At this particular time and in this specific place, God had a Son to be named Jesus, and the Son had a heavenly Father. "He will be great, and will be called the Son of the Most High . . . the holy offspring shall be called the Son of God" (Luke 1:32, 35 NASB).

The Gospel of Matthew records that Mary, a virgin, would bear a Son and call His name Jesus: "She will give birth to a son. You will name him Jesus. Give him that name because he will save his people from their sins . . . The virgin will be pregnant and will give birth to a son . . ." (Matthew 1:21, 23 ERV).

The Eternal Word, Jesus, came into existence as a human on this earth in His mother's womb after the Holy Spirit, the birth agent, overshadowed, surrounded, and empowered her to conceive. The Old Testament Scriptures foretell His birth. The New Testament relates historically His actual supernatural birth on this earth as the only begotten Son of God.

He was sent to reveal and initiate God's Divine eternal plan for mankind. ". . . Jesus would be the firstborn of many brothers and sisters" (Romans 8:29 ERV). The "many brothers and sisters" are those born of human parents who are adopted into God's family by faith and spiritual rebirth.

In his letter to the church in Rome, Paul refers to the groups of people named at that particular time and place in history. Today, more people groups and nationalities are recorded on earth. All believers are, however, one in unity with equal rights and privileges, joint heirs with Jesus, the firstborn Son of God. All are members of the family of God. No matter who you are, your ethnic group, your background, or your current situation, when you trust in Jesus as your personal Savior and Lord, you are His, the accepted, beloved child of God. "Man looks at the outward appearance, but the Lord looks at the heart" (1 Samuel 16:7 NIV).

> *"For He foreordained us (destined us, planned in love for us) to be adopted (revealed) as His own children through Jesus Christ, in accordance with the purpose of His will (because it pleased Him and was His kind intent)—(so that we might be) to the praise and the commendation of His glorious grace (favor and mercy) which He fully bestowed on us in the Beloved"* (Ephesians 1:5-6 AMPC).

You are accepted in His beloved Son Jesus Christ. You are invested and furnished with special honor and are highly favored as His own child without respect to physical characteristics or outward appearance.

- CHAPTER 13 -

JESUS LOVES YOU

Registry of New Birth

". . . Rejoice that your names are recorded in heaven" (Luke 10:20 NASB). ". . . He who conquers (is victorious) . . . I will not erase or blot out his name from the Book of Life . . ." (Revelation 3:5 AMPC). The Book of Life of the Lamb (see Revelation 13:8) is the book where the names of the righteous are registered. The Father knows His own children who have believed in the work of the sacrificial Lamb, Jesus Christ. Your name written in the Lamb's Book of Life is the testimony of your supernatural rebirth from above.

The firstborn begotten Son came into human existence; however, new believers, already physically in existence, are adopted into God's family after the born-again experience. In God's heavenly records of those spiritually reborn, there are no identifiable listings of such physical characteristics as ethnic group or gender. All are equal in the heart of God. "There is (now no distinction) neither Jew or Greek, there is neither slave nor free, there is not male and female; for you are all one in Christ Jesus" (Galatians 3:28 AMPC).

"But the firm foundation of (laid by) God stands, sure and unshaken, bearing this seal (inscription): The Lord knows those who are His . . ." (2 Timothy 2:19 AMPC). The church is the solid foundation laid by God. It consists of an assembly of born-again believers who are all individually and personally known to God. You can be secure in that knowledge of the truth of His Word about His care for and acceptance of His children. His seal guarantees your membership in His family, the household of faith, and your place in the assembly of believers, the church of the living God. It is ". . . the Holy Spirit of God . . . by Whom you were sealed (marked, branded as God's own) . . ." (Ephesians 4:30 AMPC)

The Holy Spirit of God living and dwelling in you is the proof that you became His child at the very moment of your rebirth. God's seal, the Holy Spirit, guarantees His ownership.

Dedication

Anointing with oil provides what is needed to enrich and refresh the physical body as the oil is rubbed and smeared on and into the skin. A baby is anointed with oils or lotions applied and smeared over the entire body. It is physically rubbed on to saturate and be absorbed from the outside into the skin. The desired result is to soften and refresh the skin in order to protect the child's own body. This physical anointing process is initiated, performed, and completed by the soothing human touch of a natural body in contact with another natural body.

In many cultures throughout the world, newborns are often dedicated and devoted for a particular service or purpose. By a specific act, rite, and declaration, the child is set apart or affirmed to be given over to a special intent or an expected result.

"How God anointed and consecrated Jesus of Nazareth with the (Holy) Spirit and with strength and ability and power; how He went about doing good and, in particular, curing all who were harassed and oppressed by (the power of) the devil, for God was with Him" (Acts 10:38 AMPC). Jesus Christ, the

Anointed One, was fully God and yet fully man as He walked on this earth. Yet He emptied Himself of all His godly attributes of glory, authority, power, and immortality to become like you, who can do nothing by your own power and might. All He did as a natural man was accomplished through God's supernatural anointing of the Holy Spirit.

Jesus was appointed and anointed for a specific purpose and work on this earth. ". . . The reason the Son of God was made manifest (visible) was to undo (destroy, loosen, and dissolve) the works the devil (has done)" (1 John 3:8 AMPC).

Jesus came down, born of a woman, to remove the guilt of sin by His death. With His resurrection, you are also raised to newness of life to give you power over sin during your walk on earth.

Jesus Christ, the Anointed One, came to Earth to do the will of His Father. In His first sermon, delivered in His own hometown of Nazareth, He announced His mission and ministry to the world by quoting the prophet Isaiah (Isaiah 61:1-2): "The Spirit of the Lord (is) upon Me, because He has anointed Me (the Anointed One, the Messiah) to preach the good news (the Gospel) to the poor; He has sent Me to announce release to the captives and recovery of sight to the blind, to send forth as delivered those who are oppressed (who are downtrodden, bruised, crushed, and broken down by calamity), to proclaim the accepted and acceptable year of the Lord (the day when salvation and the free favors of God profusely abound" (Luke 4:18-19 AMPC).

God the Father sent Jesus the Son to earth, empowered by the Holy Spirit upon Him to do the supernatural work He was ordained to do. He was anointed to preach the good news of the gospel to those who recognize that they have need of a Savior; to preach deliverance and to set free and liberate those held captive by sin, sickness, and death.

He came to announce that to all who accept His finished work on the cross, complete restoration and wholeness of spirit, soul, and body is possible and available through faith. He defeated Satan to recover dominion over the earth lost by the first man Adam's disobedience. He proclaimed His healing ministry to those broken, beaten, and oppressed in any aspect of their being. His mission was to bring light into the lives of those in darkness, both physically and spiritually.

Jesus prayed before His crucifixion to His Father for Himself and others: "I have brought you glory on earth by completing the work you gave me to do" (John 17:4 NIV). He came, died, was buried, resurrected, and returned victoriously to His Father in heaven. As a result, all who believe, rely on, and trust in Him are brought back into a right relationship with God as members of His family, with all resulting benefits due children of the living God and joint heirs with Jesus.

A believer is set apart for God spiritually, to be devoted to the service of God. Christians, Christ-like anointed ones, are dedicated and empowered to do the specific will of the Father. God's supernatural touch, the anointing, provides and equips you with what is needed for you to accomplish whatever He has divinely purposed to set you apart or consecrate you for a particular work.

Oil is symbolic of the Holy Spirit, from whom flows all the gifts and power needed by believers to enable you to serve others and bring glory to God. His supreme purpose, the plan of salvation, is to reconcile sinful man back to Himself and for you individually to fulfill the destiny predetermined for you.

God's ultimate act of love was to sacrifice His only begotten Son, who left the glories of heaven to take on human form in order to identify with your weaknesses, yet to live without sin. "For God so loved the world that he gave his one and only Son, that whoever believes in him shall not perish but have eternal life. For God did not send his Son into the world to condemn the world, but to save the world through him" (John 3:16-17 NIV).

Jesus Christ completed His assigned work by His crucifixion, death, burial, and resurrection. Belief and trust in His finished work is the doorway into salvation and acceptance as a child of God into His family. "For it is by grace you have been saved, through faith—and this not from yourselves, it is the gift of God—not by works, so that no one can boast. For we are God's workmanship, created in Christ Jesus to do good works, which God prepared in advance for us to do" (Ephesians 2:8-10 NIV). God has prepared beforehand the good works and actions you are to do as a born-again believer. He has already equipped you with all the gifts and abilities necessary for the specific call on your new life in Christ.

". . . You will receive power when the Holy Spirit comes on you; and you will be my witnesses . . ." (Acts 1:8 NIV). Spiritual anointing is God's divine supernatural touch on the life of a believer. It is God's Spirit in contact with his new creation spirit man: Spirit to spirit, empowerment from the inside to be manifest or evident on the outside to the physical senses. "Do not neglect the gift which is in you, (that special inward endowment) which was directly imparted to you (by the Holy Spirit) . . ." (1 Timothy 4:14 AMPC).

All of God's children are set apart, dedicated, and given power for a specific function or particular office in order to impact the lives of others for God's service and to bring Him glory and honor. "As each of you has received a gift (a particular spiritual talent, a gracious divine endowment), employ it for one another as (befits) good trustees of God's many-sided grace (faithful stewards of the extremely diverse powers and gifts granted to Christians by unmerited favor)" (1 Peter 4:10 AMPC).

As Christians, you are anointed ones, like Christ Jesus, given power to do the works of Jesus in this earthly realm. God not only predestined, planned beforehand, chose and called you to be His own, but in the power of the Holy Spirit, He has graciously prepared, enabled, and equipped you to do the work of the ministry. ". . .It is God Who confirms and makes us steadfast and establishes us . . . and has consecrated and anointed us (enduing us with the gifts of the Holy Spirit)" (2 Corinthians 1:21 AMPC).

Jesus promised that Christians would be able to have the power of attorney or the authority to use His name, and to do the works He did though the anointing of the Spirit. "I can assure you that whoever believes in me will do the same things I have done. And they will do even greater things than I have done, because I am going to the Father. And if you ask for anything in my name, I will do it for you. Then the Father's glory will be shown through the Son. If you ask me for anything in my name, I will do it" (John 14:12-14 ERV).

Jesus was one anointed to do good works. Christians are anointed to do greater works, also empowered by the Holy Spirit. "But you are . . . (God's) own purchased, special people, that you may set forth the wonderful deeds and display the virtues and perfections of Him Who called you out of darkness into His marvelous light" (1 Peter 2:9 AMPC).

Since you are, then, the children of the living God, you are to be a reflection of Him in your daily Christian walk and life so others hear, see, and experience the wonderful manifestation of His divine power, presence, and goodness.

Inheritance

A parent leaves a will to distribute material goods to others. It is a written legal declaration or contract of a person, a testator, for the manner in which he would like to have his estate disposed of or divided among his heirs after death. The parent determines his desires in advance, but may change his mind or "change his will" if he becomes displeased with any natural heir for any perceived reason. "To speak in terms of human relations . . . (if) even a man makes a last will and testament (a merely human covenant), no one sets it aside or makes it void or adds to it when once it has been drawn up and signed (ratified, confirmed)" (Galatians 3:15 AMPC).

The Bible clearly spells out all that God has prepared for His family, the inheritance that is assured to those who are His children during their lifetime and forevermore. "In Him [Christ], we also were made (God's) heritage (portion) and we obtained an inheritance; for we had been foreordained (chosen and appointed beforehand) in accordance with His purpose . . ." (Ephesians 1:11 AMPC).

"The yes to all of God's promises is in Christ. And that is why we say 'Amen' through Christ to the glory of God" (2 Corinthians 1:20 ERV). We agree with God's Word that it is trustworthy, that it stands firm, that it is immovable and fixed. So we can say, "So be it" to His promises, for surely, truly, they are ours.

> *"So Christ brings a new agreement from God to his people. He brings this agreement so that those who are chosen by God can have the blessings God promised, blessings that last forever. This can happen only because Christ died to free people from sins committed against the commands of the first agreement. When someone dies and leaves a will, there must be proof that the one who wrote the will is dead. A will means nothing while the one who wrote it is still living. It can be used only after that person's death" (Hebrews 9:15-17 ERV).*

The Bible consists of two sections, the Old Testament and the New Testament. "Testament" means agreement or contract. In this instance, it refers to the God-given covenant, contract, agreement made by God to His chosen people. First, it was His agreement with the Jews or Israelites and His desire to bless them. In the New or Renewed Testament, God offers to His chosen ones, the church, His family, a new and better covenant. It is an agreement or contract that went into effect after Christ paid the price for our sins according to the plans determined before the foundation of the world.

The last will and testament is a legally binding agreement so that heirs know exactly what belongs to them by faith, that is, as a free gift according to what He has promised. "Now if we are children, then we are heirs—heirs of God and co-heirs with Christ, if indeed we share in his sufferings in order that we may also share in his glory" (Romans 8:17 NIV).

"Praise be to the God and Father of our Lord Jesus Christ, who has blessed us in the heavenly realms with every spiritual blessing in Christ" (Ephesians 1:3 NIV). Through the last will and testament, you have already been made a beneficiary to everything that heaven has to offer, now and throughout eternity. It belongs to you and is yours through Christ Jesus and by Him only.

"So God created man in His own image, in the image and likeness of God He created him; male and female He created them. And God blessed them and said to them, 'Be fruitful, multiply, and fill the earth . . .'" (Genesis 1:27-28 AMPC). God wanted generations of natural descendants, image bearers, unique reflections of Himself to inhabit the earth and to carry out His eternal plan and purpose.

". . . Come, you blessed of My Father (you favored of God and appointed to eternal salvation), inherit (receive as your own) the kingdom prepared for you from the foundation of the world" (Matthew 25:34 AMPC). Not only are you a joint heir, sharing in the inheritance of Jesus, but you are also loved just as much as even the Father God loves His only begotten Son. He loves you, His adopted child, born of natural parents and born again spiritually through faith in Jesus. By inheritance, you get all that He receives.

". . . So that you can know and understand . . . how rich is His glorious inheritance in the saints (His set-apart ones)" (Ephesians 1:18 AMPC). God the Father makes known and clearly shows the spiritual inheritance and blessings possessed by His children and heirs made possible by the sacrificial death of Jesus.

". . . Righteousness (that state which makes a person acceptable to God) and (heart) peace and joy in the Holy Spirit" (Romans 14:17 AMPC). Righteousness is that inward condition making you acceptable to God and in right standing with Him, just as if you had never sinned. Heart peace is that blessed quietness and rest from continuous striving, work, and self-effort to achieve acceptance. Joy is that delight and gladness that results when you enjoy the calmness from bring undisturbed and independent of circumstances.

"And the effect of righteousness will be peace (internal and external), and the result of righteousness will be quietness and confident trust forever" (Isaiah 32:17 AMPC). Right standing with God results in the blessed assurance, without anxiety, when you willingly and humbly submit in dependence on Him to complete His plan and purpose for your life. He will finish what He started when He chose and called you before the foundation of the world.

". . . And so we will be with the Lord forever. Therefore encourage each other with these words" (1 Thessalonians 4:17-18 NIV). So be inspired and comforted that your heavenly Father will always be with you. From the time of your new birth and continuing throughout all eternity, forever and ever, you can enjoy a loving relationship with Him because you are His child.

If you are a born-again believer, you are a legitimate child in the royal family of God. In the natural world system, great attention is given to the birth of a legal heir to the throne. As a born-again child of the King eternal, you are, by the new birth, an heir of God and a co-heir with Jesus, with power and authority to rule and reign with Him now at this present time—not only now, but also when Jesus Christ comes again to set up His kingdom on earth.

> *"And the kingdom and the dominion and the greatness of the kingdom under the whole heavens shall be given to the people of the saints of the Most High; His kingdom is an everlasting kingdom, and all the dominions shall serve and obey Him" (Daniel 7:27 AMPC).*

- Chapter 14 -

Gifts to the Newborn

Friends and family carefully select and purchase the most appropriate gifts for the newborn child. These are presented to the mother to assist her in the care and nurture of her baby. They will be useful at various stages of its growth, development, and maturation. Gifts are freely given and are received gladly. There is great expectation by the giver that they will be beneficial and satisfactory to both mother and child to meet specific needs.

Men gave costly gifts to the child Jesus, who was sent to earth by His Father. He came to pay the penalty of death in your place, as your substitute, and to reconcile you back to a right relationship with God. Because they believed He was born to be a king, they worshiped Him and presented Him with treasures of costly gifts.

If you as a human ". . . know how to give good gifts to your children, how much more your Father, the one in Heaven, will give good things to those who ask Him" (Matthew 2:11 PNT). When you are welcomed into His family, God will accept the responsibility for you, His own child, just as humans assume their parental roles. Only God, the Father with a maternal heart, is more than enough and more than able in His ability to meet your every possible need. A good God gives good gifts to you who are His in order to fulfill His divine plan and purpose for you, and especially for you to bless others.

"Every good act of giving and every perfect gift is from above, coming down from the Father who made the heavenly lights; with him there is neither variation nor darkness caused by turning" (James 1:17 Jewish New Testament). God never changes; all good comes from Him. His love and care for you does not vary because of your past or current situation. Each child in His family is special in His sight. He has preplanned and prepared a specific work for you to complete. He has equipped you for that task because He never asks you to do anything without first enabling you to accomplish it. God's gifts to His children cannot be obtained through your own performance and resources.

God's Free Gift, Too Wonderful to Describe: Jesus

> *"For God so greatly loved and dearly prized the world that He (even) gave up His only begotten (unique) Son, so that whoever believes in (trusts in, clings to, relies on) Him shall not perish (come to destruction, be lost) but have eternal (everlasting) life" (John 3:16 AMPC).*

"Now thanks be to God for His Gift, (precious) beyond telling (His indescribable, inexpressible, free Gift)!" (2 Corinthians 9:15 AMPC). The gift above all gifts is the giving of His only begotten Son to a lost and dying world. A gift, a Person beyond description, so precious and costly that it cannot be expressed or explained. It is to be received freely because the price for your salvation has already been paid at the cross. As for Jesus Christ, the sacrificial offering, it cost all He had, the ultimate price, His own life.

> *". . . If God is for us, who (can be) against us? (Who can be our foe, if God is on our side?) He who did not withhold or spare (even) His own Son but gave Him up for us all, will He not also with Him freely and graciously give us all (other)*

things? Who shall bring any charge against God's elect (when it is) God Who justifies (that is, Who puts us in right relation to Himself? Who shall come forward and accuse or impeach those whom God has chosen? Will God, Who acquits us?)" (Romans 8:31-32 AMPC).

Gifts to the Son of God, Jesus

The news of the birth of Jesus spread so widely that some great wise men from afar, from the East, came to search for the child who was born to be ruler and leader. They came to worship and bow down before Him. When they came to the place where the child was, ". . . they saw the Child with Mary His mother, and they fell down and worshiped Him. Then opening their treasure bags, they presented to Him gifts—gold and frankincense and myrrh" (Matthew 2:11 AMPC).

Gifts were freely given to the child Jesus after His birth. Gold, frankincense, and myrrh, each one particularly suitable and appropriate to signify or point to His current purpose on earth and His future kingly role. Gold, a most valuable metal, was a gift fitting for the future King of kings and Lord of lords. Frankincense was a mineral used as an ingredient in sacred incense for sacrificial offerings in the Old Testament. Jesus Himself became the sacrificial offering or substitute for sinful man by taking the punishment of death in His own body on the cross. Myrrh, another mineral, was used for perfume, anointing oil, and embalming. This gift was acceptable as an offering to One who would be the Christ, the Anointed One, set apart by God for special service. By His death, He redeemed mankind back to a right relationship with His Father God. After His death, burial, and resurrection, He was proven to be who He said He was, the Son of God.

Frankincense and myrrh were often used together. Both were the most precious minerals or materials available in the times of the life and death of Jesus Christ. They were also considered to be worth their weight in gold and were gifts suited to be presented to the One who will rule and reign when He establishes His kingdom on the earth.

". . . God anointed and consecrated Jesus of Nazareth with the (Holy) Spirit and with strength and ability and power; how He went about doing good . . ." (Acts 10:38 AMPC). God the Father equipped Jesus the Son of man with every gift He needed to complete His work and ministry on earth. The man Christ Jesus, while ministering on earth, needed the personal presence and supernatural power of the Holy Spirit to enable Him to do the work of the ministry.

The Burial of Jesus

> ". . . Joseph of Arimathea, being a disciple of Jesus . . . came therefore, and took the body of Jesus. And there came also Nicodemus . . . and brought a mixture of myrrh and aloes, about an hundred pound weight. Then took they the body of Jesus, and wound it in linen clothes with the spices, as the manner of the Jews is to bury" (John 19:38-40 KJV).

After the death and burial of Jesus, these women came to complete the work of embalming His body: ". . . Mary Magdalene, and Mary (the mother) of James, and Salome purchased sweet-smelling spices, so that they might go and anoint (Jesus' body)" (Mark 16:1 AMPC). But when they came to the tomb, they found no body, for Jesus had risen from the dead as He had promised.

Salvation—a Gift

Your salvation—your birth from above—is a gift from God. "For it is by free grace (God's unmerited favor) that you are saved . . . through (your) faith. And this (salvation) is not of yourselves (of your own doing, it came not through your own striving), but it is the gift of God; not because of works . . . lest any man should boast. (It is not the result of what anyone can possibly do, so no one can pride himself in it or take glory to himself)" (Ephesians 2:8-9 AMPC).

Salvation is deliverance from sin and its consequences, and reconciliation and restoration back to fellowship with a holy God. It is a free gift from God resulting from your personal confession of faith in the finished work on the cross of God's own Son, Jesus Christ. It comes through the sacrificial death of the sinless, righteous man for unrighteous, sinful mankind.

It involves all the benefits and provisions for every aspect of your new life in Christ and includes health, safety, victory, preservation, freedom, defense, and welfare for your total being: spirit, soul, and body. Salvation is not dependent on your own ability or effort but on what Jesus accomplished for you in His death on the cross for you by His death and resurrection. It comes by what He did and not by your deeds.

The Gift of Eternal Life

> *"For the wages which sin pays is death, but the (bountiful) free gift of God is eternal life through (in union with) Jesus Christ our Lord" (Romans 6:23 AMPC).*

Eternal life is not merely living eternally, for so will both believers and unbelievers. Eternal life is knowledge resulting from a personal, loving relationship. It comes from close communion and fellowship with another person. This results only when quality time is experienced, sharing together in total trust and reliance. It occurs when two walk and talk together in agreement, just as Adam and Eve were in union with God in the garden of Eden.

"And this is eternal life: that people can know you, the only true God, and that they can know Jesus Christ, the one you sent" (John 17:3 ERV). To know means to experience and be directly familiar with another person. It comes only through a continued personal relationship. It is not just head knowledge or mental assent or agreement, but total commitment one to another.

"And when he [Jesus] was gone forth into the way, there came one running, and kneeled to him, and asked him, 'Good Master, what shall I do that I may inherit eternal life?'" (Mark 10:17 KJV). You do not—and cannot—do anything, achieve, or earn by working to receive an inheritance. It is a gift to be received by faith.

"The thief comes only in order to steal and kill and destroy. I came that they may have and enjoy life, and have it in abundance (to the full, till it overflows)" (John 10:10 AMPC). Jesus prayed to His Father before His crucifixion: "And this is eternal life: (it means) to know (to perceive, recognize, become acquainted with, and understand) You, the only true and real God, and (likewise) to know Him, Jesus (as the) Christ (the Anointed One, the Messiah), Whom You have sent" (John 17:3 AMPC).

Intimacy, fellowship, a personal close communion with God the Father and Jesus Christ the Son is your inheritance when you trust in the finished work of Christ on the cross. This is freely given that you enjoy this relationship, with all its benefits and blessings, continuously throughout this time, now and in the world to come. You will be certain that you know Him personally when you obey His commands for your life.

Your Inheritance Guaranteed by God the Holy Spirit

"And you also were included in Christ when you heard the word of truth, the gospel of your salvation. Having believed you were marked in Him with a seal, the promised gift of the Holy Spirit, who is a deposit guaranteeing our inheritance until the redemption of those who are God's possessions to the praise of His glory" (Ephesians 1:13-14 NIV).

Children of God received the indwelling Holy Spirit as evidence of present salvation. The Holy Spirit is also a pledge and down payment on our complete realization and possession of the inheritance, the redemption of our bodies, resurrected and equipped to function in the new Heaven and restored Earth.

You are stamped with a seal confirming ownership by God Who has adopted you into His family. You can be secure because a seal cannot be tampered with because of the authority of God, the Holy Spirit stands behind it, assuring you that you will receive all God promised you, the fullness and completion of redemption.

Gift—Righteousness—Right Standing with God

As Paul writes to the believers in Rome, "Blessed and happy and to be envied are those whose iniquities are forgiven and whose sins are covered up and completely buried. Blessed and happy and to be envied is the person of whose sin the Lord will take no account nor reckon it against him" (Romans 4:7-8 AMPC). "For if because of one man's trespass (lapse, offense) death reigned through that one, much more surely will those who receive (God's) overflowing grace (unmerited favor) and the free gift of righteousness (putting them into right standing with Himself) reign as kings in life through the one Man Jesus

Christ (the Messiah, the Anointed One)" (Romans 5:17 AMPC).

Because of Adam's disobedience in believing God's Word (Genesis 3:1-24) man was translated from innocent obedience to a position of guilty disobedience. Because the first man, Adam, sinned, only another man, sinless, could legally take the place and accept the punishment you deserved as Adam's descendant.

> *"But when the proper time had fully come, God sent His Son, born of a woman . . . to purchase the freedom of (to ransom, to redeem, to atone for) . . . that we might be adopted and have sonship conferred upon us (and be recognized as God's sons)" (Galatians 4:4-5 AMPC).*

Personal Gifts to Enjoy

". . . God, Who richly and ceaselessly provides us with everything for (our) enjoyment" (1 Timothy 6:17 AMPC). He will give you the desires of your heart when you make Him your priority. You please your Father when you put Him first and foremost in your life.

"For God's gifts and His call are irrevocable. (He never withdraws them when once they are given, and He does not change His mind about those to whom He gives His grace or to whom He sends His call)" (Romans 11:29 AMPC). All true believers will be saved. Even before God laid the foundation of the world, you were called, chosen, and predetermined to become adopted children. He will shower gifts on you, as His beloved children.

Everything good has its source in God. The love of God motivates sacrificial giving for the benefit of man. He longs to give you the desires of your heart. Those desires are the same ones He Himself initially placed there. He has lavishly poured out the God-kind of love into your heart by the Holy Spirit. He gives you the gifts and talents to complete all that He has called you to do. He has gifted you with an exact portion of faith, that firm conviction and confident reliance on His Word and His ability to accomplish His divine purposes as promised. His gift of grace, unearned, undeserved, and unmerited favor, regard, and loving-kindness is adequate for you to attain the destiny God has already planned and purposed for you.

Gifts for His Body, the Church

The church, God's universal family, is a living, breathing, growing organism of born-again believers. They assemble together throughout the world out of every nation, language, people, and kingdom. As preplanned, at the time of rebirth from above, each member of the Godhead gives the appropriate gifts for each new child of God. The gifts are to prepare believers for serving others and for the work of ministry. They build up, encourage, and comfort other family members until all reach Christian unity and maturity.

The Gift of Forgiveness

"Faith is what makes real the things we hope for. It is proof of what we cannot see" (Hebrews 11:1 ERV). It is the conviction of the truthfulness of God. Grace is God's love, mercy, and compassion for you. It is His willingness to show you His favor, which you have not earned. You have access to all God has. It is His great desire to freely bless you. It is His overwhelming longing that your sins be blotted and wiped out just as if they had never happened, erased completely from the consciousness. He wants to treat you and relate to you as though sin had never occurred. "I, even I, am He Who blots out and cancels your transgressions, for My own sake, and I will not remember your sins" (Isaiah 43:25 AMPC).

"For You, O Lord, are good, and ready to forgive (our trespasses, sending them away, letting them go completely and forever); and You are abundant in mercy and loving-kindness to all those who call upon You" (Psalm 86:5 AMPC).

"In Christ we are made free by his blood sacrifice. We have forgiveness of sins because of God's rich grace. God gave us that grace fully and freely. With full wisdom and understanding he let us know his secret plan. This was what God wanted, and he planned to do it through Christ. God's goal was to finish his plan when the right time came. He planned that all things in heaven and on earth be joined together with Christ as the head" (Ephesians 1:7-10 ERV).

"The Lord your God is in the midst of you, a Mighty One, a Savior (Who saves)! . . . He will rest (in silent satisfaction) and in His love He will be silent and make no mention (of past sins, or even recall them) . . ." (Zephaniah 3:17 AMPC). He not only forgives, but He also promises to forget when you ask. So there is no need for you or others to continually remind yourselves of your mistakes.

Ministry Gifts From Jesus

Christ, the ascended Lord, gave varied gifts. He appointed apostles, prophets, evangelists, pastors, and teachers. ". . . He made some to be apostles, some to be prophets, some to go and tell the Good News, and some to care for and teach God's people. Christ gave these gifts to prepare God's holy people for the work of serving, to make the body of Christ stronger. This work must continue until we all joined together in what we believe and in what we know about the Son of God . . ." (Ephesians 4:11-13 ERV).

These gifts are given to insure that God's children grow from infancy to maturity and completeness as found in Christ. These are specific people who are gifted to minister to His body of believers, the assembly of born-again ones, the church of the living God.

Spiritual Gifts from the Holy Spirit: Manifestation Gifts

Spiritual gifts are "special endowments of supernatural energy" (1 Corinthians 12:1 AMPC). "There are different kinds of spiritual gifts, but they are all from the same Spirit. There are different ways to serve, but we serve the same Lord. And there are different ways that God works in people, but it is the same God who works in all of us to do everything. Something from the Spirit can be seen in each person. The Spirit gives this to each one to help others" (1 Corinthians 12:4-7 ERV).

He gives to each person exactly as He wishes for the profit of everyone and for the common good. These gifts are given according to God's will, not because people earn or merit them or of their own accord or their own will to have them.

These spiritual gifts include the following: ". . . the word of wisdom . . . the word of knowledge . . . faith . . . gifts of healing . . . the effecting of miracles . . . prophecy . . . the distinguishing of spirits . . . various kinds of tongues, and . . . the interpretation of tongues" (1 Corinthians 12:8-10 NASB).

These are the works that Jesus did during His earthly ministry. Believers, family members, joint heirs will operate in the same anointing and power of the Holy Spirit sent to indwell and empower them to continue the work.

> *"I tell you the truth, anyone who has faith in me will do what I have been doing . . . because I am going to the Father" (John 14:12 NIV).*

Motivational Gifts from God

Motivational gifts are those that impel you and are incentives to your choice of action. What are you passionate about?

> "... They [the crowds] followed Him [Jesus] (by land) on foot from the towns. When He went ashore and saw a great throng of people, He had compassion (pity and deep sympathy) for them and cured their sick" (Matthew 14:13-14 AMPC).

> "... You have heard of the endurance of Job, and you have seen the Lord's (purpose and how He richly blessed him in the) end, inasmuch as the Lord is full of pity and compassion and tenderness and mercy" (James 5:11 AMPC).

> "But love your enemies and be kind and do good (doing favors so that someone derives benefit from them) ... but considering nothing as lost and despairing of no one ... and you will be sons of the Most High, for He is kind and charitable and good to the ungrateful and the selfish and wicked. So be merciful (sympathetic, tender, responsive, and compassionate) even as your Father is (all these)" (Luke 6:35-36 AMPC).

> "So we, numerous as we are, are one body in Christ (the Messiah) and individually we are parts one of another (mutually dependent on one another). Having gifts (faculties, talents, qualities) that differ according to the grace given us, let us use them..." (Romans 12:5-6 AMPC).

> "... Whoever has the gift of prophecy should use that gift in a way that fits the kind of faith

they have. Whoever has the gift of serving should serve. Whoever has the gift of teaching should teach. Whoever has the gift of comforting others should do that. Whoever has the gift of giving to help others should give generously. Whoever has the gift of leading should work hard at it. Whoever has the gift of showing kindness to others should do it gladly" (Romans 12:6-8 ERV).

- Chapter 15 -

Past, Present, Future

". . . I kneel before the Father, from whom his whole family in heaven and on earth derives its name" (Ephesians 3:14-15 NIV). The family gets their true name and existence from the Father.

The Apostle Paul writes about God's extended family and His relationship to all under His care and provision: ". . . We are made right with God through faith" (Romans 3:28 ERV). ". . . The Scriptures say, 'Abraham believed God, and because of this he was accepted as one who is right with God'" (Romans 4:3 ERV).

People throughout the ages were accepted into God's family by faith, by believing and relying on God's Word and His promise. "Faith is what makes real the things we hope for. It is proof of what we cannot see. God was pleased with the people who lived a long time ago because they had faith like this. Faith helps us understand that God created the whole world by his command. This means that the things we see were made by something that cannot be seen" (Hebrews 11:1-3 ERV).

The following is a "Faith Hall of Fame" of Biblical heroes of the past who are examples for encouragement and inspiration for those who follow. They are those who walked in faith and depended on God's faithfulness. You can be motivated and influenced by such historical examples as Abel, Enoch, Noah,

Abraham, Sarah, Jacob, Moses, Rahab, Gideon, Barak, Samson, Jephthah, David, Samuel, and others.

This list includes imperfect beings with human frailties, but who believed God and gained His approval by their active faith. God no longer sees them as murderers, prostitutes or children of prostitutes, liars, cheaters and deceivers, thieves, adulterers, womanizers, or abusers of alcohol. God loved them even when they were in unbelief and practicing sinful behavior. But, after they believed God's Word, that active faith resulted in their becoming in right standing with Him. It was credited to them for righteousness. They changed their lives to conform to their inward condition.

"It is a great blessing when people are forgiven for the wrong they have done, when their sins are erased!" (Romans 4:7-8 ERV). It is a great blessing when the Lord accepts people as if they are without sin. So it will be with you or anyone, no matter your past! He will receive you when you trust Him with your present and with your future.

> *"We have all these great people around us as examples. Their lives tell us what faith means. So we, too, should run the race that is before us and never quit. We should remove from our lives anything that would slow us down and the sin that so often makes us fall. We must never stop looking to Jesus. He is the leader of our faith, and he is the one who makes our faith complete . . ."* (Hebrews 12:1-2 ERV).

You can follow the example of the firstborn in the family of God: your elder brother Jesus, whose death on the cross resulted in your salvation. "Yes, God loved the world so much that he gave his only Son, so that everyone who believes in him would not be lost but have eternal life" (John 3:16 ERV). Believers are children (or sons) of God by spiritual rebirth and adoption into the family of God. "How great is the love the Father has lavished on us, that we should be called children of God! . . . Now we are children of God . . ." (1 John 3:1-2 NIV).

Extended Family of Believers

> *"And let us keep paying attention to one another, in order to spur each other on to love and good deeds, not neglecting our congregational meetings, as some have made a practice of doing, but, rather, encouraging each other . . ." (Hebrews 10:24-25 Jewish New Testament).*

Presently, assembling together with other born-again believers, your brethren in God's family, is necessary for continued growth in your Christian walk. You will have many opportunities to rejoice and be glad together. There will also be times when believers will need the comforting and consoling care that each can give to another. Family members build up and edify each other in love.

As God's children gather together in an atmosphere of thanksgiving, worshiping, and praising Him for His goodness and mercy, it is wonderfully pleasing to Him as Father. When you lift up the name of Jesus as Savior and Lord, He is glorified. When you acknowledge the indwelling Holy Spirit, you recognize His divine work in the world and in your own life. When you submit yourselves to godly church leadership and teaching, you will learn life-changing Biblical truths necessary for you to grow and mature as a child of God.

Jesus talks about the future in the Gospel of Matthew: "And the Good News I have shared about God's kingdom will be told throughout the world. It will be spread to every nation . . ." (Matthew 24:14 ERV). Your extended family will include people out of every kingdom, tongue, people, and nation who will hear and believe the Word of truth. They will be those who believe in their hearts that Jesus, the Son of God, paid the penalty for their sins on the cross, died, and was raised from the dead. They will agree with God's Word that they are forgiven and cleansed when they make Jesus the One in control of their lives.

Extended Family: Angelic Allies—Heavenly Hosts, Sons of God

You are not alone in the universe! Angels are God's created spirit beings without number. ". . . And they numbered ten thousand times ten thousand and thousands of thousands" (Revelation 5:11 AMPC). The angelic host are called sons of God by divine creation before He laid the foundations of the earth. They were observers along with the starry host as they celebrated and sang praises to God for His magnificent creative work: "When the morning stars sang together and all the sons of God shouted for joy" (Job 38:7 AMPC).

God has commissioned heavenly armies who faithfully serve Him to accomplish His will, plans, and purposes for your life. "Are not the angels all ministering spirits (servants) sent out in the service (of God for the assistance) of those who inherit salvation?" (Hebrews 1:14 AMPC). They are called "Sons of God" in Job 38:7 and also "Sons of the Mighty" who inhabit heaven and are the sent ones. They are readily available as powerful allies, invisible messengers, working on behalf of God's chosen people and the born-again children who populate the earthly realm. "For He will give His angels (especial) charge over you to accompany and defend and preserve you in all your ways (of obedience and service). They shall bear you up in their hands, lest you dash your foot against a stone" (Psalm 91:11-12 AMPC).

The angels are divinely organized types and have differing ranks, roles, and responsibilities. They bring answers to the prayers of believers. They assist, protect, defend, deliver, and are dispensed at the spoken Word of God by man. They minister to those who are heirs of salvation, a position they themselves cannot attain. They are commissioned to go forth to respond to God's commands and to do those things that please Him.

Their voices are lifted in song as they gather around the throne of God to praise and worship Him for His faithfulness and wondrous works. ". . . Gratefully praise the Lord, you His angels, you mighty ones who do His commandments, hearkening to the voice of His word . . . gratefully praise the Lord, all you His hosts, you His ministers who do His pleasure" (Psalm 103:20-21 AMPC).

They marvel at His mercies and boundless, unconditional love for man, God's highest creation. As the Psalmist David asks God in awesome wonder: "When I view and consider Your heavens, the work of Your fingers, the moon and the stars, which You have ordained and established, what is man that You are mindful of him, and the son of (earthbound) man that You care for him? . . . You have crowned him with glory and honor. You made him to have dominion over the works of Your hands; You have put all things under his feet (Psalm 8:3-5 AMPC).

Man holds a special place in God's plan. He was personally present in Christ Jesus when He assumed the physical form and nature of humans, lived on earth among men, and gave His life to redeem sinful man back to God. Those angelic host who serve, guide, watch over and protect, keep, assist, and communicate with God's crowning achievement, mankind, are also part of the Father's extended family and eternal kingdom, which includes both human and angelic members, those who now inhabit the earthly realm as well as the heavenly realm.

They are brought and accepted into God's family by various means including divine creation, faith in God's promise, spiritual rebirth, and adoption or supernatural physical birth as with His only unique begotten Son Jesus! They are from the past, now in the present, and those who will be offspring in the future. They exist as spiritual beings and in fleshly form; the invisible and invisible, the currently seen and the unseen.

John writes about a vision of things to come: "And I saw heaven opened, and behold a white horse; and he that sat upon him was called Faithful and True, and in righteousness he doth judge and make war . . . And the armies which were in heaven followed him upon white horses . . ." (Revelation 19:11, 14 KJV). Christ will return to the earth with all redeemed and resurrected believers from throughout the ages. In addition, all the angelic host, the armies of heaven, called sons of God, will also accompany Christ at His second coming when He will overcome His enemies and restore His Father's kingdom.

- Chapter 16 -

A Family Affair

Families often gather together joyfully to celebrate special occasions as weddings, birthdays, and holidays. Reunions or larger extended gatherings unite multi-generational family members, bringing them together from greater distances for food and fellowship.

God the Father desires that His family be gathered with Him, so He will send His Son, our Brother Jesus Christ, back to assemble all of His children together. Those who have died in Christ will be raised or resurrected first, and then the living believers will also be caught up with them and meet together in the air with Jesus for a great family reunion in heaven.

In our redeemed bodies, we will receive our full inheritance. When we see Jesus, we will be like Him, as He is. "He will change our humble bodies and make them like his own glorious body. Christ can do this by his power, with which he is able to rule everything" (Philippians 3:21 ERV).

". . . (As surely as) there is a physical body, there is also a spiritual body" (1 Corinthians 15:44 AMPC). A physical body perishes, dies and decays, but the spiritual bodies of God's children will be resurrected and never again subject to decay. They will be raised at this time in power and strength, in honor and glory.

Family Reunion in the Air

Although we live presently in this physical world, our citizenship is in heaven where our Father dwells, and our Lord and Savior, the man Christ Jesus, is now seated at God's right hand in his changed, glorified, resurrected body. At God's appointed time, He will send His Son, Jesus, who will descend from heaven to meet His other family members in the air. They will be instantly snatched up, just as a protective parent removes a child from impending danger or peril.

Jesus comforted His followers before He was offered up on the cross, completed His work, and was resurrected to return to His Father in heaven: "Do not let your hearts be troubled (distressed, agitated). You believe in and adhere to and trust in and rely on God; believe in and adheres to and trust in and rely also on Me . . . I will come back again and will take you to Myself, that where I am you may be also" (John 14:1, 3 AMPC). Jesus is referring to the gathering or rapture of New Testament saints, who will be caught up and translated to meet the Lord Jesus in the air to be forever with Him.

"We believe that Jesus died, but we also believe that he rose again. So we believe that God will raise to life through Jesus any who have died and bring them together with him when he comes . . . Those of us who are still living when the Lord comes again will join him, but not before those who have already died. The Lord himself will come down from heaven with a loud command, with the voice of the archangel, and with the trumpet call of God. And the people who have died and were in Christ will rise first. After that we who are still alive at that time will be gathered up with those who have died. We will be taken up in the clouds and meet the Lord in the air. And we will be with the Lord forever. So encourage each other with these words" (1 Thessalonians 4:14-18 ERV).

These scriptures detail the coming of the Lord Jesus Christ for believers, his family, to take them back with Him to heaven. Because Jesus has been resurrected, raised from the dead, all men will also be assured of resurrection: some to spend eternity with the Father, others to eternal separation, those who have not received by faith His Son Jesus as Savior and Lord.

Jesus will keep His promise to depart from His Father's side to come back for believers. They will all be caught away together with Him in the air for a glorious family reunion. Christ comforted His followers when He told them that He would return again and receive them to Himself. You will never be separated from Him again because where He is, you will be there also.

> *"But the Lord says, 'Your people have died, but they will live again. The bodies of my people will rise from death . . . It shows that a new time is coming, when the earth will give birth to the dead who are in it'"* (Isaiah 26:19 ERV).

In the physical birth of a child, just at the right time, the body of the newborn baby is propelled from its place in the mother's womb into a new life. So it shall be that the earth will be unable to contain the bodies of those who are dead in Christ. Their eternal spirits will be joined with new resurrected spiritual bodies to be caught up in the air together with those in Christ who are alive at that time.

Great Gathering—The Birth of Christ's Earthly Physical Kingdom

The followers of Jesus asked about the return of Christ to the earth for the final restoration of His earthly, physical kingdom. "They said, 'Tell us when these things will happen. And what will happen to prepare us for your coming and the end of time?'" (Matthew 24:3 ERV).

He will be the head and will establish peace and harmony among nations. God the Father and Jesus Christ the Son will live eternally with other family members. This perfect kingdom on the new earth will be a result of being birthed into being. As with every physical or natural birth, travail and labor pains precede the spiritual actual birth and delivery process.

> *"Jesus answered . . . 'Many people will come and use my name. They will say, 'I am the Messiah.' And they will fool many people. You will hear about wars that are being fought . . . But don't be afraid. These things must happen before the end comes. Nations will fight against other nations. Kingdoms will fight against other kingdoms. There will be times when there is no food for people to eat. And there will be earthquakes in different places. These things are only the beginning of troubles, like the first pains of a woman giving birth"* (Matthew 24:4-8 ERV).

Christ Comes Back to Earth With the Called-Out Ones

> *"Even so it is that Christ, having been offered to take upon Himself and bear as a burden the sins of many once and once for all, will appear a second time, not to carry any burden of sin nor to deal with sin, but to bring full salvation those who are (eagerly, constantly, and patiently) waiting for and expecting Him"* (Hebrews 9:28 AMPC).

The sin problem had been addressed at His first coming when He was offered up on the cross. His second coming to the earth will gloriously accomplish and usher in complete salvation, the eternal blessings promised for those who look for and await His second coming to establish His kingdom on the restored earth. "But we look for new heavens and a new earth according to His promise, in which righteousness (uprightness, freedom from sin, and right standing with God) is to abide" (2 Peter 3:13 AMPC).

Homecoming

"Behold, I will create new heavens and a new earth. The former things will not be remembered, nor will they come to mind" (Isaiah 65:17 NIV). God's entire creation will be delivered and liberated from its bondage to corruption and decay. It has been groaning in painful travail, as a woman in childbirth, until the time when it will be set free. All creation will then also partake of the liberty that the children of God enjoy.

> *"Then I saw a new sky (heaven) and a new earth, for the former sky and the former earth had passed away (vanished) and there no longer existed any sea. And I saw the holy city, the new Jerusalem, descending out of heaven from God, all arrayed like a bride beautified and adorned for her husband; then I heard a mighty voice from the throne and I perceived its distinct words, saying, 'See! The abode of God is with men, and He will live (encamp, tent) among them, and they shall be His people, and God shall personally be with them and be their God. God will wipe away every tear from their eyes; and death shall be no more, neither shall there be anguish (sorrow and mourning) nor grief nor pain any more, for the old conditions and the former order of things have passed away"* (Revelation 21:1-4 AMPC).

The Scriptures speak of the world that was, the world that is now, and the world to come. In this instance, in the world to come, in the eternal city on the restored earth, God will come down to live and dwell together with men for all eternity. ". . . See, the Lord is coming with thousands upon thousands of his holy ones" (Jude 14 NIV).

May the Lord "strengthen and confirm and establish your hearts faultlessly pure and unblamable in holiness in the sight of our God and Father, at the coming of our Lord Jesus Christ (the Messiah) with all His saints (the holy and glorified people of God)! Amen, (so be it)!" (1 Thessalonians 3:13 AMPC).

The willful disobedience of the earth's first parents, Adam and Eve, affected all descendants. Their sin and rebellion resulted in separation from God and from the joy of close fellowship in His presence. But a merciful, loving God had a preordained plan for mankind and for you personally to be reconciled back to Himself. It was through the sacrificial death of His own Son, Jesus Christ. Through Him, peace between God and man has been restored.

> *"For the grace of God (His unmerited favor and blessing) has come forward (appeared) for the deliverance from sin and the eternal salvation for all mankind" (Titus 2:11 AMPC).*

> *"But all things are from God, Who through Jesus Christ reconciled us to Himself (received us into favor, brought us into harmony with Himself) . . ." (2 Corinthians 5:18 AMPC).*

Restoration

". . . I have nourished and brought up children, and they have rebelled against me" (Isaiah 1:2 KJV). God often expresses His loving-kindness in terms of His maternal care for a specific nation, a special city, and for His chosen people. He also has an eternal divine plan for the redemption of the entire created universe and all its inhabitants. Here, He refers specifically to Judah and Jerusalem as His children who revolted and sinned against His authority. As natural children often rebel against parental authority, so did the nation and people who were destined to forward God's purposes for mankind.

However, God's original plans will be fulfilled eventually. Because of His long-suffering and tenderhearted mercies, His willingness to forgive and restore, He will reconcile back to Himself all who completely trust in him. ". . . Then you will be called 'The Good and Faithful City.' God is good and does what is right, so he will rescue Zion and the people who come back to him (Isaiah 1:26-27 ERV). The good and faithful city is Jerusalem, the future capital city of Israel and also of the entire world that is to come.

Isaiah the prophet responds with God's answers to the King of Judah, Hezekiah's prayer on behalf of Jerusalem, the royal city of God. This capital city was surrounded and in danger of invasion and expected defeat by the evil, boastful king of Assyria, a very powerful and cruel nation. This was the Lord's message against the king of Assyria: "'The virgin daughter Zion does not think you are important . . . Daughter Jerusalem shakes her head at you and laughs behind your back . . . You were speaking against the Holy One of Israel . . . You sent your officers to insult the Lord . . . I heard your proud insults . . . Then I will turn you around and lead you back the way you came . . . He will not come into this city. The Lord says this! I will protect this city and save it. I will do this for myself and for my servant David" (Isaiah 37:22-24, 29, 34-35 ERV).

Those who put complete trust in God can request and expect that help will come from Him in times of trouble. The Father's divine plan to establish His eternal kingdom on this earth will prevail. His kingdom will come, and His will and purposes will be accomplished on earth as in heaven. He will establish the rule and reign of His beloved Son Jesus Christ. He will be personally present with His family in the restored perfect home he has prepared for you. So will those who are His forever be with the Lord.

In the book of Lamentations, the earthly city of Jerusalem is pictured as a woman. It describes her misery and suffering after the destruction of the city. She is suffering the consequences of her rebellion and sin against God's purposes. "The beauty of Daughter Zion has gone away" (Lamentations 1:6 ERV). "Look how the Lord has covered Daughter Zion with the cloud of his anger" (Lamentations 2:1 ERV).

Zion is often used as another name for the city of Jerusalem. Judah describes the nation named after one of the tribes of Israel. Jerusalem, the city, is called "the Virgin Daughter of Judah" (Lamentations 1:15 NIV). "What can I say for you? With what can I compare you, O Daughter of Jerusalem. To what can I liken you, that I may comfort you, O Virgin Daughter of Zion?" (Lamentations 2:13 NIV). In these passages, she is referred to as "Daughter of Zion," Virgin Daughter of Judah," and "Daughter of Jerusalem."

"Be in pain, and labour to bring forth, O Daughter of Zion, like a woman in travail . . . There shalt thou be delivered; there the Lord shall redeem thee from the hand of thine enemies" (Micah 4:10 KJV). They were to go into captivity and be judged. But after this time of distress and destruction, the God of restoration will bring salvation to His chosen people.

The Heavenly City—Mother of Children of Faith

"The Scriptures say that Abraham had two sons. The mother of one son was a slave woman, and the mother of the other son was a free woman. Abraham's son from the slave woman was born in the normal human way. But the son from the free woman was born because of the promise God made to Abraham. This true story makes a picture for us. The two women are like the two agreements between God and his people. One agreement is the law that God made on Mount Sinai. The people who are under this agreement are like slaves. The mother named Hagar is like that agreement. So Hagar is like Mount Sinai . . . She is a picture of the earthly . . . city of Jerusalem . . . But the heavenly Jerusalem that is above is like the free woman, who is our mother" (Galatians 4:22-26 ERV).

The new heavenly Jerusalem, the capital of the universe, the city of the living God, will descend from heaven to Planet Earth above the earthly city of Jerusalem. The earthly city represents the old covenant of law that came by Moses and is one of works and self-effort, sin, and death. It was abolished and cast out, as was Hagar the handmaiden and her son.

While the earthly city is referred to as "Daughter of Jerusalem," the heavenly city of Jerusalem is called "Mother." The heavenly city represents the new covenant that came by Jesus Christ at Mount Calvary and is now in force because Christ is the One who, at the cross, set free all who come to Him by faith. Christians, believers, will be the inhabitants of the city of God and are His children by the power and authority of God's promise to Abraham. This is the eternal dwelling place where Father God will live with His family.

After Christ returns to the earth with the saints who will rule and reign with Him, there will be a great homecoming back to the restored earth originally created as a perfect dwelling place for man. God will restore the broken relationship with Him that had resulted from Adam's rebellion. The heavenly Father will dwell with men in the holy city after it descends from the new heaven. God's people will see His face and enjoy unhindered fellowship and worship. All those who are His own will experience His presence and comforting care forever.

All of God's family will be reunited and live together in a redeemed world in loving, peaceful harmony.

> *"He who is victorious shall inherit all these things, and I will be God to him and he shall be My son" (Revelation 21:7 AMPC).*

God prepares a perfect eternal habitat for His family of overcoming and born-again believers.

> *"Now to the King eternal, immortal, invisible, the only God, be honor and glory for ever and ever. Amen" (1 Timothy 1:17 NIV).*